**NOTHING
TO ENVY**

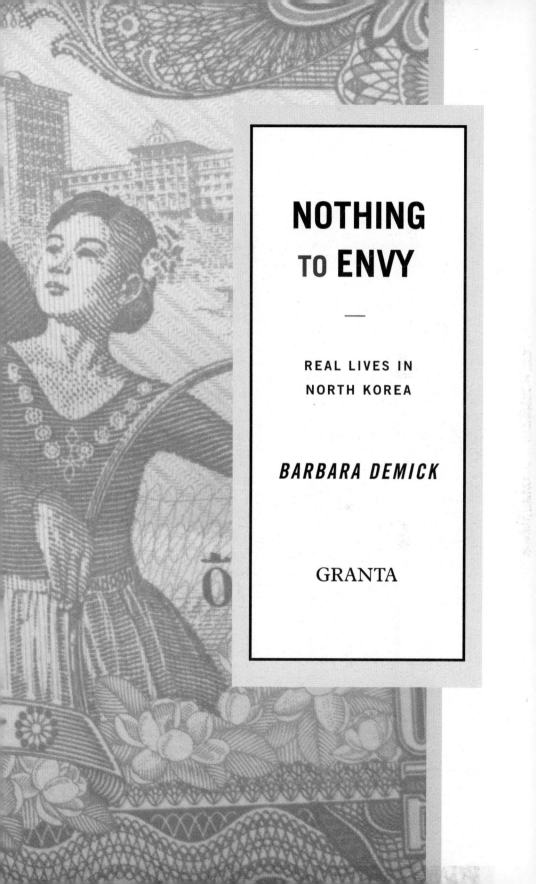

NOTHING
TO ENVY

—

REAL LIVES IN
NORTH KOREA

BARBARA DEMICK

GRANTA

Granta Publications, 12 Addison Avenue, London W11 4QR

First published in Great Britain by Granta Books 2010
First published in the USA in 2010 by Spiegel & Grau

A CIP catalogue record for this book
is available from the British Library.
1 3 5 7 9 10 8 6 4 2

ISBN 978 1 84708 014 1

Book design by Barbara M. Bachman

Printed in the UK by
CPI William Clowes Beccles NR34 7TL

For
Nicholas,
Gladys, and
Eugene

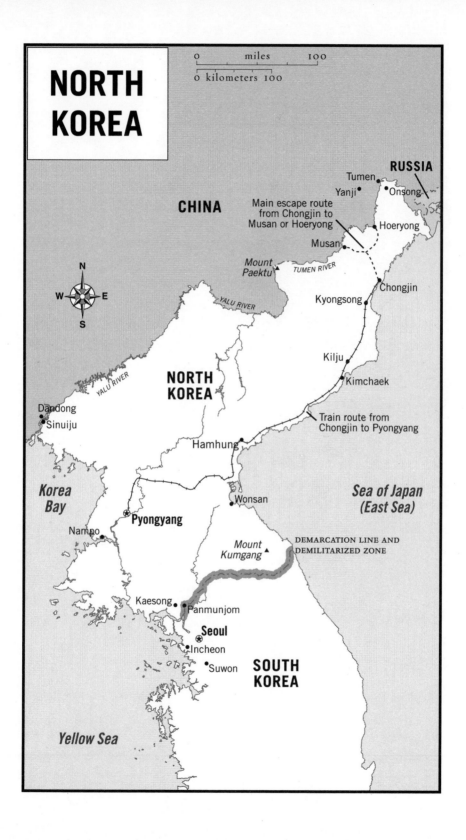

IN 2001 I MOVED TO SEOUL AS A CORRESPONDENT FOR THE *Los Angeles Times*, covering both Koreas. At the time, it was exceedingly difficult for an American journalist to visit North Korea. Even after I succeeded in getting into the country, I found that reporting was almost impossible. Western journalists were assigned "minders" whose job it was to make certain that no unauthorized conversations took place and visitors hewed to a carefully selected itinerary of monuments. There was no contact permitted with ordinary citizens. In photographs and on television, North Koreans appeared to be automatons, goose-stepping in formation at military parades or performing gymnastics en masse in homage to the leadership. Staring at the photographs, I'd try to discern what was behind those blank faces.

In South Korea, I began to talk to North Koreans who had defected, escaping to South Korea or China, and a picture of real life in the Democratic People's Republic of Korea began to emerge. I wrote a series of articles for the *Los Angeles Times* that focused on former residents of Chongjin, a city located in the northernmost reaches of the country. I believed that I could verify facts more easily if I spoke to numerous people about one place. I wanted that place to be far from the well-manicured sights that the North Korean government shows to foreign visitors—even if it meant I would be writing about a place that was off limits. Chongjin is North Korea's third-largest city and one of the places that were hardest hit by the famine of the mid-1990s. It is also almost entirely closed to foreigners. I had the good fortune to meet many wonderful people from Chongjin who were both articulate and generous with their time. *Nothing to Envy* grew out of that original series of articles.

This book is based on seven years of conversations with North Koreans. I have altered only some of the names to protect those still living in North Korea. All of the dialogue is drawn from the accounts of one or more people present. I have attempted as best I can to corroborate the stories I was told and to match them with publicly reported events. The descriptions of places that I haven't visited personally come from defectors, photographs, and videos. So much about North Korea remains impenetrable that it would be folly to claim I've gotten everything right. My hope is that one day North Korea will be open and we will be able to judge for ourselves what really happened there.

NOTHING
TO ENVY

CHAPTER 1

HOLDING HANDS IN THE DARK

Satellite photo of North and South Korea by night.

I F YOU LOOK AT SATELLITE PHOTOGRAPHS OF THE FAR EAST by night, you'll see a large splotch curiously lacking in light. This area of darkness is the Democratic People's Republic of Korea.

Next to this mysterious black hole, South Korea, Japan, and now China fairly gleam with prosperity. Even from hundreds of miles above, the billboards, the headlights and streetlights, the neon of the fast-food chains appear as tiny white dots signifying people going about their business as twenty-first-century energy consumers. Then, in the middle of it all, an expanse of blackness nearly as large as England. It is baffling how a nation of 23 million people can appear as vacant as the oceans. North Korea is simply a blank.

North Korea faded to black in the early 1990s. With the collapse of the Soviet Union, which had propped up its old Communist ally with cheap fuel oil, North Korea's creakily inefficient economy collapsed. Power stations rusted into ruin. The lights went out. Hungry people scaled utility poles to pilfer bits of copper wire to swap for food. When the sun drops low in the sky, the landscape fades to gray and the squat little houses are swallowed up by the night. Entire villages vanish into the dusk. Even in parts of the showcase capital of Pyongyang, you can stroll down the middle of a main street at night without being able to see the buildings on either side.

When outsiders stare into the void that is today's North Korea, they think of remote villages of Africa or Southeast Asia where the civilizing hand of electricity has not yet reached. But North Korea is not an undeveloped country; it is a country that has fallen out of the developed world. You can see the evidence of what once was and what has been lost dangling overhead alongside any major North Korean road—the skeletal wires of the rusted electrical grid that once covered the entire country.

North Koreans beyond middle age remember well when they had more electricity (and for that matter food) than their pro-American cousins in South Korea, and that compounds the indignity of spending their nights sitting in the dark. Back in the 1990s, the United States offered to help North Korea with its energy needs if it gave up its nuclear weapons program. But the deal fell apart after the Bush administration accused the North Koreans of reneging on their promises. North Koreans complain bitterly about the darkness, which they still blame on the U.S. sanctions. They can't read at night. They can't watch television. "We have no culture without electricity," a burly North Korean security guard once told me accusingly.

But the dark has advantages of its own. Especially if you are a teenager dating somebody you can't be seen with.

When adults go to bed, sometimes as early as 7:00 P.M. in winter, it is easy enough to slip out of the house. The darkness confers measures of privacy and freedom as hard to come by in North Korea as electricity. Wrapped in a magic cloak of invisibility, you can do what you like without worrying about the prying eyes of parents, neighbors, or secret police.

I met many North Koreans who told me how much they learned to love the darkness, but it was the story of one teenage girl and her boyfriend that impressed me most. She was twelve years old when she met a young man three years older from a neighboring town. Her family was low-ranking in the byzantine system of social controls in place in North Korea. To be seen in public together would damage the boy's career prospects as well as her reputation as a virtuous young woman. So their dates consisted entirely of long walks in the dark. There was nothing else to do anyway; by the time they started dating in earnest in the early 1990s, none of the restaurants or cinemas were operating because of the lack of power.

They would meet after dinner. The girl had instructed her boyfriend not to knock on the front door and risk questions from her older sisters, younger brother, or the nosy neighbors. They lived squeezed together in a long, narrow building behind which was a common outhouse shared by a dozen families. The houses were set off from the street by a white wall, just above eye level in height. The boy found a spot behind the wall where nobody would notice him as the light seeped out of the day. The clatter of the neighbors washing the dishes or using the toilet masked the sound of his footsteps. He would wait hours for her, maybe two or three. It didn't matter. The cadence of life is slower in North Korea. Nobody owned a watch.

The girl would emerge just as soon as she could extricate herself from the family. Stepping outside, she would peer into the darkness, unable to see him at first but sensing with certainty his presence. She wouldn't bother with makeup—no one needs it in the dark. Sometimes she just wore her school uniform: a royal blue skirt cut modestly below the knees, a white blouse and red bow tie, all of it made from a crinkly synthetic material. She was young enough not to fret about her appearance.

At first, they would walk in silence, then their voices would gradually rise to whispers and then to normal conversational levels as they left the village and relaxed into the night. They maintained an arm's-length distance from each other until they were sure they wouldn't be spotted.

Just outside the town, the road headed into a thicket of trees to the grounds of a hot-spring resort. It was once a resort of some renown; its 130-degree waters used to draw busloads of Chinese tourists in search of cures for arthritis and diabetes, but by now it rarely operated. The entrance featured a rectangular reflecting pond rimmed by a stone wall. The paths cutting through the grounds were lined with pine trees, Japanese maples, and the girl's favorites—the ginkgo trees that in autumn shed delicate mustard-yellow leaves in the shape of perfect Oriental fans. On the surrounding hills, the trees had been decimated by people foraging for firewood, but the trees at the hot springs were so beautiful that the locals respected them and left them alone.

Otherwise the grounds were poorly maintained. The trees were untrimmed, stone benches cracked, paving stones missing like rotten teeth. By the mid-1990s, nearly everything in North Korea was worn out, broken, malfunctioning. The country had seen better days. But the imperfections were not so glaring at night. The hot-springs pool, murky and choked with weeds, was luminous with the reflection of the sky above.

The night sky in North Korea is a sight to behold. It might be the most brilliant in Northeast Asia, the only place spared the coal dust, Gobi Desert sand, and carbon monoxide choking the rest of the continent. In the old days, North Korean factories contributed their share to the cloud cover, but no longer. No artificial lighting competes with the intensity of the stars etched into its sky.

The young couple would walk through the night, scattering ginkgo leaves in their wake. What did they talk about? Their families, their classmates, books they had read—whatever the topic, it was endlessly fascinating. Years later, when I asked the girl about the happiest memories of her life, she told me of those nights.

This is not the sort of thing that shows up in satellite photographs. Whether in CIA headquarters in Langley, Virginia, or in the East Asian studies department of a university, people usually analyze North Korea from afar. They don't stop to think that in the middle of this black hole, in this bleak, dark country where millions have died of starvation, there is also love.

BY THE TIME I met this girl, she was a woman, thirty-one years old. Mi-ran (as I will call her for the purposes of this book) had defected six years earlier and was living in South Korea. I had requested an interview with her for an article I was writing about North Korean defectors.

In 2004, I was posted in Seoul as bureau chief for the *Los Angeles Times*. My job was to cover the entire Korean peninsula. South Korea was easy. It was the thirteenth-largest economic power, a thriving if sometimes raucous democracy, with one of the most aggressive press corps in Asia. Government officials gave reporters their mobile telephone numbers and didn't mind being called at off-hours. North Korea was at the other extreme. North Korea's communications with the outside world were largely confined to tirades spat out by the Korean Central News Agency, nicknamed the "Great Vituperator" for its ridiculous bombast about the "imperialist Yankee bastards." The United States had fought on South Korea's behalf in the 1950–53 Korean War, the first great conflagration of the Cold War, and still had forty thousand troops stationed there. For North Korea, it was as though the war had never ended, the animus was so raw and fresh.

U.S. citizens were only rarely admitted to North Korea and American journalists even less frequently. When I finally got a visa to visit Pyongyang in 2005, myself and a colleague were led along a well-worn path of monuments to the glorious leadership of Kim Jong-il and his late father, Kim Il-sung. At all times, we were chaperoned by two skinny men in dark suits, both named Mr. Park. (North Korea takes the precaution of assigning two "minders" to foreign visitors, one to watch the other so that they can't be bribed.) The minders spoke the same stilted rhetoric of the official news service. ("Thanks to our dear leader Kim Jong-il" was a phrase inserted with strange regularity into our conversations.) They rarely made eye contact when they spoke to us, and I wondered if they believed what they said. What were they really thinking? Did they love their leader as much as they claimed? Did they have enough food to eat? What did they do when they came home from work? What was it like to live in the world's most repressive regime?

If I wanted answers to my questions, it was clear I wasn't going to get them inside North Korea. I had to talk to people who had left—defectors.

In 2004, Mi-ran was living in Suwon, a city twenty miles south of Seoul, bright and chaotic. Suwon is home to Samsung Electronics and a cluster of manufacturing complexes producing objects most North Koreans would be stumped to identify—computer monitors, CD-ROMs, digital televisions, flash-memory sticks. (A statistic one often sees quoted is that the economic disparity between the Koreas is at least four times greater than that between East and West Germany at the time of German reunification in 1990.) The place is loud and cluttered, a cacophony of mismatched colors and sounds. As in most South Korean cities, the architecture is an amalgam of ugly concrete boxes topped with garish signage. High-rise apartments radiate for miles away from a congested downtown lined with Dunkin' Donuts and Pizza Huts and a host of Korean knock-offs. The backstreets are filled with love hotels with names like Eros Motel and Love-Inn Park that advertise rooms by the hour. The customary state of traffic is gridlock as thousands of Hyundais—more fruit of the economic miracle—try to plow their way between home and the malls. Because the city is in a perpetual state of gridlock, I took the train down from Seoul, a thirty-minute ride, then crawled along in a taxi to one of the few tranquil spots in town, a grilled beef-ribs restaurant across from an eighteenth-century fortress.

At first I didn't spot Mi-ran. She looked quite unlike the other North Koreans I had met. There were by that time some six thousand North Korean defectors living in South Korea and there were usually telltale signs of their difficulty in assimilating—skirts worn too short, labels still attached to new clothes—but Mi-ran was indistinguishable from a South Korean. She wore a chic brown sweater set and matching knit trousers. It gave me the impression (which like many others would prove wrong) that she was rather demure. Her hair was swept back and neatly held in place with a rhinestone

barrette. Her impeccable appearance was marred only by a smatter-
ing of acne on her chin and a heaviness around the middle, the result of being three months pregnant. A year earlier she had married
a South Korean, a civilian military employee, and they were expecting their first child.

I had asked Mi-ran to lunch in order to learn more about North
Korea's school system. In the years before her defection, she had
worked as a kindergarten teacher in a mining town. In South Korea
she was working toward a graduate degree in education. It was a serious conversation, at times grim. The food on our table went uneaten as she described watching her five- and six-year-old pupils die
of starvation. As her students were dying, she was supposed to
teach them that they were blessed to be North Korean. Kim Il-sung,
who ruled from the time the peninsula was severed at the end of
World War II until his death in 1994, was to be revered as a god, and
Kim Jong-il, his son and successor, as the son of a god, a Christ-like
figure. Mi-ran had become a harsh critic of the North Korean system of brainwashing.

After an hour or two of such conversation, we veered into what
might be disparaged as typical girl talk. There was something about
Mi-ran's self-possession and her candor that allowed me to ask more
personal questions. What did young North Koreans do for fun?
Were there any happy moments in her life in North Korea? Did she
have a boyfriend there?

"It's funny you ask," she said. "I had a dream about him the other
night."

She described the boy as tall and limber with shaggy hair flopping
over his forehead. After she got out of North Korea, she was delighted to discover that there was a South Korean teen idol by the
name of Yu Jun-sang who looked quite like her ex-boyfriend. (As a result, I have used the pseudonym Jun-sang to identify him.) He was
smart, too, a future scientist studying at one of the best universities
in Pyongyang. That was one of the reasons they could not be seen in
public.

There are no love hotels in North Korea. Casual intimacy between the sexes is discouraged. Still, I tried to pry gently about how
far the relationship went.

Mi-ran laughed.

"It took us three years to hold hands. Another six to kiss," she said. "I would never have dreamed of doing anything more. At the time I left North Korea, I was twenty-six years old and a school-teacher, but I didn't know how babies were conceived."

Mi-ran admitted she frequently thought about her first love and felt some pangs of remorse over the way she left. Jun-sang had been her best friend, the person in whom she confided her dreams and the secrets of her family. But she had nonetheless withheld from him the biggest secret of her life. She never told him how dis-gusted she was with North Korea, how she didn't believe the prop-aganda she passed on to her pupils. Above all, she never told him that her family was hatching a plan to defect. Not that she didn't trust him, but in North Korea, you could never be too careful. If he told somebody who told somebody . . . well, you never knew—there were spies everywhere. Neighbors denounced neighbors, friends denounced friends. Even lovers denounced each other. If anybody in the secret police had learned of their plans, her entire family would have been carted away to a labor camp in the moun-tains.

"I couldn't risk it," she told me. "I couldn't even say good-bye."

After our first meeting, Mi-ran and I spoke frequently about Jun-sang. She was a happily married woman and, by the time I saw her next, a mother, but still her speech raced and her face flushed when-ever his name came up. I got the feeling she was pleased when I brought up the subject, as it was one she could not discuss with any-one else.

"What happened to him?" I asked.

She shrugged. Fifty years after the end of the Korean War, North and South Koreans still have no proper communication. In this re-gard, it is nothing like East and West Germany or any other place for that matter. There is no telephone service between North and South Korea, no postal service, no e-mail.

Mi-ran had many unanswered questions herself. Was he married? Did he still think of her? Did he hate her for leaving without saying good-bye? Would Jun-sang consider Mi-ran a traitor to the mother-land for having defected?

"Somehow I think he'd understand, but I have no way, really, of knowing," she answered.

MI-RAN AND JUN-SANG met when they were in their early teens. They lived on the outskirts of Chongjin, one of the industrial cities in the northeast of the peninsula, not far from the border with Russia.

The North Korean landscape is perfectly depicted by the black brushstrokes of Oriental painting. It is strikingly beautiful in places—from an American frame of reference, it could be said to resemble the Pacific Northwest—but somehow devoid of color. The palette has a limited run from the dark greens of the firs, junipers, and spruce to the milky gray of the granite peaks. The lush green patchwork of the rice paddies so characteristic of the Asian countryside can be seen only during a few months of the summer rainy season. The autumn brings a brief flash of foliage. The rest of the year everything is yellow and brown, the color leached away and faded.

The clutter that you see in South Korea is entirely absent. There is almost no signage, few motor vehicles. Private ownership of cars is largely illegal, not that anyone can afford them. You seldom even see tractors, only scraggly oxen dragging plows. The houses are simple, utilitarian, and monochromatic. There is little that predates the Korean War. Most of the housing stock was built in the 1960s and 1970s from cement block and limestone, doled out to people based on their job and rank. In the cities there are "pigeon coops," one-room units in low-rise apartment buildings, while in the countryside, people typically live in single-story buildings called "harmonicas," rows of one-room homes, stuck together like the little boxes that make up the chambers of a harmonica. Occasionally, door frames and window sashes are painted a startling turquoise, but mostly everything is whitewashed or gray.

In the futuristic dystopia imagined in 1984, George Orwell wrote of a world where the only color to be found was in the propaganda posters. Such is the case in North Korea. Images of Kim Il-sung are depicted in the vivid poster colors favored by the Socialist Realism style of painting. The Great Leader sits on a bench smiling benevolently at a group of brightly dressed children crowding around him. Rays of yellow and orange emanate from his face: He is the sun.

Red is reserved for the lettering of the ubiquitous propaganda signs. The Korean language uses a unique alphabet made up of circles and lines. The red letters leap out of the gray landscape with urgency. They march across the fields, preside over the granite cliffs of the mountains, punctuate the main roads like mileage markers, and dance on top of railroad stations and other public buildings.

LONG LIVE KIM IL-SUNG.

김일성 만세!

KIM JONG-IL, SUN OF THE 21ST CENTURY.

21세기의 태양 김정일 장군 만세!

LET'S LIVE OUR OWN WAY.

우리 식으로 살자.

WE WILL DO AS THE PARTY TELLS US.

당이 결심하면 우리는 한다!

WE HAVE NOTHING TO ENVY IN THE WORLD.

세상에 부럼 없어라.

Until her early teens, Mi-ran had no reason not to believe the signs. Her father was a humble mine worker. Her family was poor, but so was everyone they knew. Since all outside publications, films, and broadcasts were banned, Mi-ran assumed that nowhere else in the world were people better off, and that most probably fared far worse. She heard many, many times on the radio and television that South Koreans were miserable under the thumb of the pro-American puppet leader Park Chung-hee and, later, his successor, Chun Doo-hwan. They learned that China's diluted brand of communism was less successful than that brought by Kim Il-sung and that millions of Chinese were going hungry. All in all, Mi-ran felt she was quite lucky to have been born in North Korea under the loving care of the fatherly leader.

In fact, the village where Mi-ran grew up was not such a bad place in the 1970s and 1980s. It was a cookie-cutter North Korean village of about one thousand people, stamped out by central planning to be indistinguishable from other such villages, but its location was fortuitous. The East Sea (the Sea of Japan) was only six miles away, so locals could occasionally eat fresh fish and crab. The village lay just beyond the smokestacks of Chongjin and so had the advantages of proximity to the city as well as open space on which to grow vegetables. The terrain was relatively flat, a blessing in a country where level ground for planting is scarce. Kim Il-sung kept one of his many vacation villas at the nearby hot springs.

Mi-ran was the youngest of four girls. In 1973, when she was born, this was as much a calamity in North Korea as it was in nineteenth-century England when Jane Austen wrote in *Pride and Prejudice* about the plight of a family with five daughters. Both North and South Koreans are steeped in Confucian traditions in which boys carry on the family line and care for elderly parents. Mi-ran's parents were ultimately spared the tragedy of having no sons with the birth of one three years after Mi-ran, but it meant their youngest daughter was the forgotten child of the family.

They lived in a single unit of a harmonica house, befitting Mi-ran's father's status. The entrance led directly into a small kitchen that doubled as a furnace room. Wood or coal would be shoveled into a hearth. The fire it produced was used both to cook and to heat the home by means of an underfloor system known as *ondol*. A sliding door separated the kitchen from the main room where the entire family slept on mats that were rolled up during the day. The birth of the boy swelled the family size to eight—the five children, their parents, and a grandmother. So Mi-ran's father bribed the head of the people's committee to give them an adjacent unit and allow them to cut a door into the adjoining wall.

In a larger space, the sexes became segregated. At mealtime, the women would huddle together over a low wooden table near the kitchen, eating cornmeal, which was cheaper and less nutritious than rice, the preferred staple of North Koreans. The father and son ate rice at their own table.

"I thought this was just the way life naturally is," Mi-ran's brother, Sok-ju, would tell me later.

If the older sisters noticed, they didn't make a fuss, but Mi-ran would burst into tears and rail against the injustice.

"Why is Sok-ju the only one who gets new shoes?" she demanded. "Why does Mama only take care of Sok-ju and not me?"

They would hush her up without answering.

It wasn't the first time she would rebel against the strictures placed on young women. In North Korea at the time, girls weren't supposed to ride bicycles. There was a social stigma—people thought it unsightly and sexually suggestive—and periodically the Workers' Party would issue formal edicts, making it technically illegal. Mi-ran ignored the rule. From the time she was eleven years old she would take the family's single bicycle, a used Japanese model, on the road to Chongjin. She needed to get away from the oppression of her little village, to go anywhere at all. It was an arduous ride for a child, about three hours uphill, only part of the way on an asphalt road. Men would try to pass her on their bicycles, cursing her for her audacity.

"You're going to tear your cunt," they would scream at her.

Sometimes a group of teenage boys would career into her path trying to knock her off the bicycle. Mi-ran would scream back, matching obscenity with obscenity. Eventually she learned to ignore them and keep on pedaling.

THERE WAS ONLY one reprieve for Mi-ran in her hometown—the cinema.

Every town in North Korea, no matter how small, has a movie theater, thanks to Kim Jong-il's conviction that film is an indispensable tool for instilling loyalty in the masses. In 1971, when he was thirty years old, Kim Jong-il got his first job, overseeing the Workers' Party's Bureau of Propaganda and Agitation, which ran the country's film studios. He published a book in 1973, *On the Art of Cinema*, in which he expounded on his theory that "revolutionary art and literature are extremely effective means for inspiring people to work for the tasks of the revolution."

Under Kim Jong-il's direction, the Korean Feature Film Studio on the outskirts of Pyongyang was expanded to a 10-million-square-foot lot. It churned out forty movies per year. The films were mostly dramas with the same themes: The path to happiness was self-sacrifice and suppression of the individual for the good of the collective. Capitalism was pure degradation. When I toured the studio lot in 2005, I saw a mock-up of what was supposed to be a typical street in Seoul, lined with run-down storefronts and girly bars.

No matter that the films were pure propaganda, Mi-ran loved going to the movies. She was as much a cinephile as one could be growing up in a small town in North Korea. From the time she was old enough to walk to the theater herself, she begged her mother for money to buy tickets. Prices were kept low—just half a won, or a few cents, about the same as a soft drink. Mi-ran saw everything she could. Some movies were deemed too risqué for children, such as the 1985 film *Oh My Love* in which it was suggested that a man and a woman kissed. Actually, the leading lady modestly lowered her parasol so moviegoers never saw their lips touch, but that was enough to earn the film the equivalent of an R rating. Hollywood films were, of course, banned from North Korea, as were virtually all other foreign films, with the exception of an occasional entry from Russia. Mi-ran especially liked the Russian films because they were less propagandistic than North Korean ones and more romantic.

Perhaps it was inevitable that a dreamy girl who went to the cinema for on-screen romance should have found there for herself the real thing.

They met in 1986, when there was still enough electricity to run the movie projectors. The culture hall was the most imposing structure in town, built in a rather grandiose style popular in the 1930s, when Korea was occupied by Japan. Two stories high, big enough to accommodate a mezzanine, the theater had a huge portrait of Kim Il-sung covering its facade. The dimensions were dictated by regulations that all images of the Great Leader be commensurate with the size of the building. The culture hall served as a cinema, theater, and lecture hall. On public holidays, such as Kim Il-sung's birthday, it would host contests to name the citizens who best followed the example of the Great Leader. The rest of the time the theater showed movies, a fresh film arriving every few weeks from Pyongyang.

Jun-sang was every bit as crazy about the movies as Mi-ran. As soon as he heard there was a new film, he rushed to be first to see it. The film on this particular occasion was *Birth of a New Government*. It was set in Manchuria during World War II, where Korean Communists led by a young Kim Il-sung had been organized to resist the Japanese colonial occupation. The anti-Japanese resistance was as familiar a theme in North Korean cinema as cowboys and Indians was in early Hollywood. The movie was expected to draw big crowds because it starred a popular actress.

Jun-sang got to the theater early. He secured two tickets, one for himself and one for his brother. He was pacing around outside when he spotted her.

Mi-ran was standing toward the back of a crowd surging its way toward the box office. Movie audiences in North Korea tend to be young and rowdy. This crowd was especially rough. The bigger kids had pushed their way to the front of the line and formed a cordon blocking the younger ones from the box office. Jun-sang moved in to take a better look at the girl. She was stamping her feet with frustration and looked like she might cry.

The North Korean standard of beauty calls for pale skin, the whiter the better, a round face, and bow-shaped mouth, but this girl looked nothing like that. Her facial features were long and pronounced, her nose high-bridged, and her cheekbones well defined. To Jun-sang, she looked almost foreign and a little wild. Her eyes flashed with anger at the melee at the box office. She didn't seem like other girls, who made self-effacing gestures and covered their mouths when they laughed. Jun-sang sensed in her a spirited impatience, as if she hadn't been beaten down by life in North Korea. He was immediately enchanted.

At fifteen, Jun-sang was naggingly aware that he was interested in girls in a generalized way, but had never focused on a particular girl—until now. He had seen enough movies to be able to step out of himself and envision what this first encounter with her might look like if it were unfolding on-screen. He would later remember the moment in a dreamlike Technicolor, with a mystical glow around Mi-ran.

"I can't believe there is a girl like that in this little town," he told himself.

He walked around the perimeter of the crowd a couple of times to get a better look and debated what to do. He was a scholar, not a fighter. It wouldn't do to try to push his way back to the box office. Then an idea lodged in his mind. The movie was about to start, and his brother wasn't there yet. If he sold her the extra movie ticket, she would have to sit next to him since the tickets were for assigned seats. He circled her again, formulating in his mind the exact words he would use to offer her the ticket.

In the end, he couldn't muster the courage to speak to a girl he didn't know. He slipped into the movie theater. As the screen filled with the image of the movie's heroine galloping across a snowy field, Jun-sang thought of the opportunity he had let pass. The actress played a fierce resistance fighter who wore her hair tomboy-short and rode her horse across the Manchurian steppe, proclaiming revolutionary slogans. Jun-sang couldn't stop thinking of the girl outside the theater. When the credits rolled at the end of the movie, he rushed outside to look for her, but she was gone.

CHAPTER 2

TAINTED BLOOD

Refugees from the Korean War on the move.

AT FIFTEEN, JUN-SANG WAS A LANKY AND STUDIOUS BOY. SINCE childhood he had scored the best grades in his class in math and science. His father, something of a frustrated intellectual, was ambitious for his children, especially his talented eldest son. It was his dream that the boy would get out of the provinces and further his schooling in Pyongyang. If Jun-sang came home after 9:00 P.M. or fell behind in his homework, his father was quick to pull out a stick he kept for the express purpose of beating intransigent children. The boy would need to maintain top grades through high school and pass two weeks of rigorous examinations in Chongjin to secure a place in a competitive school such as Kim Il-sung University. Although he was just starting his first year of high school, Jun-sang was already on a career trajectory that didn't leave room for dating or sex. The imperatives of puberty would have to wait.

Jun-sang tried to push aside the errant thoughts that would disrupt his concentration at the most inconvenient moments. But try as he might, he could not dislodge the image of the girl with the cropped hair stamping her feet. He didn't know anything about her. What was her name? Was she as beautiful as he remembered? Or was it just memory playing tricks on him? How would he even find out who she was?

As it happened, it was surprisingly easy to track her down. Mi-ran was the kind of girl young men noticed, and her short hair was distinctive enough that a description to a couple of friends yielded her identity. A boy in Jun-sang's boxing class happened to live just two doors away in the same strip of harmonica housing. Jun-sang chatted up the boy, prodding him for bits of information and recruiting him as a personal spy. The neighborhood buzzed with gossip about Mi-ran and her sisters. People often remarked that each was more beautiful than the next. They were tall, a highly prized quality in North Korea, and talented, too. The oldest was a singer, another one painted. They were all athletic, excelling in volleyball and basketball. Such beautiful and clever girls. It was a pity, then, the neighborhood gossips would add, that their family background was so disgraceful.

The problem was their father, a gaunt and quiet man who, like many others in the neighborhood, was employed in the mines. He worked as a carpenter, repairing wooden support beams inside a mine that produced kaolin, a clay used for making pottery. The only thing conspicuous about this bland soul was his sobriety. While other miners chugged down copious quantities of a gut-curdling brew made of corn and, if they could afford it, *soju,* the Korean rice liquor, Mi-ran's father never touched a drop. He didn't want to consume anything that would loosen his tongue and cause him to talk about his past.

Mi-ran's father, Tae-woo, was born in 1932 in a place that later became a part of South Korea, the enemy state. No matter how long they've been away, Koreans describe their home as the place where their paternal ancestors were born. Tae-woo came from South Chungchong province, far on the other side of the peninsula near the Yellow Sea coast. This is gentle countryside of emerald green rice paddies, the terrain as hospitable as Chongjin's is forbidding. His village was on the outskirts of Seosan, a small town that consisted of little more than a row of houses along a spine of dry land cutting through the checkerboard of rice paddies. Back in the 1940s, everything was made out of mud and straw, even the balls that the boys used to kick down the street. Rice was the soul and the sustenance of the village. Growing rice was backbreaking work, with the plowing, seeding, and transplanting all done by hand. Nobody in the village was rich, but Tae-woo's family was just a notch or two better off than the others. Their thatched-roof house was a little larger. The family had 2,000 *pyong* of land, a Korean measure equivalent to 1.6 acres. They supplemented their income by running a small mill where neighbors could bring their rice and barley to grind. Mi-ran's grandfather's status was high enough that he had two wives, a practice not uncommon at the time, although only the first marriage was recognized by law. Tae-woo was the firstborn to the second wife and the only boy. He had two adoring younger sisters who used to follow him around the village, much to his annoyance but to the delight of his friends as the girls grew into beautiful teenagers.

Tae-woo wasn't the biggest kid in the pack, but he was a natural leader. When the boys played war games, Tae-woo got to be the general. His friends would call him a little Napoleon. "He was straightforward and decisive. He would say things firmly and people would listen," said Lee Jong-hun, a childhood friend who still lives in the village. "He was smart, too."

Tae-woo attended elementary school and later middle school, through the age of fifteen, which was standard for the sons of farmers. The language of instruction was Japanese. Japan had annexed Korea in 1910 and deposed the last of the Korean emperors, after which it went about methodically stamping out Korean culture and superimposing its own. During the early years of the occupation, the older men in the village had been forced to cut off the long braid that Korean males traditionally wore bound in a topknot and covered with a black hat. They were made to take Japanese names. The Japanese levied heavy taxes, taking 50 percent or more of the rice harvest, claiming it was necessary to support the war they were waging in the Pacific. Young men and women were shipped off to Japan to contribute to the war effort, while girls were forced into prostitution, becoming what were euphemistically known as "comfort women" who sexually serviced the troops. The rice farmers loathed the Japanese. They couldn't do anything without Japanese approval.

On August 15, 1945, Emperor Hirohito announced Japan's surrender over the radio. It took several days for the news to reach the village. When the boys heard the news, they ran to the barracks where the Japanese were garrisoned and found that they had pulled out, abruptly leaving their personal belongings behind. The occupation was over. The villagers didn't have the money for a celebration, but they ran jubilant in the streets, congratulating one another and cheering.

"*Mansei Chosun,*" they cried. Long live Korea!

The Koreans believed they were once again in control of their own destiny. They would reclaim their country.

As the Japanese emperor read his statement over the radio, across the globe in Washington, D.C., two young army officers huddled over a National Geographic Society map, wondering what to do about Korea. Nobody in Washington knew much about this obscure Japanese colony. While elaborate plans had been drawn up for the postwar occupation of Germany and Japan, Korea was an afterthought. The Japanese had ruled for thirty-five years, and with their abrupt withdrawal there would be a dangerous power vacuum. The United States was concerned that the Soviet Union might seize Korea as a staging ground on the way to the bigger prize of Japan. Despite the World War II alliance, distrust of the Soviet Union was growing in Washington. Soviet troops had already entered Korea from the north the week before Japan's surrender and were poised to keep going. The Americans sought to appease the Soviets by giving them the northern half of Korea to administer in what was supposed to be a temporary trusteeship. The officers, one of whom was Dean Rusk, later to become secretary of state, wanted to keep the capital, Seoul, in the U.S. sector. So the two army officers looked for a convenient way to divide the peninsula. They slapped a line across the map at the 38th parallel.

The line bore little relationship to anything in Korean history or geography. The little thumb jutting out of China that is the Korean peninsula is a well-delineated landmass with the Sea of Japan to the east, the Yellow Sea to the west, and the Yalu and Tumen Rivers forming the boundary with China. Nothing about it suggests that there is a natural place to carve it in two. For the 1,300 years prior to the Japanese occupation, Korea had been a unified country governed by the Chosun dynasty, one of the longest-lived monarchies in world history. Before the Chosun dynasty, there were three kingdoms vying for power on the peninsula. Political schisms tended to run north to south, the east gravitating naturally toward Japan and the west to China. The bifurcation between north and south was an entirely foreign creation, cooked up in Washington and stamped on the Koreans without any input from them. One story has it that the secretary of state at the time, Edward Stettinius, had to ask a subordinate where Korea was.

Koreans were infuriated to be partitioned in the same way as the Germans. After all, they had not been aggressors in World War II, but victims. Koreans at the time described themselves with a self-deprecating expression, saying they were "shrimp among whales," crushed between the rivalries of the superpowers.

Neither superpower was willing to cede ground to allow for an independent Korea. The Koreans themselves were splintered into more than a dozen rival factions, many with Communist sympathies. The temporary demarcations on the map soon hardened into facts on the ground. In 1948, the Republic of Korea was created under the leadership of the seventy-year-old Syngman Rhee, a crusty conservative with a PhD from Princeton. Kim Il-sung, an anti-Japanese resistance fighter backed by Moscow, quickly followed suit by declaring his state the Democratic People's Republic of Korea—North Korea. The line along the 38th parallel would solidify into a 155-mile-long, 2.5-mile-wide thicket of concertina wire, tank traps, trenches, embankments, moats, artillery pieces, and land mines.

With both sides claiming to be the legitimate government of Korea, war was inevitable. Before dawn on Sunday morning, June 25, 1950, Kim Il-sung's troops stormed across the border with Soviet-supplied tanks. They quickly captured Seoul and swept southward until all that was left of South Korea was a pocket around the south-eastern coastal city of Pusan. The daring amphibious landing at Incheon of forty thousand U.S. troops under the command of General Douglas MacArthur in September reversed the Communist gains. Besides the United States and South Korea, troops of fifteen nations joined a U.N. coalition—among them Britain, Australia, Canada, France, and the Netherlands. They recaptured Seoul and headed north to Pyongyang and beyond. As they approached the Yalu River, however, Chinese Communist forces entered the war and pushed them back. Two more years of fighting produced only frustration and stalemate. By the time an armistice was signed on July 27, 1953, nearly three million people were dead and the peninsula lay in ruins. The border remained more or less along the 38th parallel. Even by the dubious standards of twentieth-century warcraft, it was a futile and unsatisfying war.

Tae-woo was eighteen years old when the Communists invaded. He was the main source of support for his mother and sisters, his father having died before the war began. The South Koreans were ill-prepared for the invasion, with only sixty-five thousand under arms—roughly one quarter the troop strength of the North Koreans. They would need all the able-bodied men they could get. Some of the rice farmers were sympathetic to the North because they'd heard a rumor that the Communists would give them free land. Their economic situation hadn't improved since the defeat of the Japanese. But most of the young men were apolitical. "We didn't know left from right in those days," Lee Jong-hun recalled. Whatever their political persuasions, they had no choice but to enlist in the South Korean army.

Tae-woo eventually rose to the rank of sergeant. His unit's last battle took place near the village of Kimhwa, twenty-five miles north of the 38th parallel. Kimhwa (later renamed Kumhwa) made up one point in what the U.S. military had nicknamed the "Iron Triangle," a strategic valley surrounded by granite mountains. (Pyongyang and

Chorwon made up the other two points.) It had witnessed some of the heaviest fighting in this late stage of the war as the Chinese tried to nudge the front line southward in anticipation of an armistice. On the night of July 13, 1953, three divisions of Chinese troops—about sixty thousand soldiers—launched a surprise attack against U.N. and South Korean troops. At about 7.30 P.M. the Communist forces started bombing the U.N. positions; at around 10:00 P.M. they fired flares so the soldiers would see the "hills and valleys come alive with thousands of enemy soldiers," a U.S. soldier later recalled about the attack. Bugles sounded from all sides and they could see the Chinese troops running toward them. "We were incredulous. It was like a scene unfolding in a motion picture," a former American soldier said. It had been raining steadily for a week and the hills "streamed with blood and water."

Tae-woo, by this time assigned to a medical unit, was carrying a South Korean soldier on a stretcher when the unit was surrounded by the Chinese. It was only two weeks before the signing of the armistice, but he, along with approximately five hundred other soldiers from the South Korean army's Capital Division, were taken as prisoners of war.

His life as a South Korean was effectively over. Mi-ran's father never discussed what happened to him in captivity. One would expect that conditions for him were no better than for other POWs held by the Communists. Huh Jae-suk, a fellow POW who later escaped, wrote in his memoir that the men were housed in squalid camps where they were not permitted to bathe or brush their teeth. Their hair became infested with lice; untreated wounds swarmed with maggots. They were fed one meal of rice and saltwater a day.

After the armistice, there was a prisoner exchange in which the Communist forces released 12,773 prisoners, among them 7,862 South Koreans. Thousands more, maybe tens of thousands, were never sent home, among them Tae-woo. They were loaded onto trains at Pyongyang station that they thought were heading south toward home, but instead went north toward the coal-rich mountains that hugged the Chinese border, according to Huh's memoir. Under the name Construction Unit of the Interior Department, new POW camps had been built near the mines. Coal mining in North

Korea was not only dirty but exceedingly dangerous, since the mines frequently collapsed or caught fire. "The life of a POW was worth less than a fly," Huh wrote. "Every day that we walked into the mines, I shuddered with fear. Like a cow walking to the slaughterhouse, I never knew if I would emerge alive."

In 1956, the North Korean cabinet issued an order that allowed the South Korean prisoners of war to be issued certificates of North Korean citizenship. It meant that the worst was over, but also that they were never going home. The worst were in the coal mines, which were hastily dug and subject to frequent collapses and fires. Tae-woo was sent to an iron-ore mine in Musan, a gritty town on the North Korean side of the Chinese border in North Hamgyong province. The men were all former South Koreans and lived together in a dormitory.

One of the workers at the dormitory was a woman, nineteen years old and single—a virtual old maid. She was too angular to be considered pretty, but there was something in her purposeful manner that was appealing; she radiated strength in mind and body. She was eager to get married, if only to get away from her mother and sisters, with whom she was living. Marriageable men were scarce after the war. The manager of the dormitory introduced her to Tae-woo. Though he was no taller than she, he was soft-spoken, a gentlemanly quality coming through from under the black grit of the coal mine. She felt a rush of pity for this young man who was so alone in the world. They married that same year.

Tae-woo quickly assimilated into North Korean life. It was easy enough for him to blend in. The Koreans were one people—*han nara*, one nation, as they liked to say. They looked the same. The Pyongyang accent was often ridiculed for its similarity to the guttural dialect of Pusan. The chaos of the war years had thoroughly mixed the Korean population. Fearing persecution by the Communists, tens of thousands of Koreans from north of the 38th parallel had fled south—among them landlords, businessmen, Christian clergymen, and Japanese collaborators. A smaller number of Communist sympathizers fled north. Countless others with no political agenda were simply pushed up or down as they fled the fighting.

Who could tell who was a North Korean and who was a South

Korean? Soon after his marriage, Tae-woo and his new bride were transferred to another mine near Chongjin where he knew nobody. There was no reason for anyone to suspect anything unusual in his background, but it was in the peculiar nature of North Korea that somebody always did know.

After the war, Kim Il-sung made it his first order of business to weed out foe from friend. He started at the top with potential rivals for the leadership. He disposed of many of his comrades in arms who had led the struggle from Manchuria to unseat the Japanese occupiers. He ordered the arrest of the founding members of the Communist Party in South Korea. They had been invaluable during the war; now that they'd served their purpose they could be discarded. Throughout the 1950s, many more were purged in what was increasingly coming to resemble an ancient Chinese empire with Kim Il-sung the unchallenged master of the realm.

Kim Il-sung then turned his attention to ordinary people. In 1958, he ordered up an elaborate project to classify all North Koreans by their political reliability, ambitiously seeking to reorganize an entire human population. While the Chinese Red Guard also rooted out "capitalist roaders" during the Cultural Revolution of the 1960s and 1970s, it resulted in a chaotic reign of terror in which neighbor denounced neighbor. The North Koreans were methodical to a fault. Each person was put through eight background checks. Your *songbun*, as the rating was called, took into account the backgrounds of your parents, grandparents, and even second cousins. The loyalty surveys were carried out in various phases with inspiring names. "Intensive Guidance by the Central Party" was the first announced phase. The classifications became more refined in subsequent phases, such as the "Understanding People Project," between 1972 and 1974.

Despite the twentieth-century lingo of social engineering, this process was akin to an updating of the feudal system that had stifled Koreans in prior centuries. In the past, Koreans were bound by a caste system nearly as rigid as that of India. Noblemen wore white shirts and high black horsehair hats, while slaves wore wooden tags around their necks. The old class structure drew heavily on the teachings of the Chinese philosopher Confucius, who believed that humans fit strictly into a social pyramid. Kim Il-sung took the least humane elements of Confucianism and combined them with Stalin-ism. At the top of the pyramid, instead of an emperor, resided Kim Il-sung and his family. From there began a downward progression of fifty-one categories that were lumped into three broad classes—the core class, the wavering class, and the hostile class.

The hostile class included the *kisaeng* (female entertainers who, like the Japanese geisha, might provide a bit more for high-paying clients), fortune-tellers, and *mudang* (shamans, who were also in the lower classes during the dynastic period). Also included were the po-litically suspect, as defined by a white paper on human rights in North Korea based on testimony of defectors living in South Korea.

> People from families of wealthy farmers, merchants, industri-alists, landowners, or those whose private assets have been completely confiscated; pro-Japan and pro-U.S. people; reac-tionary bureaucrats; defectors from the South . . . Buddhists, Catholics, expelled public officials, those who helped South Korea during the Korean War.

As a former South Korean soldier, Tae-woo's ranking was toward the bottom of the heap—not the very bottom, because those people (about 200,000, or 1 percent of the population) were permanently banished to labor camps modeled after the Soviet gulag. North Ko-reans of the lower ranks were banned from living in the showcase capital of Pyongyang or the nicer patches of countryside toward the south where the soil was more fertile and the weather warmer. Tae-woo couldn't dream of joining the Workers' Party, which, like the Communist Party in China and the Soviet Union, controlled the plum jobs.

People of his rank would be closely watched by their neighbors. North Koreans are organized into what are called the *inminban*—literally, "people's group"—cooperatives of twenty or so families whose job it is to keep tabs on one another and run the neighbor-hood. The *inminban* have an elected leader, usually a middle-aged woman, who reports anything suspicious to higher-ranking authori-ties. It was almost impossible for a North Korean of low rank to im-prove his status. Personal files were locked away in local offices of the Ministry for the Protection of State Security and, for extra safe-keeping, just in case someone dared to think of tampering with the records, in the mountainous Yanggang province. The only mobility within the class system was downward. Even if you were in the core class—reserved for relatives of the ruling family and party cadres—you could get demoted for bad behavior. But once in the hostile class, you remained there for life. Whatever your original stain, it was permanent and immutable. And just like the caste system of old Korea, family status was hereditary. The sins of the father were the sins of the children and the grandchildren.

The North Koreans called these people *beulsun*—"tainted blood," or impure.

Mi-ran and her four siblings would carry that taint in their blood. They had to expect that their horizons would be as limited as those of their father.

AS A CHILD, Mi-ran was unaware of the catastrophe that had be-fallen her even before she was born. Her parents thought it best if they said nothing at all to the children about their father's roots in South Korea. What was the point in burdening them with the knowledge that they would be barred from the best schools and the best jobs, that their lives would soon reach a dead end? Why would they bother to study hard, to practice their musical instruments or compete in sports?

North Koreans aren't informed of their classification, so it wasn't immediately obvious that there was something wrong with the fam-ily, but the children themselves suspected something peculiar about their father. He was an odd, solitary figure who seemed to carry a ponderous burden. He had no known relatives. It was not only that he wouldn't speak of the past, he hardly spoke at all. He gave mono-syllabic answers to questions; he kept his voice to a whisper. Tae-woo looked happiest when he was working with his hands, fixing something around the house, intent on a project that gave him an excuse not to speak.

There was no trace of the bossy little boy who strutted around playing general. His wife, from whom the daughters inherited their height and athleticism, did all the talking for him. If the children needed to be disciplined, if there was a complaint to be made to a neighbor, it was his wife who did it. If he had any opinions, he kept them to himself. On the occasions that they could get a newspaper, a luxury in North Korea, he would read in silence by the light of their single lamp with its 40-watt bulb. What he thought of the latest great achievement of Kim Il-sung, as touted in *Rodong Sinmun,* the official Workers' Party newspaper, or in *Hambuk Daily,* the local paper, he would not say. Had he come to believe in North Korea? Was he convinced?

Mi-ran often found her father's passivity maddening. Only later did she understand this was a survival mechanism. It was as though he had hammered down his own personality to avoid drawing undue attention to himself. Among the thousands of former South Korean soldiers who tried to assimilate into North Korean society, many slipped up. Mi-ran's mother later told her that four of her father's buddies in the mines, fellow South Koreans, had been executed for minor infractions, their bodies dumped in mass graves. Being a member of the hostile class meant you would never get the benefit of the doubt. A sarcastic inflection when referring to Kim Il-sung or a nostalgic remark about South Korea could get you in serious trouble. It was especially taboo to talk about the Korean War and who started it. In the official histories (and there was nothing but official history in North Korea), it was the South Korean Army that invaded, acting on orders from the Americans, not the North Korean Army storming across the 38th parallel. "The U.S. imperialists gave the Syngman Rhee puppet clique an order to unleash a Korean War," goes the account in *Rodong Sinmun.* Anybody who remembered what really happened on June 25, 1950 (and which Korean could forget?), knew it was wise to keep one's mouth shut.

As the children approached adolescence, the obstacles presented by their father's background began to loom larger. By age fifteen mandatory schooling is completed and students begin applying to high schools. Those not admitted are assigned to a work unit, a factory, a coal mine, or the like. But Mi-ran's siblings were confident they would be among those chosen to further their education. They were smart, good-looking, athletic, well liked by teachers and peers.

Had they been less talented, rejection might have gone down more easily.

Her eldest sister, Mi-hee, had a lovely soprano voice. Whether she was belting out one of the syrupy folk songs so beloved by Koreans or a paean to Kim Il-sung, the neighbors would come to listen. She was often asked to perform at public events. Singing is a highly valued talent in North Korea since few people have stereos. Mi-hee was so pretty that an artist came to sketch her portrait. She had every expectation that she would be selected to attend a performing arts high school. She wailed for days when she was rejected. Their mother must have known the reason, but she nevertheless marched to the school to demand an explanation. The headmaster was sympathetic, but unhelpful. She explained that only students with better *songbun* could secure placement in performing arts schools.

Mi-ran didn't have any particular artistic or athletic talent like her older sisters, but she was a good student and she was beautiful. When she was fifteen years old, her school was visited by a team of serious-looking men and women in somber suits. These were the *okwa,* members of the fifth division of the Central Workers' Party, recruiters who scoured the country looking for young women to serve on the personal staff of Kim Il-sung and Kim Jong-il. If selected, the girls would be sent off to a military-style training camp, before being assigned to one of the leadership's many residences around the country. Once accepted, they would not be permitted to visit their homes, but their families would be compensated with expensive gifts. It wasn't exactly clear what jobs these girls did. Some were said to be secretaries, maids, and entertainers; others were rumored to be concubines. Mi-ran had heard all about this from a friend whose cousin had been one of those chosen.

"You know, Kim Jong-il and Kim Il-sung, they're just men, like any others," Mi-ran's friend whispered to her. Mi-ran nodded knowingly, embarrassed to admit she was utterly mystified. North Korean girls her age didn't know what a concubine was, only that whatever you might do to serve the leadership would be a tremendous honor. Only the smartest and prettiest girls would be selected.

When the recruiters walked into the classroom, the students sat upright at their desks and waited quietly. The girls sat two to a desk, in long rows. Mi-ran wore her middle school uniform. On her feet were canvas exercise shoes. The recruiters wove in between the rows of desks, pausing from time to time to take a closer look. They slowed down when they came to Mi-ran's desk.

"You, stand up," one of the recruiters commanded. They beckoned her to follow them to the teachers' lounge. When she got there, four other girls were waiting. They looked over her files, measured her. At five foot three, Mi-ran was one of the tallest girls in the class. They peppered her with questions: How were her grades? What was her favorite subject? Was she healthy? Did anything hurt? She answered their questions calmly and, she thought, correctly.

That was the last she heard of them. Not that she really wanted to be taken away from her family, but rejection always stung.

By then, the children had come to realize that their family background was the problem. They began to suspect that their father had come from the other side of the border, because he had no relatives in the North, but under what circumstances? They assumed he must have been a committed Communist who had heroically run away to enlist with Kim Il-sung's troops. Mi-ran's brother finally forced the truth to the surface. An intense young man with permanently furrowed brows, Sok-ju had spent months cramming for an exam to win admission to the teachers' college. He knew every answer perfectly. When he was told he had failed, he angrily confronted the judges to demand an explanation.

The truth was devastating. The children had been thoroughly inculcated in the North Korean version of history. The Americans were the incarnation of evil and the South Koreans their pathetic lackeys. They'd studied photographs of their country after it had been pulverized by U.S. bombs. They'd read about how sneering American and South Korean soldiers drove their bayonets into the bodies of innocent civilians. Their textbooks at school were full of stories of people burned, crushed, stabbed, shot, and poisoned by the enemy. To learn that their own father was a South Korean who had fought with the Yankees was too much to bear. Sok-ju got drunk for the first time in his life. He ran away from home. He stayed at a friend's house for two weeks until the friend convinced him he had to return.

"He's still your father, you know," the friend urged him. Sok-ju took the words to heart. He knew, like any other Korean boy, especially an only son, that he had to revere his father. He went home and fell to his knees, begging for forgiveness. It was the first time he saw his father cry.

WHILE THE CHILDREN were slow to discover the truth about their father, they may have been the last to know. The gossips in the neighborhood had long spread the rumor that he was a South Korean soldier, and the *inminban,* the people's group, had been told to keep a watchful eye on the family. Almost as quickly as Jun-sang discovered the name of the girl he spotted at the movie theater, he heard the gossip. Jun-sang was well aware that a liaison with a girl of Mi-ran's status could hurt his prospects. He was not cowardly, but he was a dutiful son, as much a creature of the Confucian system as any other North Korean. He believed he was put on this earth to serve his father, and it was his father's ambition that he attend university in Pyongyang. He would need not only top grades, but impeccable conduct. The smallest indiscretion could derail him because his own family background was problematic, too.

Jun-sang's parents were both born in Japan, part of a population of ethnic Koreans that numbered about two million at the end of World War II. They were a cross section of Korean society—elites who had gone there to study, people who had been forcibly conscripted to help the Japanese war effort, and migrant workers. Some had gotten rich, but they were always a minority, often despised. They ached to return to the homeland, but which homeland? After the partition of Korea, the Koreans in Japan divided into two factions—those who supported South Korea and those who sympathized with North Koreans. The pro–North Koreans affiliated with a group called Chosen Soren, the General Association of Korean Residents in Japan.

For these nationalists, North Korea looked to be the true motherland because it had severed itself from the Japanese colonial past, whereas Syngman Rhee's pro-U.S. government had elevated many Japanese collaborators. And until the late 1960s, the North Korean economy looked to be much stronger. North Korean propaganda conjured up images of rosy-cheeked children playing in the fields and brand-new farm equipment hauling in abundant harvests in the miraculous new country that flourished under the wise leadership of Kim Il-sung. Today, the bright-colored posters of this genre are easy to dismiss as socialist kitsch, but back then, they proved, for many, convincing.

More than eighty thousand people were sucked in by the pitch, Jun-sang's grandparents among them. His paternal grandfather was a member of the Japanese Communist Party and had even served time in a Japanese prison for his left-wing beliefs. Too old and infirm himself to be of use to the new country, he instead sent his oldest son. Jun-sang's father landed on the shores of this brave new world in 1962 after a twenty-one-hour ferry ride across the Sea of Japan. Because he was an engineer, his skills were in great demand and he was assigned to a work unit at a factory near Chongjin. A few years later, he met an elegant young woman who had come with her parents from Japan around the same time. Jun-sang's father was homely, with sloping shoulders and pitted skin, but he was intelligent and literate. His family would say he looked like a pirate, but spoke like a poet. With kindness and persistence, he managed to woo this delicate beauty until she accepted his proposal of marriage.

Jun-sang's parents had managed to keep enough of their money to enjoy a better quality of life than most North Koreans. They had wangled for themselves a freestanding house—a luxury that afforded them a garden in which to grow vegetables. Until the 1990s, North Koreans weren't allowed to cultivate their own plots of land. Inside the house were five substantial wooden wardrobes stuffed with quality Japanese-made quilts and clothing. (North Koreans sleep on mats on the floor in the traditional Asian style, rolling up their bedding during the day and stuffing it into cabinets.) North Koreans tended to rank themselves by the number of wardrobes in their home, and five meant that you were prosperous indeed. They had more appliances than any of their neighbors—an electric fan, a television, a sewing machine, an eight-track tape player, a camera, and even a refrigerator—a rarity in a country where hardly anybody had enough fresh food to keep cold.

Most unusual, though, was that Jun-sang had a pet—a Korean breed called the poongsan, a shaggy white-haired dog that resembles a spitz. Although some Koreans in the countryside kept dogs as farm animals, raising them in large part to eat in a spicy dog-meat stew called *boshintang,* it was unheard of to have a dog as a household pet. Who could afford an extra mouth to feed?

In fact, Japanese Koreans, who were known as *kitachosenjin,* after the Japanese term for North Korea, Kita Chosen, lived in a world apart. They had distinctive accents and tended to marry one another. Although they were far from rich by Japanese standards, they were wealthy compared with ordinary North Koreans. They had arrived in the new country with leather shoes and nice woolen sweaters, while North Koreans wore canvas on their feet and shiny polyester. Their relatives regularly sent them Japanese yen, which could be used in special hard-currency shops to buy appliances. Some had even brought over automobiles, although soon enough they would break down for lack of spare parts and have to be donated to the North Korean government. Years after they arrived, Japanese Koreans received regular visits from their relatives who would travel over on the *Mangyongbong-92* ferry with money and gifts. The ferry was operated by the pro-regime Chosen Soren and its visits to North Korea were encouraged as a way of bringing currency into the country. The regime skimmed off a portion of the money sent by relatives. Yet for all their wealth, the Japanese Koreans occupied a lowly position in the North Korean hierarchy. No matter that they were avowed Communists who gave up comfortable lives in Japan, they were lumped in with the hostile class. The regime couldn't trust anyone with money who wasn't a member of the Workers' Party. They were among the few North Koreans permitted to have contact with the outside, and that in itself made them unreliable; the strength of the regime came from its ability to isolate its own citizens completely.

The new immigrants from Japan quickly shed their idealism. Some of the early immigrants who arrived in North Korea wrote letters home warning others not to come, but those letters were intercepted and destroyed. Many of the Japanese Koreans, including some prominent in Chosen Soren, ended up being purged in the early 1970s, the leaders executed, their families sent to the gulag.

Jun-sang had overheard his parents whispering these stories. When they came to take you away, there was no warning. A truck would pull up outside your house late at night. You'd get maybe an hour or two to pack up your belongings. Jun-sang lived with a fear that was so internalized that he wasn't able to articulate it, but it was ever-present. He knew by instinct to watch what he said.

He was also careful not to provoke envy. He wore thick woolen socks from Japan whereas most children had no socks at all, but he kept his feet tucked under long pants, hoping nobody would notice. He would later describe himself as a sensitive animal with big twitching ears, always on the alert for predators.

For all their warm sweaters, appliances, and blankets, Jun-sang's family was no more at ease than Mi-ran's. His mother, who had been a pretty and popular teenager when she'd left Japan, grew increasingly wistful about her lost girlhood as she aged. After the birth of her four children, she never recovered her health. In the evening, Jun-sang's father would sit and smoke, sighing glumly. It was not that they thought anyone was listening—one of the advantages of a free-standing house was a certain degree of privacy—but they wouldn't dare give voice to what they really felt. They couldn't come out and say that they wanted to leave this socialist paradise to go back to capitalist Japan.

So the unspoken hung over the household: the realization sank in deeper with each passing day that a terrible mistake had been made in going to North Korea. Returning to Japan was impossible, they knew, so they had to make the best of a bad situation. The only way to redeem the family would be to play the system and try to climb the social ladder. The family's hopes rested on Jun-sang. If only he could get himself to university in Pyongyang, perhaps he would eventually be permitted to join the Workers' Party and then the family might be forgiven their bourgeois Japanese past. The constant pressure left Jun-sang nervous and indecisive. He fantasized about the girl he'd seen at the movie theater and debated whether to approach her, but ended up doing nothing.

CHAPTER 3

THE TRUE BELIEVER

The USS *Missouri* firing on Chongjin, October 1950.

CHONGJIN IS A CITY WITH A BAD REPUTATION, AN UNDESIRABLE place to live even by North Korean standards. The city of 500,000 is wedged between a granite spine of mountains zigzagging up and down the coast and the Sea of Japan, which Koreans call the East Sea. The coastline has the rugged beauty of Maine, and its glistening waters run deep and cold, but fishing is treacherous without a sturdy boat. The wind-whipped mountains support few crops, and temperatures in the winter can plunge to 40 degrees below (Fahrenheit). Only the land around the low-lying coast can grow rice, the staple food around which Korean culture revolves. Historically, Koreans have measured their success in life by their proximity to power—part of a long Asian tradition of striving to get off the farm and close to the imperial palace. Chongjin is practically off the map of Korea, so far north that it is nearer to the Russian city of Vladivostok than to Pyongyang. Even today, the drive between Chongjin and Pyongyang, just 250 miles apart, can take three days over the unpaved mountain roads, with dangerous hairpin turns.

During the Chosun dynasty, when the Korean capital was even farther away—on the site of present-day Seoul—officials who incurred the wrath of the emperor were exiled to this outlying fringe of the realm. Perhaps as a result of all these malcontents in the gene pool, what is now North Hamgyong province is thought to breed the toughest, hardest-to-subdue Koreans anywhere.

Until the twentieth century, this northernmost province of Korea, extending all the way to the Tumen River, its border with China and Russia, was sparsely populated and of little economic significance. The province's human population was most likely outnumbered by tigers in centuries past, the beasts that still terrify small children in Korean folktales. Today, though, the animals themselves are long gone. All that changed when the Japanese set their sights on empire building. North Hamgyong province lay right in the pathway of Japan's eventual push toward Manchuria, which it would occupy in the run-up to World War II. The Japanese also coveted the largely unexploited coal and iron-ore deposits around Musan and they would need to ship their booty from the occupied peninsula back home. Chongjin, just a small fishing village (the name comes from the Chinese characters for "clear river crossing"), was transformed into a port that could handle three million tons of freight each year. During the occupation (1910–45), the Japanese built massive steelworks at Chongjin's port, and farther south they developed Nanam, a planned city with a rectangular street grid and large modern buildings. The Imperial Japanese Army's 19th infantry division, which assisted in the invasion of eastern China, was headquartered there. Farther down the coast, they built virtually from scratch the city of Hamhung as the headquarters of massive chemical factories producing everything from gunpowder to fertilizer.

After the Communists came to power in the 1950s, they rebuilt the factories that had been bombed in the successive wars and reclaimed them as their own. Chongjin's Nippon Steel became Kimchaek Iron and Steel, the largest factory in North Korea. Kim Il-sung pointed to the industrial might of the northeast as a shining example of his economic achievements. To this day, Chongjin residents know little of their city's history—indeed, it seems to be a place without any past at all—because the North Korean regime does not credit the Japanese for anything. Within the Democratic People's Republic of Korea, Chongjin's prestige and population continued to grow, making it by the 1970s the second-largest city in the country, with a population of 900,000. (The population is believed to have since slipped to about 500,000, making Chongjin the third-largest city, behind Hamhung.)

Chongjin, the "city of iron," as it was sometimes called, was a city of increasing economic and strategic importance with its steel and iron works. Its factories made watches, televisions, synthetic fibers, pharmaceuticals, machine tools, tractors, plows, steel plates, and munitions. Crabs, squid, and other marine products were fished for export. The port was taken over for shipbuilding. Up and down the coast, the North Koreans took over the Japanese military installations and built bases for missiles that would be aimed at Japan. And yet the surrounding villages remained dumping grounds for exiles—members of the hostile and wavering classes, like Mi-ran's father, were settled in the mining towns. A city of this importance, however, could not be left to unreliable people. The regime needed loyal cadres from the core classes to make sure that Chongjin toed the party line. Chongjin had its own ruling elite. They lived in close proximity—although not side by side—with the outcasts. The interplay between these two populations at the extreme ends of North Korean society would give Chongjin a unique dynamic.

SONG HEE-SUK WAS one of the true believers. A factory worker and mother of four, she was a model citizen of North Korea. She spouted the slogans of Kim Il-sung without a flicker of doubt. She was a stickler for rules. Mrs. Song (as she would call herself later in life; North Korean women do not take their husband's surnames) was so enthusiastic in her embrace of the regime one could almost imagine her as the heroine of a propaganda film. In her youth, she looked the part, too—the quintessential North Korean woman. She

THE TRUE BELIEVER | 39

was a type preferred by casting directors at Kim Jong-il's film studios: she had a face as plump as a dumpling, which made her look well fed even when she wasn't, and a bow-shaped mouth that made her look happy even when she was sad. Her button of a nose and bright, earnest eyes made her look trusting and sincere—and in fact she was.

Well past the point when it should have been obvious that the system had failed her, she remained unwavering in her faith. "I lived only for Marshal Kim Il-sung and for the fatherland. I never had a thought otherwise," she told me the first time we met.

Mrs. Song was born on the last day of World War II, August 15, 1945. She grew up in Chongjin near the railroad station, where her father worked as a mechanic. When the Korean War broke out, the station became a major bombing target as the American-led U.N. forces tried to break the Communists' supply and communications lines along the coast. The USS *Missouri* and other battleships plied the waters of the Sea of Japan, firing into Chongjin and other coastal cities. U.S. warplanes roared overhead, terrifying the children. Sometimes they flew so low Mrs. Song could see the pilots. During the daytime, Mrs. Song's mother would drag her six small children up to the mountains to keep them out of harm's way. By night, they'd return to sleep in a shelter the neighbors had dug outside their house. Mrs. Song used to tremble under her thin blanket, snuggling next to her mother and siblings for protection. One day her mother left the children alone to find out how their father was doing. The night before there had been heavy bombing and one of the factories that made railroad parts had been demolished. She came back weeping, falling to her knees, lowering her head to the ground. "Your father has been killed," she wailed, gathering the children around her.

Her father's death gave Mrs. Song a pedigree as the child of a "martyr of the Fatherland Liberation War." The family even got a certificate. It also stamped her psyche with the indelible anti-Americanism that was so central to the country's ideology. Having spent her impressionable years in the chaos of war, she was ready to embrace the meticulous ordering of her life by the Workers' Party. And she certainly was poor enough to qualify as a member of the downtrodden underclass that Kim Il-sung claimed to represent. It was only fitting that a girl with such impeccable Communist credentials would make an excellent marriage. She was introduced to her future husband by a Workers' Party official. Her intended, Chang-bo, was also a party member—she wouldn't have dreamed of marrying a man who wasn't. His father had a good war record as a member of the North Korean intelligence; his younger brother had already joined the North Korean Ministry of Public Security. Chang-bo was a graduate of Kim Il-sung University and was headed for a career in journalism, a highly prestigious profession in North Korea since journalists were considered the mouthpieces of the regime. "Those who write in accordance with the party's intention are heroes," Kim Jong-il proclaimed.

Chang-bo was a strapping man, exceptionally tall for a North Korean of his generation. Mrs. Song was barely five feet and could nestle under his arm like a little bird. It was a good match. This handsome, politically correct young couple would have easily qualified to live in Pyongyang. Because Pyongyang is the only North Korean city frequented by foreigners, the regime goes to great lengths to ensure that its inhabitants make a good impression with their appearance and are ideologically sound. Instead, it was decided that the couple was needed to fill out the ranks of the stalwarts in Chongjin and so they were settled there with certain privileges in the best neighborhood in town.

For all the supposed egalitarianism of North Korea, real estate is doled out according to the same hierarchical principles as the class-background registers. The less-desirable neighborhoods are in the south near the coal and kaolin mines where the working stiffs lived in squat whitewashed harmonica houses. Farther north, everything becomes more imposing. As the main road runs through Nanam, the buildings are taller, some up to eighteen stories, the height of modernity at the time they were built. The builders even left shafts for elevators, although they never got around to installing the elevator cabs themselves. The architectural designs for many of the postwar apartments came from East Germany, with adaptations for Korean culture. Between the stories, extra space was provided for the Korean underfloor heating system, and apartment buildings were equipped with loudspeakers in the individual units to broad-cast community notices.

Chongjin is far from the modernity of Pyongyang, but it has its own aura of power. Now the capital of North Hamgyong province, it has large administrative offices for the province and Workers' Party. The bureaucratic center is laid out in an orderly grid. There is a university, a metallurgy college, a mining college, an agricultural college, an arts college, a foreign languages college, a medical school, three teachers' colleges, a dozen theaters, and a museum of revolutionary history devoted to the life of Kim Il-sung. Across from the east port is the Chonmasan Hotel for foreign visitors and near that a Russian consulate. The streets and squares in the city center were designed in the ostentatiously oversized style favored in Moscow and other Communist cities that conveys the power of the regime over the individual.

The main thoroughfare known simply as Road No. 1 running the width of the city is so broad it could easily accommodate six lanes of traffic if there were that many cars in Chongjin. On both sides, spaced at regular intervals like sentries on guard duty, are large plane and acacia trees, the lower part of the trunks painted white. The white paint is variously said to keep away insects, protect the tree against harsh temperatures, or to assert that the tree is government property and cannot be chopped for firewood. The curbs are also painted white. Interspersed between the trees are the familiar red signposts with propaganda slogans and behind them soaring street lamps that are seldom switched on. The sidewalks are as broad as the Champs-Élysées—this is supposed to be a grand boulevard, after all—although many pedestrians choose to walk in the road since there is little traffic. There are no traffic lights, instead uniformed traffic police who perform robotic calisthenics with their arms to direct the few cars. The main road comes to a T-stop in front of the North Hamgyong Province Theater, a grand building topped by a twelve-foot-high portrait of Kim Il-sung. Behind the theater, the city comes to an abrupt end where it is hemmed in by Mount Naka to the northeast. These days, the mountainside is dotted with graves and most of the trees have been chopped for firewood, but it still makes for a pleasant setting. In fact, Chongjin's downtown, even today, makes a positive first impression, but a closer inspection reveals that chunks of concrete have fallen off the buildings, the streetlights all tilt precariously in different directions, and the trams are cratered with dents, but the few visitors to Chongjin whiz by so quickly that these sights are easily missed.

Mrs. Song's apartment was on the second floor of an eight-story building that had no elevators. When she first saw it Mrs. Song was amazed to learn that the building had indoor plumbing—regular people like her had never seen anything so modern in the 1960s. Heating radiated up from under the floor as in a traditional Korean house, but it came from water heated by a hydroelectric plant and piped through the building. The young couple didn't have much in the way of furniture, but they had two separate rooms, one for themselves and another for their growing number of children. Their first daughter, Oak-hee, was born in 1966, followed two years later by another daughter and then another. North Korean medicine was sufficiently developed by this time that most urban women gave birth in the hospital, but Mrs. Song, despite her soft appearance, was built of strong stuff. She delivered all her children by herself without even the help of a midwife. One was born on the side of the road—Mrs. Song had been walking home with a basket of laundry. With the first birth, her mother-in-law cooked her a soup with slimy ribbons of seaweed, a traditional Korean recipe to help a new mother recover her iron. The next time her mother-in-law—disappointed by the birth of another girl—threw the seaweed at Mrs. Song to make the soup herself. After the third girl, she stopped speaking to her.

"You're doomed to have nothing but girls," she snapped as her parting shot.

Mrs. Song persevered. The fourth child arrived one afternoon when she was home alone in the apartment. She had left work early that day because her belly was hurting, but she hated to be idle, so she began to scrub the floors. A sharp pain surged through her body and she rushed toward the bathroom. A boy, at last. Mrs. Song was redeemed in the eyes of her family. This time her mother-in-law cooked the seaweed soup.

Chang-bo was on a business trip and received a message the next day. He caught the first train home, stopping on the way to buy a child's bicycle—a gift for the brand-new baby.

Despite having four children and keeping house, Mrs. Song worked full-time six days a week at the Chosun Clothing factory in Pohang as a clerk in the bookkeeping department of the factory's day-care center. Women were expected to keep the factories going, since North Korea was perpetually short of men—an estimated 20 percent of working-age men were in the armed services, the largest per capita military in the world. Mrs. Song usually went to work with one baby strapped to her back and one or two others dragging along behind her. Her children basically grew up at the day-care center. She was supposed to work eight hours with a lunch break and nap in the middle of her shift. After work, she had to spend several more hours in ideological training in the factory's auditorium. One day the lecture might be about the struggle against U.S. imperialism; another time it might be about Kim Il-sung's exploits (actual or exaggerated) fighting the Japanese during World War II. She had to write essays on the latest pronouncements of the Workers' Party or analyze the day's editorials in the *Hambuk Ilbo* newspaper. By the time she got home, it would be 10:30 P.M. She would do her housework and cooking, then get up before dawn to prepare herself and her family for the day ahead before leaving home at 7:00 A.M. She seldom slept more than five hours. Some days were harder than others. On Wednesday mornings, she had to report to work early for mandatory meetings of the Socialist Women's Federation. Friday nights she stayed especially late for self-criticism. In these sessions, members of her work unit—the department to which she was assigned—would stand up and reveal to the group anything they had done wrong. It was the Communist version of the Catholic confessional. Mrs. Song would usually say, in all sincerity, that she feared she wasn't working hard enough.

Mrs. Song believed what she said. All those years of sleep deprivation, all those lectures and self-criticisms—the very same tools used in brainwashing or interrogations—had wiped out any possibility of resistance. She had been molded into one of Kim Il-sung's improved human beings. Kim Il-sung's goal wasn't merely to build a new country; he wanted to build better people, to reshape human nature. To that end, he created his own philosophical system, *juche,* which is commonly translated as "self-reliance." *Juche* drew on Marx's and Lenin's ideas about the struggle between landlord and peasant, between rich and poor. It similarly declared that man, not God, shaped his own fate. But Kim Il-sung rejected traditional Communist teachings about universalism and internationalism. He was a Korean nationalist in the extreme. He instructed Koreans that they were special—almost a chosen people—and that they no longer had to rely on their more powerful neighbors, China, Japan, or Russia. The South Koreans were a disgrace because of their dependence on the United States. "Establishing *juche* means, in a nutshell, being the master of revolution and reconstruction in one's own country. This means holding fast to an independent position, rejecting dependence on others, using one's own brains, believing in one's own strength, displaying the revolutionary spirit of self-reliance," he expounded in one of his many treatises. This was seductive to a proud people whose dignity had been trampled by its neighbors for centuries.

Once in power, Kim Il-sung retooled the ideas developed during his time as an anti-Japanese guerrilla fighter as instruments of social control. He instructed North Koreans that their power as human beings came from subsuming their individual will to that of the collective. The collective couldn't go off willy-nilly doing whatever the people chose through some democratic process. The people had to follow an absolute, supreme leader without question. That leader, of course, was Kim Il-sung himself.

And still it was not enough; Kim Il-sung also wanted love. Murals in vivid poster colors showed him surrounded by pink-cheeked children looking on with adoration as he bestowed on them a pearly-toothed, ear-to-ear grin. Toys and bicycles clutter the background of these images—Kim Il-sung didn't want to be Joseph Stalin; he wanted to be Santa Claus. His dimpled cheeks made him appear more cuddly than other dictators. He was to be regarded as a father, in the Confucian sense of commanding respect and love. He wanted to ingratiate himself into North Korean families as their own flesh and blood. This kind of Confucian communism bore greater resemblance to the culture of imperial Japan, where the emperor was the sun to which all subjects bowed, than to anything envisioned by Karl Marx.

To a certain extent, all dictatorships are alike. From Stalin's Soviet Union to Mao's China, from Ceaușescu's Romania to Saddam Hussein's Iraq, all these regimes had the same trappings: the statues looming over every town square, the portraits hung in every office, the wristwatches with the dictator's face on the dial. But Kim Il-sung took the cult of personality to a new level. What distinguished him in the rogues' gallery of twentieth-century dictators was his ability to harness the power of faith. Kim Il-sung understood the power of religion. His maternal uncle was a Protestant minister back in the pre-Communist days when Pyongyang had such a vibrant Christian community that it was called the "Jerusalem of the East." Once in power, Kim Il-sung closed the churches, banned the Bible, deported believers to the hinterlands, and appropriated Christian imagery and dogma for the purpose of self-promotion.

Broadcasters would speak of Kim Il-sung or Kim Jong-il breathlessly, in the manner of Pentecostal preachers. North Korean newspapers carried tales of supernatural phenomena. Stormy seas were said to be calmed when sailors clinging to a sinking ship sang songs in praise of Kim Il-sung. When Kim Jong-il went to the DMZ, a mysterious fog descended to protect him from lurking South Korean snipers. He caused trees to bloom and snow to melt. If Kim Il-sung was God, then Kim Jong-il was the son of God. Like Jesus Christ, Kim Jong-il's birth was said to have been heralded by a radiant star in the sky and the appearance of a beautiful double rainbow. A swallow descended from heaven to sing of the birth of a "general who will rule the world."

North Korea invites parody. We laugh at the excesses of the propaganda and the gullibility of the people. But consider that their indoctrination began in infancy, during the fourteen-hour days spent in factory day-care centers; that for the subsequent fifty years, every song, film, newspaper article, and billboard was designed to deify

Kim Il-sung; that the country was hermetically sealed to keep out anything that might cast doubt on Kim Il-sung's divinity. Who could possibly resist?

IN 1972, ON THE occasion of his sixtieth birthday, a traditional milestone in Korean culture, the Workers' Party began distributing lapel pins of Kim Il-sung. Before long, the entire population was required to wear them on the left breast, over the heart. In Mrs. Song's home, as in every other, a framed portrait of Kim Il-sung hung on an otherwise bare wall. People were not permitted to put anything else on that wall, not even pictures of their blood relatives. Kim Il-sung was all the family you needed—at least until the 1980s, when portraits of Kim Jong-il, named secretary of the Workers' Party, were hung alongside those of his father. Later came a third portrait, of the father and son together. The North Korean newspapers liked to run "human interest stories" about heroic citizens who lost their lives rescuing the portraits from fire or flood. The Workers' Party distributed the portraits free of charge along with a white cloth to be stored in a box beneath them. It could be used only to clean the portraits. This was especially important during the rainy season, when specks of mold would creep under the corners of the glass frame. About once a month, inspectors from the Public Standards Police would drop by to check on the cleanliness of the portraits.

Mrs. Song didn't need the threat of an inspection to clean her portraits. Even in the mad scramble of the mornings, rolling up the bed mats, making lunches, hustling the children out the door, she would give the portraits a quick swab with the cloth. Other women disliked wearing their Kim Il-sung pins because they often made holes and rust stains on their clothing, but not Mrs. Song. One day after she'd changed clothes in a hurry, she ran out without her badge and was stopped by a teenager wearing an armband that identified him as part of the Maintenance of Social Order brigade. These were Socialist Youth League vigilantes who made spot checks to see if people were wearing their badges. First offenders were usually forced to attend extra ideological lectures and got a black mark on their record. But Mrs. Song was so genuinely horrified to realize she'd left the badge at home that the boy let her go with just a warning.

Mrs. Song tried to live her life according to Kim Il-sung's teachings, which she had memorized during all those evenings in the factory's study hall. Even her everyday conversation was peppered with their aphorisms. "Loyalty and filial devotion are the supreme qualities of a revolutionary" was a particularly handy quote for taming a rebellious child. The children were never to forget that they owed everything to the national leadership. Like other North Korean children, they didn't celebrate their own birthdays, but those of Kim Il-sung on April 15 and Kim Jong-il on February 16. These days were national holidays and they were often the only days people would get meat in their ration packages. Later, after the energy crisis began, these were the only days there was electricity. A few days before each birthday, the Workers' Party would distribute to every child more than two pounds of sweets. It was a truly impressive gift for kids, all kinds of cookies, jellies, chocolates, and chewing gums. These treats weren't to be eaten until the day of the birthday, but some mothers ignored that, though Mrs. Song went by the book. When the time came, the children lined up in front of the portraits to express their gratitude. In unison, they would bend from the waist, bowing deeply, with feeling.

"Thank you, dear father Kim Il-sung," the children repeated as their mother looked on with satisfaction.

Years later, Mrs. Song looked back at this time with nostalgia. She considered herself lucky. Chang-bo proved to be a good husband. He didn't sleep around. He didn't hit Mrs. Song or the children. He enjoyed his drink, but was a cheerful drunk, cracking jokes as the laughter rippled down his increasingly ample belly. They were a happy family full of love. Mrs. Song loved her three daughters, her son, her husband, and, at times, even her mother-in-law. And she loved Kim Il-sung.

Mrs. Song would take away from those years a few cherished memories. There was the very occasional Sunday when neither she nor Chang-bo reported to work, when the children were not in school and they could spend time together as a family. Twice, in those years, they managed to go to the beach, which was only a few miles from their apartment. Nobody in the family could swim, but they walked on the sand, picking up clams, which they took home and steamed for dinner. Once, when her son was eleven years old, she took him to Chongjin's zoo. It was a place she had visited on a school trip. She remembered seeing tigers, elephants, bears, and a wolf when she'd gone as a child, but now there were only a few birds left. Mrs. Song never went back.

The complications began when Mrs. Song's children reached adolescence. The most difficult of the four was her oldest daughter. Oak-hee was the spitting image of Mrs. Song—she was built compact and round, buxom and pretty. But on Oak-hee the same plump lips were fixed in a petulant pout. Her personality was all sharp edges. Instead of her mother's forgiving nature, she had a keen sense of outrage and seemed permanently aggrieved. As the oldest daughter of a working mother absent from the house from dawn until late at night, Oak-hee had to assume much of the housework, and she didn't do it cheerfully. Oak-hee wasn't a martyr like her mother. She couldn't tolerate the small stupidities that made life so grueling. It wasn't that she was lazy so much as rebellious. She refused to do anything she thought pointless.

She complained about the "volunteer work" that North Korean teenagers were expected to perform out of their patriotic duty. Starting at the age of twelve, kids were mobilized in battalions and sent out to the countryside for rice planting and transplanting and weeding. She dreaded springtime, when she had to hoist buckets of soil and spray pesticides that stung her eyes. While the other kids were cheerfully singing "Let Us Safeguard Socialism" as they marched, Oak-hee glowered in silence.

The absolute worst was when it came to collecting "night soil" from the toilets in the apartment building. North Korea was chronically short of chemical fertilizer and needed to use human excrement since there were few farm animals. Each family had to provide a bucketful each week, delivered to a warehouse miles away. In exchange, you were given a chit certifying that you'd done your duty and that chit would later be traded for food. This foul-smelling chore was usually assigned to the older children, so Oak-hee set her considerable imagination to finding a short cut. Actually, it turned out to be easy to cheat. The warehouse where the full buckets were submitted was not guarded (after all, who wanted to steal a bucket of shit?). Oak-hee figured out that she could sneak in, grab a full bucket, and then submit it as her own and collect her chit.

Oak-hee cheerfully boasted about the ruse when she got home. Mrs. Song was furious over the deception. She'd always known that Oak-hee was the most clever of her four children—she could read by the age of three and impressed their relatives by memorizing long passages from Kim Il-sung's writings. But the incident with the night soil confirmed her mother's fears that Oak-hee was an individualist who lacked the collective spirit. How was she to survive in a society where everybody was supposed to march in step?

After Oak-hee finished high school, Mrs. Song's husband used his connections to get her a job with a construction company's propaganda department. Oak-hee had to write up reports about work teams that were exceeding their quotas and the remarkable progress that the company was making building roads. The company had its own sound truck, actually a broken-down army van with slogans plastered on its side ("Let us model the whole society on the *juche* idea"). As the truck cruised by construction sites, Oak-hee would take the microphone and read her reports, broadcasting the achievements of the company through screechy loudspeakers. It was a fun job that didn't require any heavy lifting and, like any position in the propaganda department, carried some prestige.

Mrs. Song and her husband sought to further secure Oak-hee's future by finding her a suitable husband in the Workers' Party. Mrs. Song hoped to find someone just like her own husband, so she instructed Chang-bo to look around for a younger version of himself. While he was taking a train to Musan on a business trip, he sat next to an engaging young man. Choi Yong-su came from a good family in Rajin, a city just north of Chongjin. He was a civilian employee of the Korean People's Army, a musician who played the trumpet. Anybody with a military position above the rank and file had some clout in North Korea and was sure to get into the party. Chang-bo thought the young man looked promising and invited him home to visit.

Oak-hee and Yong-su got married in 1988 in the traditional North Korean style—in front of the statue of Kim Il-sung, who symbolically presided over all marriages in the absence of clergy. They put on their best clothes—she a beige jacket and black trousers, and Yong-su a dark suit—and stood stiffly side by side to pose for a photograph in front of the towering bronze statue. They deposited a bouquet of flowers and considered their union to have been blessed in spirit by the Great Leader. They went back to the family apartment to gorge themselves on a banquet prepared by Mrs. Song. The tradition was to have two receptions, at the homes of the bride and groom, a bit of a competition for each family to show off. These were expensive affairs since neighbors and co-workers were invited and the bride's family had to provide a cupboard full of quilts, kitchenware, a mirror, and makeup table, and if the family was wealthy, perhaps a sewing machine or appliances. Mrs. Song was feeling insecure; she knew Yong-su's family was of a higher class, so she went all out to make a good impression. She'd laid out tables full of food—rice cakes, pollack, boiled octopus, fried tofu, hairy crab, and three varieties of dried squid. It was the most lavish meal the family would ever eat together and it might have been the high point of the marriage.

Yong-su turned out to have a taste for *neungju,* a cheap home-brewed corn liquor. After downing a few cups, his lighthearted musician's charm would vanish and a mean streak would overtake him. The swagger that Oak-hee at first found seductive now felt menacing. The young couple had moved into their own apartment near the railroad station, but Oak-hee often ran back home. One day she would show up with a black eye, the next with a split lip. Within six months of the marriage, Yong-su got into a fight with a co-worker and was expelled from the military band. He was sent to work at the iron-ore mines at Musan. He now had no chance of joining the Workers' Party. You had to apply for membership in your twenties and undergo review by your party secretary. Without party membership, Yong-su's career path would be limited. Oak-hee, who was by then in a difficult pregnancy, had to give up her job. Her situation was more precarious than ever.

—

NOT LONG AFTER, Mrs. Song's son began to give her grief too. Unlike Oak-hee, he had always been the model child. Nam-oak was a sturdy boy who resembled his father, muscular with an impressive height of five foot nine. He rarely raised his voice or quarreled. Whatever his parents or older sisters instructed, he would do without complaint. Oak-hee marveled that the same set of parents could have produced a child so unlike herself. "He's so quiet you don't even know he's there," she would say about her kid brother. Nam-oak was only a middling student, but he excelled at sports. He was happiest playing by himself, kicking a ball again and again against the concrete wall of the apartment building. At the age of eleven, a coach measured the length of his forearms and legs and tapped him for a special athletic school in Chongjin. It was in keeping with the Communist approach to competitive sports that the regime—not the families—decided which children would be plucked out of regular schooling to be groomed for the national teams. Nam-oak did well enough that at fourteen he was sent to Pyongyang to train in boxing.

For the next seven years, Nam-oak was permitted to come home only twice a year, each time for a twelve-day vacation. Mrs. Song barely saw him. He was never one to cry on her shoulder like her daughters, but now he seemed like a complete stranger. Then she got wind of a disturbing rumor. Nam-oak had a girlfriend in Chongjin, a woman five years older than himself. When he came home from Pyongyang, he would often stay in her apartment. This was scandalous on two counts: North Korean men didn't as a rule date older women, and premarital sex was strongly discouraged. Nam-oak could be kicked out of school or expelled from the Socialist Youth League, thereby ruining his chances for future entry into the Workers' Party. As the only son, he carried the responsibility of making a good match and continuing the family line. Mrs. Song and her husband tried to question him, but all they got was uncomfortable silence. Nam-oak became increasingly alienated from his own family, sometimes not even bothering to visit on vacations.

Next, Chang-bo had a brush with the law. One night he and Mrs. Song were home watching the television news with some neighbors. Mrs. Song and her husband were among the few families in their apartment building to own their own television set. In 1989, televisions cost the equivalent of three months' salary, about $175, and you weren't allowed to buy one without special permission from your work unit. They were usually bestowed by the government in the name of Kim Il-sung as a reward for extraordinary service. Chang-bo got theirs because his father had been an intelligence officer who had infiltrated the south during the Korean War. The set was manufactured by the Japanese company Hitachi, but had a Korean brand name, *Songnamu*, meaning "pine tree." Televisions and radios in North Korea are preset so that they can receive only official government channels. Still, the programming was relatively entertaining. Besides the usual speeches of Kim Il-sung, on a typical weeknight you might have sports, concerts, television dramas, and movies produced by Kim Jong-il's film studio. On weekends, you might get a Russian movie as a special treat. Mrs. Song and her husband were proud of their television. They usually left the door open to their apartment when it was on so that neighbors could wander in and watch with them. It was in keeping with the collective spirit of the times.

The program that got Chang-bo in trouble was an innocuous business report about a shoe factory producing rubber boots for the rainy season. The camera panned over crisply efficient workers on an assembly line where the boots were being produced by the thousands. The narrator raved about the superb quality of the boots and reeled off the impressive production statistics.

"Hah. If there are so many boots, how come my children never got any?" Chang-bo laughed aloud. The words tumbled out of his mouth before he could consider the consequences.

Mrs. Song never figured out which neighbor blabbed. Her husband's remark was quickly reported to the head of the *inminban*, the neighborhood watchdogs, who in turn passed on the information to the Ministry for the Protection of State Security. This ominously named agency is effectively North Korea's political police. It runs an extensive network of informers. By the accounts of defectors, there is at least one informer for every fifty people—more even than East Germany's notorious Stasi, whose files were pried open after German reunification.

Spying on one's countrymen is something of a national pastime. There were the young vigilantes from the Socialist Youth League like the one who stopped Mrs. Song for not wearing a badge. They also made sure people weren't violating the dress code by wearing blue jeans or T-shirts with Roman writing—considered a capitalist indulgence—or wearing their hair too long. The party issued regular edicts saying that men shouldn't allow the hair on top of their head to grow longer than five centimeters—though an exemption was granted for balding men, who were permitted seven centimeters. If a violation was severe, the offender could be arrested by the Public Standards Police. There were also *kyuch'aldae,* mobile police units who roamed the streets looking for offenders and had the right to barge into people's houses without notice. They would look for people who used more than their quota of electricity, a lightbulb brighter than 40 watts, a hot plate, or a rice cooker. During one of the surprise inspections, one of the neighbors tried to hide their hot plate under a blanket and ended up setting their apartment on fire. The mobile police often dropped in after midnight to see if there were any overnight guests who might have come to visit without travel permits. It was a serious offense, even if it was just an out-of-town relative, and much worse if the guest happened to be a lover. But it wasn't just the police and the volunteer leagues who did the snooping. Everybody was supposed to be vigilant for subversive behavior and transgressions of the rules. Since the country was too poor and the power supply too unreliable for electronic surveillance, state security relied on human intelligence—snitches. The newspapers would occasionally run feature stories about heroic children who ratted out their parents. To be denounced by a neighbor for bad-mouthing the regime was nothing extraordinary.

Chang-bo's interrogation lasted three days. The agents yelled and cursed at him, although they never beat him—at least that's what he told his wife. He claimed afterward that his gift with language helped him talk his way out of the bind. He cited the truth in his defense.

"I wasn't insulting anybody. I was simply saying that I haven't been able to buy those boots and I'd like to have some for my family," Chang-bo protested indignantly.

He made a convincing case. He was a commanding figure with his potbelly and his stern expression. He looked like the epitome of a Workers' Party official. The political police in the end decided not to push the case and released him without charges.

When he returned home, he got a tongue-lashing from his wife that was almost harsher than the interrogation. It was the worst fight of their marriage. For Mrs. Song, it was not merely that her husband had been disrespectful of the government; for the first time in her life, she felt the stirrings of fear. Her conduct had always been so impeccable and her devotion so genuine that it never occurred to her that she might be vulnerable.

"Why did you say such nonsense when there were neighbors in the apartment? Didn't you realize you could have jeopardized everything we have?" she railed at him.

In fact, they both realized how lucky they were. If not for Chang-bo's excellent class background and his party membership, he would not have been let off so lightly. It helped, too, that Mrs. Song had at various times been head of the *inminban* in the building and commanded some respect from the state security officers. Chang-bo's offhand remark was precisely the kind of thing that could result in deportation to a prison camp in the mountains if the offender didn't have a solid position in the community. They had heard of a man who cracked a joke about Kim Jong-il's height and was sent away for life. Mrs. Song personally knew a woman from her factory who was taken away for something she wrote in her diary. At the time, Mrs. Song hadn't felt any pity for the woman. "The traitor probably deserved what she got," she'd said to herself. Now she felt embarrassed for having thought such a thing.

The incident seemed to blow over. Chastened by the experience, Chang-bo was more careful about what he said outside the family, but his thoughts were running wild. For many years, Chang-bo had been fighting off the doubts that would periodically creep into his consciousness. Now those doubts were gelling into outright disbelief. As a journalist, Chang-bo had more access to information than ordinary people. At the North Hamgyong Provincial Broadcasting Company, where he worked, he and his colleagues heard uncensored news reports from the foreign media. It was their job to sanitize it for domestic consumption. Anything positive that happened in capitalist countries or especially South Korea, which in 1988 hosted the Summer Olympics, was downplayed. Strikes, disasters, riots, murders—elsewhere—got plenty of coverage.

Chang-bo's job was to report business stories. He toured collective farms, shops, and factories with a notebook and tape recorder, interviewing the managers. Back in the newsroom, he would write his stories in fountain pen (there were no typewriters) about how well the economy was doing. He always put a positive spin on the facts, although he tried to keep them at least plausible. By the time they were edited by his superiors in Pyongyang, however, any glimmer of the truth was gone. Chang-bo knew better than anyone that the supposed triumphs of the North Korean economy were fabrications. He had good reason to scoff at the report about the rubber boots.

He had one trusted friend from the radio station who shared his increasing disdain for the regime. When the two of them got together, Chang-bo would open a bottle of Mrs. Song's *neungju* and, after a few drinks, they would let rip their true feelings.

"What a bunch of liars!" Chang-bo would say in an emphatic tone, taking care just the same not to speak loudly enough for the sound to carry through the thin plaster walls between the apartments.

"Crooks, all of them."

"The son is even worse than the father."

Oak-hee eavesdropped on her father and his friend. She nodded quietly in agreement. When her father noticed, he at first tried to shoo her away. Eventually he gave up. Swearing her to secrecy, he took her into his confidence. He told her that Kim Il-sung was not the anti-Japanese resistance fighter he claimed to be so much as a puppet of the Soviet Union. He told her that South Korea was now among the richest countries in Asia; even ordinary working people owned their own cars. Communism, he reported, was proving a failure as an economic system. China and the Soviet Union were now embracing capitalism. Father and daughter would talk for hours, always taking care to keep their voices at a whisper in case a neighbor was snooping around. And, at such times, they always made sure that Mrs. Song, the true believer, was not at home.

CHAPTER 4

FADE TO BLACK

The industrial district of Chongjin.

As THE YEAR 1990 OPENED, THE BERLIN WALL HAD BEEN reduced to chunks of rubble hawked by souvenir vendors in a soon-to-be-reunited Germany. The Soviet Union was being wrenched apart at the seams. Mao Zedong's face was an iconic image on kitschy watches that American tourists bought in Beijing. The former Communist dictator of Romania, Nicolae Ceaușescu, not coincidentally a close personal friend of Kim Il-sung's, had recently been executed by a firing squad. Statues of Lenin were being pulled off their pedestals and smashed to pieces. Communist Party cadres around the world were gobbling up Big Macs for lunch and washing them down with Coca-Cola. In the hermit kingdom of North Korea, however, life carried on as it always had.

To the extent that North Korea's censors allowed in reports of communism's demise, they were watered down and twisted with a distinctive spin. As far as the *Rodong Sinmun* was concerned, the troubles elsewhere in the Communist bloc were due to the inherent weakness of the people. (The North Korean press always liked to allude to the genetic superiority of Koreans.) The Eastern Europeans and the Chinese weren't as strong by nature or as disciplined. They had deviated from the true path of socialism. If they had a genius on the order of Kim Il-sung to guide them, their Communist systems would be intact and thriving. In keeping with his teachings about self-reliance, North Koreans had to ignore what other countries were doing and continue on their own path.

So Mrs. Song squeezed her eyes shut, willing herself blind to the unmistakable signs that something was amiss. At first the clues were small, barely noticeable. The lightbulb that blinked out for a few seconds, then minutes, then hours, then days. The electricity became increasingly sporadic until you could expect only a few hours, a few nights a week. The running water stopped. Mrs. Song quickly figured out that when the water came on she'd better fill up as many buckets and pots as she could. But it was never enough for washing because the water pumps in the building ran on electricity and the water ran out before the power came back on. She collected plastic jugs and took them down the block to a public pump. Fetching water became part of her morning routine. It went on the chore list after folding the bedding and dusting the portraits of Kim Il-sung. Although she no longer had small children in the house, she had to get up earlier than ever before. The electric tram that she took to work down Road No. 1 was operating infrequently and when it came it would be so overcrowded that people hung off a ladder on the back. Mrs. Song didn't want to jostle with all the young men on the tram to get a place, so she usually walked. It took her one hour on foot.

Chongjin's factories girded the coastline, stretching for nearly eight miles from Pohang in the north down to Nanam, the former Japanese military base, which was now headquarters for the 6th Army division of the Korean People's Army. The biggest factories were Chongjin Steel and Kimchaek Iron and Steel, Chemical Textile, Second Metal Construction, May 10 Coal Mine Machinery, and the Majon Deer Company, which produced a medicine made from deer antlers. Mrs. Song worked at the northern end of the industrial strip at the Chosun Clothing factory, part of the largest national clothing company. The Chongjin branch employed two thousand people, almost all women—the exception being the top managers and the truck drivers. North Koreans spend most of their lives in uniform, so that was what the factory churned out—standardized uniforms for students, shop clerks, train conductors, laborers, and of course uniforms for factory workers. They were made out of Vinalon, a stiff, shiny synthetic material unique to North Korea. The North Koreans were so proud of this material, invented by a Korean scientist in 1939, that they called it the *juche* fiber. Most of it was produced 175 miles down the coast in Hamhung.

Beginning in 1988, though, the shipments of fabric were delayed. Mrs. Song and the other workers were told the problem was in Hamhung. Either they had run out of the anthracite coal that was one of the raw materials in vinalon or they didn't have enough electricity at the factory—Mrs. Song never got a clear answer. But without fabric, you couldn't make uniforms.

The seamstresses spent their days sweeping the floors and polishing the equipment, waiting for the next delivery of fabric. The factory was uncannily quiet. Where once you heard the clattering of the sewing machines, now the only sound was the whisking of brooms.

To keep the women gainfully employed, the factory management launched what were euphemistically called "special projects." In fact, they were scavenging for anything that could be sold or bartered for food. One day, the women would march in formation to the railroad track with bags and shovels to collect dog shit to be used for fertilizer. Other days it would be scrap metal. At first it was only the seamstresses who were sent, but soon Mrs. Song and the other women from the day-care center had to join in as well. They'd do it in shifts—half the women from the center would stay with the kids while the other half would be sent to scavenge.

"Even if the road is harsh, we'll protect the party," they had to sing as they went out on their excursions, the managers trying to prop up the group's morale.

Some days they went to the beach to collect scrap metal from the effluent that came gushing out of pipes under the shadow of the giant steelworks. Mrs. Song didn't like getting her feet wet—not even at the beach next to the Chongjin Youth Park where they collected clams when her children were young. Like most North Koreans of her generation, she didn't know how to swim. Even though the water was shallow, Mrs. Song shuddered. She had to roll up her pants to the knees, wading through the ocean waters with only canvas shoes on her feet and a basket for sifting the metal as though panning for gold. At the end of the day, the supervisors would weigh the metal to make sure each unit had gotten its quota.

All the women were trying to figure out how to wriggle out of these unpleasant excursions. They didn't dare quit their jobs, even though they were getting almost no pay. In North Korea, if you skipped work, you wouldn't get the coupons you needed to trade in for food. And if you stayed out a whole week without good reason, you could get sent to a detention center.

Some of the women concocted family emergencies. Or they got notes from their doctor saying they couldn't come in to work. It was all done with a wink and a nod. The supervisors didn't inspect the notes too closely because they knew the women had nothing to do. Mrs. Song, on the other hand, wouldn't dream of bringing in one of the fake notes. It felt wrong to her. She showed up for work punctually as before. Since the seamstresses weren't coming in, there were no children in the day-care center. The bosses tried to fill the day by scheduling extra lectures on Kim Il-sung, but with blackouts occurring more frequently, the light was often too dim inside the factory. After years of working fifteen-hour days, Mrs. Song finally got a chance to rest. She took long naps at her desk, resting her cheek against the wood, wondering how much longer it could go on like this.

One day, the manager called Mrs. Song and her co-workers in for a chat. The manager was a woman Mrs. Song respected, a party member and devout Communist, a true believer like herself. In the past, he'd always reassured the workers that the shipment of fabric was expected any day from Hamhung. Now she cleared her throat awkwardly and spoke with embarrassment. The situation was not likely to improve in the near future. These women, the die-hards like Mrs. Song who were still coming to work, well, maybe they shouldn't bother anymore.

"You *ajumma*," she said, using a Korean word for "auntie," commonly used for married women, "should think about finding some other way to bring food home for your families."

Mrs. Song was horrified. The manager wasn't referring to prostitution, though she might as well have been. She was suggesting she work on the black market.

LIKE EVERY OTHER Communist country, North Korea had black markets. Although it was technically illegal to buy and sell most commodities privately, the rules changed frequently and were often ignored. Kim Il-sung had given dispensation for people to grow vegetables in their gardens and sell them, so people set up a makeshift market in an empty lot behind Mrs. Song's apartment complex. It wasn't much more than a collection of tarpaulins laid out in the dirt with meager offerings of radishes and cabbage. Occasionally people would sell old clothes, chipped pottery, used books. Anything newly manufactured couldn't be sold at the market. Those products were restricted to state stores. Grain sales were prohibited, too, and anybody caught selling rice would receive a prison sentence.

Mrs. Song thought the whole atmosphere of the black market was sleazy. The vendors were mostly older women, some grandmothers. Mrs. Song would see them squatting on their haunches over their grubby vegetables, yelling out prices to customers in a most undignified fashion. Some of the women even smoked pipes, despite taboos in North Korea against women smoking. Mrs. Song was disgusted by these old *halmoni*, these grandmothers. The very idea of selling at a market was repugnant. This was no place for a proper Communist!

In fact, proper Communists didn't shop, period. Kim Il-sung had created about as anticonsumerist a culture as could exist in the twentieth century. Elsewhere in Asia, markets teeming with humanity and merchandise abounded. Not in North Korea. The most famous stores in the country were Pyongyang's two department stores—Department Store No. 1 and Department Store No. 2, they were called—and their merchandise was about as exciting as their names. When I saw the stores on a visit to Pyongyang in 2005, I could see Chinese-made bicycles on the first floor, but it was unclear whether the merchandise was really for sale or just on display to impress foreigners. Visitors to Pyongyang in the 1990s reported that the stores sometimes put plastic fruit and vegetables on display for foreign window-shoppers.

North Koreans were not supposed to shop because in theory everything they needed was supplied by the government in the name of Kim Il-sung's benevolence. They were supposed to get two sets of clothing each year—one for summer and one for winter. New clothes were dispensed by your work unit or school, often on Kim Il-sung's birthday, reinforcing his image as the source of all good things. Everything was pretty much standard issue. Only vinyl or canvas shoes were provided, as leather ones were a tremendous luxury and only people with some outside source of income could afford them. The clothes came out of garment factories like Mrs. Song's. The favored fabric was Vinalon, which didn't hold dye very well, so there was a limited palette: drab indigo for factory workers uniforms, black or gray for office workers. Red was reserved for the scarves that children wore around their necks until the age of thirteen as part of their obligatory membership in the Young Pioneers.

Not only was there no shopping, there was virtually no money. North Korean jobs paid salaries so nominal they were more like allowances. Mrs. Song's monthly salary amounted to 64 North Korean won, which at the official exchange rate amounted to $28, but in reality wasn't even enough to buy a single nylon sweater. You could pay only for incidentals, such as movies, haircuts, bus tickets, and newspapers. For men, cigarettes. For women, makeup—which, surprisingly, they wore in ample quantity. Red lipstick gave the women a retro look like 1940s movie stars and pink blush gave a healthy glow to skin made sallow by the long winters. Each neighborhood of Chongjin had its own cluster of state-run shops that were identical to the cluster in the next neighborhood. North Korean women paid attention to their appearance: Mrs. Song would skip breakfast rather than go to work without makeup. Her hair was naturally curly, but other women her age got their hair permed at a hair salon that looked like an assembly line, with a row of barber chairs on one side for men and another on the other side for women. Hairdressers were all state employees who worked for an agency called the Convenience Bureau. It was also responsible for bicycle and shoe repairmen.

There was a food shop, a stationery shop, a clothing shop. Unlike in the Soviet Union, you seldom saw long lines in North Korea. If you wanted to make a major purchase—say, to buy a watch or a record player—you had to apply to your work unit for permission. It wasn't just a matter of having the money.

The crowning achievement of the North Korean system was subsidized food. Like the campaign pledge of a chicken in every pot often attributed to Herbert Hoover, Kim Il-sung had promised North Koreans daily meals of rice and meat soup. Rice, especially white rice, was a luxury in North Korea. It was a magnanimous promise that was impossible to fulfill for all but the elite. However, the public distribution system did supply the population with a mixture of grains in amounts that were carefully calibrated in accordance with rank and work. Coal miners doing hard labor were to get 900 grams of grain daily, while factory workers like Mrs. Song got 700 grams. The system also dispensed other staples in the Korean diet, such as soy sauce, cooking oil, and a thick red bean paste called *gochujang*. On national holidays, such as the Kim family birthdays, there might be pork or dried fish.

The best part was the cabbage, distributed in the autumn for making kimchi. The spicy preserved cabbage is the Korean national dish, the only vegetable product in the traditional diet during the long winters and as integral to the culture as rice. The North Korean regime understood you couldn't keep Koreans happy without kimchi. Each family got 70 kilograms (154 pounds) per adult and 50 kilos (110 pounds) per child, which for Mrs. Song came to 410 kilos after her mother-in-law came to live with her. The cabbage was pickled with salt, spiced with lots of red pepper, sometimes bean paste or baby shrimp. Mrs. Song also made radish and turnip kimchi. She would spend weeks preparing it, and would store it in tall earthen jars. Chang-bo had to help her carry them down to the basement, where each family had a storage bin. The tradition was to bury kimchi pots in the garden, so that they would stay cold but not frozen.

In the apartment building, they improvised by packing dirt around the urns. When they were done, they closed up the bin with their strongest padlock. Kimchi thieves were common in Chongjin. Even in a society as collectivist as North Korea, no one wanted to share their kimchi with a stranger.

NORTH KOREA wasn't the workers' paradise that the propaganda claimed, but Kim Il-sung's achievements were not insignificant. In the first two decades after the 1945 partition of the peninsula, the north was richer than the capitalist south. In the 1960s, when Korean scholars bandied about the term "economic miracle," they meant North Korea. Merely to feed the population in a region with a long history of famine was an accomplishment, all the more so given that the crude partition of the peninsula had left all the better farmland on the other side of the divide. Out of the wreckage of a country that had lost almost all of its infrastructure and 70 percent of its housing stock in the war, Kim Il-sung created what appeared to be a viable, if Spartan, economy. Everybody had shelter and clothing. In 1949, North Korea claimed to be the first Asian country to have nearly eliminated illiteracy. Foreign dignitaries who visited in the 1960s, often arriving by train across the Chinese border, gushed over the obviously superior living standards of the North Koreans. In fact, thousands of ethnic Koreans in China fled the famine caused by Mao Zedong's disastrous "Great Leap Forward" to return to North Korea. North Korea put tile roofs on the houses, and every village was wired for electricity by 1970. Even a hard-bitten CIA analyst, Helen-Louise Hunter, whose reports on North Korea from the 1970s were later declassified and published, grudgingly admitted she was impressed by Kim Il-sung's North Korea.

As Communist countries went, it seemed more like Yugoslavia than Angola. It was a point of pride within the Communist bloc. People pointed to North Korea's gains—especially relative to South Korea—as proof that communism was *actually* working.

Or was it? So much of the supposed North Korean miracle was illusory, based on propaganda claims that couldn't be substantiated.

The North Korean regime didn't publish economic statistics, at least none that could be trusted, and took great pains to deceive visitors and even themselves. Supervisors routinely fabricated statistics on agricultural production and industrial output because they were so fearful of telling their own bosses the truth. Lies were built upon lies, all the way to the top, so it is in fact conceivable that Kim Il-sung himself didn't know when the economy crashed.

For all its arrogant rhetoric about *juche* and self-sufficiency, North Korea was utterly dependent on the kindness of its neighbors. The country got subsidized oil, rice, fertilizer, pharmaceuticals, industrial equipment, trucks, and cars. X-ray machines and incubators came from Czechoslovakia; architects from East Germany. Kim Il-sung skillfully played the Soviet Union and China against each other, using their rivalry to extract as much aid as possible. Like an old-style emperor, he commanded tribute from neighboring realms: Stalin personally sent an armored limousine, Mao sent a complete train carriage.

Kim Il-sung or Kim Jong-il, who by the 1980s was increasingly assuming his father's duties, offered "on-the-spot guidance" to address the country's woes. Father and son were experts in absolutely everything, be it geology or farming. "Kim Jong-il's on-site instructions and his warm benevolence are bringing about a great advance in goat breeding and output of dairy products," the Korean Central News Agency opined after Kim Jong-il visited a goat farm near Chongjin. One day he would decree that the country should switch from rice to potatoes for its staple food; the next he would decide that raising ostriches was the cure for North Korea's food shortage. The country lurched from one harebrained scheme to another.

An enormous share of the country's wealth was squandered on the military. North Korea's defense budget eats up 25 percent of its gross national product—as opposed to an average of less than 5 percent for industrialized countries. Although there had been no fighting in Korea since 1953, the country kept one million men under arms, giving this tiny country, no bigger than Pennsylvania, the fourth-largest military in the world. The North Korean propaganda machine kept hysteria at a high level, ginning up incessant reports of imminent invasion by the imperialist warmongers.

Kim Jong-il, who had been rapidly rising through the Politburo as he was being groomed for the succession, was named supreme commander of the North Korean armed forces in 1991. A few years later, billboards would go up around the country next to the *juche* monuments, introducing a new catchword, *songun*, or "military first," and stating that the Korean People's Army was at the center of all policy decisions. The younger Kim had long since outgrown his dabblings in cinema and turned his attention to bigger toys— nuclear weapons and long-range missiles.

Ever since the U.S. bombing of Hiroshima at the end of World War II, Kim Il-sung had dreamed of making his country a nuclear power, and research had been under way since the 1960s at a Soviet-designed nuclear compound at Yongbyon, in the mountains north of Pyongyang. But it was Kim Jong-il who put the nuclear program on the fast track, apparently believing it would boost North Korea's standing and his own at a time when its international prestige was flagging. Instead of rebuilding aging factories and infrastructure, North Korea put its money into expensive secret weapons projects, claiming the need for a "nuclear deterrent" against American aggression. By 1989, North Korea was developing a reprocessing plant at Yongbyon to produce weapons-grade plutonium from the fuel rods of its nuclear reactors, and by the early 1990s the CIA was assessing that it had enough for one or two nuclear bombs. "Kim Jong-il didn't care if he bankrupted the rest of the country. He saw the missiles and nuclear weapons as the only way to maintain power," Kim Dok-hong, a high-ranking defector from Pyongyang, told me in an interview in Seoul in 2006.

North Korea's timing was terrible. Kim Jong-il realized that the Cold War was over, but he didn't seem to grasp that his old Communist patrons were more interested in making money than bankrolling an anachronistic dictatorship with nuclear ambitions. The economy of his archrival, South Korea, had edged ahead in the mid-1970s; by the next decade, North Korea had been left in the dust. Never mind Communist solidarity, China and the Soviet Union wanted to do business with the likes of Hyundai and Samsung, not with state-owned enterprises in the North that didn't pay their bills on time. In 1990, the year before it collapsed, the Soviet Union established diplomatic relations with South Korea in a devastating blow to North Korea's world standing. China followed suit two years later.

Creditors were increasingly fed up with North Korea's failure to repay loans that had amounted to an estimated $10 billion by the early 1990s. Moscow decided that North Korea would have to pay prevailing world prices for Soviet imports rather than the lower "friendship" prices charged Communist allies. In the past, the Chinese, who provided three quarters of North Korea's fuel and two thirds of its food imports, used to say they were close as "lips and teeth" to North Korea; now they wanted cash up front.

Soon the country was sucked into a vicious death spiral. Without cheap fuel oil and raw material, it couldn't keep the factories running, which meant it had nothing to export. With no exports, there was no hard currency, and without hard currency, fuel imports fell even further and the electricity stopped. The coal mines couldn't operate without electricity because they required electric pumps to siphon water. The shortage of coal worsened the electricity shortage. The electricity shortage further lowered agricultural output. Even the collective farms couldn't operate properly without electricity. It had never been easy to eke out enough harvest from North Korea's hardscrabble terrain for a population of 23 million, and the agricultural techniques developed to boost output relied on electrically powered artificial irrigation systems and on chemical fertilizers and pesticides produced at factories that were now closed for lack of fuel and raw materials. North Korea started running out of food, and as people went hungry, they didn't have the energy to work and so output plunged even further. The economy was in a free fall.

North Korea was (and remains as of this writing in 2009) the last place on earth where virtually all staples are grown on collective farms. The state confiscates the entire harvest and then gives a portion back to the farmer. But as harvests withered in the early 1990s, the farmers themselves were going hungry and began stashing some of the harvest away—there were stories from the countryside of roofs that collapsed under the weight of grain hidden away in the eaves. The farmers also neglected the collective fields for their private "kitchen gardens" next to their houses or small, steep plots they carved out of the side of uncultivated mountain slopes. Driving through the North Korean countryside, you could clearly see the contrast between the private gardens bursting with vegetables, bean poles soaring skyward, vines drooping with pumpkins, next to the collective fields with their stunted, haphazard rows of corn that had been planted by so-called volunteers doing their patriotic duty.

The people who stood the most to lose were the city folk who had no land on which to grow their own food.

For as long as she was married, Mrs. Song had gone every fifteen days with two plastic shopping bags to the same food distribution center. It was right in the neighborhood, tucked between two apartment complexes. This wasn't like a supermarket where you plucked what you wanted from the shelf; the women waited in line outside an unmarked storefront with a big metal gate that swung open. Everybody had their assigned days—Mrs. Song's were the third and the eighteenth—but still there was often a wait of several hours. Inside there was a small, unheated room with white concrete walls, and a cheerless woman sitting behind a small table covered with ledger books. Mrs. Song would hand over her ration book, a small sum of money, and coupons from the garment factory certifying that she had fulfilled her work duty. The clerks would calculate her entitlements: 700 grams each per day for her and Chang-bo; another 300 grams for her mother-in-law, since retired people got less; and 400 for each child still living at home. If anybody in the family was traveling, the rations for the days out of town would be deducted. Once the calculations were made, the clerk would pick up the official seal and with a self-important thump pound it into the red ink and onto receipts in triplicate, one of which she'd give to Mrs. Song. At the back of the warehouse, where they stored big vats of rice, corn, barley, and flour, another clerk would weigh out the rations and put them into Mrs. Song's plastic bags.

It was always a surprise what might be in the bag, sometimes a little more, sometimes a little less. Looking back years later, Mrs. Song couldn't pinpoint when it happened—1989, 1990, 1991—that her rations faded away. When they handed the bag back to her, Mrs. Song didn't need to peek inside to confirm her disappointment. The bag was lighter than it used to be. They were being systematically shortchanged. One month she might get only twenty-five days' worth of food, another month ten. Despite Kim Il-sung's promises, rice was a luxury item for North Koreans. More often now, there was only corn and barley. Cooking oil had always come sporadically, but now it was never in the bag. Mrs. Song wasn't the type to complain, not that she could have if she wanted to.

"If I made a fuss, they would have just come and taken me away," she said later.

The North Korean government offered a variety of explanations, from the patently absurd to the barely plausible. People were told that their government was stockpiling food to feed the starving South Korean masses on the blessed day of reunification. They were told that the United States had instituted a blockade against North Korea that was keeping out food. That was not true, but it was believable. North Korea in early 1993 had threatened to pull out of the Nuclear Non-Proliferation Treaty and President Bill Clinton was threatening sanctions. It was convenient for Kim Il-sung to deflect blame. He could point the finger at the United States—North Korea's favorite scapegoat. "The people of Korea have long suffered from the blockade and sanctions of the U.S. imperialists," opined *Rodong Sinmun*.

Koreans like to think of themselves as tough—and so they are. The propaganda machine launched a new campaign, playing up Korean pride by recalling a largely apocryphal fable from 1938–39 in which Kim Il-sung commanded a small band of anti-Japanese guerrillas "fighting against thousands of enemies in 20 degrees below zero, braving through a heavy snowfall and starvation, the red flag fluttering in front of the rank." The Arduous March, as they called it, would later become a metaphor for the famine. *Rodong Sinmun* urged North Koreans to invoke the memories of Kim Il-sung's sacrifice to strengthen themselves against hunger.

No force on earth can bar the Korean people from making an onward march for victory in the revolutionary spirit of the "arduous march" and the DPRK will always remain a powerful nation.

Enduring hunger became part of one's patriotic duty. Billboards went up in Pyongyang touting the new slogan, "Let's Eat Two Meals a Day." North Korean television ran a documentary about a man whose stomach burst, it was claimed, from eating too much rice. In any case, the food shortage was temporary—agricultural officials quoted in the newspapers reported that bumper crops of rice were expected in the next harvest.

When the foreign press reported on food shortages in the North in 1992, the North Korean news service was indignant.

> The state supplies the people with food at a cheap price so that people do not know how much rice costs. This is the reality of the northern half of Korea. All people live a happy life without any worries about food in our land.

If North Koreans paused to contemplate the obvious inconsistencies and lies in what they were told, they would find themselves in a dangerous place. They didn't have a choice. They couldn't flee their country, depose their leadership, speak out, or protest. In order to fit in, the average citizen had to discipline himself not to think too much. Then there was the natural human survival instinct to be optimistic. Like German Jews in the early 1930s, who told themselves it couldn't get any worse, the North Koreans deceived themselves. They thought it was temporary. Things would get better. A hungry stomach shouldn't believe a lie, but somehow it did.

Along with the new propaganda campaign, the regime stepped up its extensive network of domestic surveillance. The more there was to complain about, the more important it was to ensure that nobody did.

Since the early 1970s, Mrs. Song had served periodically as *inminbanjang*, the head of her neighborhood group. Each year, the neighbors had to elect a leader, usually a married, middle-aged woman. Mrs. Song was well suited to the post because she was energetic, organized, loyal, and had what Koreans call good *nunji*, which might be loosely translated as "intuition." She got along well with everybody. She had to make chore lists, assigning who among the fifteen families in her unit would clear sidewalks and trim grass in front of the building, collect and recycle garbage. She was also supposed to report any suspicious activity.

Mrs. Song was assigned to a single agent from the Ministry for the Protection of State Security. Comrade Kang was a woman a few years older than Mrs. Song and married to a Workers' Party official who was said to have connections in Pyongyang. Every few months, they would meet up at the district office or Comrade Kang would come to Mrs. Song's apartment to enjoy a cup of home-brewed corn whiskey while getting reports from the neighborhood. Mrs. Song never had much to tell her. Life in the apartment building was uneventful. Nobody got in trouble—except for the one incident when Chang-bo complained about the boots.

But then Comrade Kang became more persistent. As the food distribution became less frequent, she wanted to know if people were bad-mouthing the regime.

"Are they complaining about the food? What are they saying?" the agent demanded. She had been waiting for Mrs. Song in front of the building and had cornered her in the entrance.

"They don't say anything," protested Mrs. Song. It was true. In fact, Mrs. Song had noticed that conversations suddenly stopped whenever she walked into an apartment, leaving an awkward hush in any room she entered. Everybody knew the *inminbanjang* had to report to national security.

Comrade Kang wasn't satisfied.

"You should complain first. You ask why is there no distribution of food. See what their reaction is," she hissed, looking around to make sure nobody in the hallway overheard what she was suggesting.

Mrs. Song nodded weakly, eager to slip away. She had no intention of complying. She knew that none of her neighbors were engaged in subversive activities. They weren't enemies of the state. And she was simply too tired to worry about ideology.

The lack of food sapped her energy. She was preoccupied all the time, her mind spinning as she tried to crunch numbers that simply wouldn't add up. She was trying to figure out how to get food for her family. The clothing factory had stopped operating entirely in 1991, and for the entire last year she had received no money, only food coupons, which were now useless since the public distribution center had no food. In the past, Mrs. Song's husband used to get extra gifts of food for working overtime—sometimes oil, crackers, tobacco, or liquor—but that had pretty much stopped. The shelves at the state stores were empty.

After her factory closed, Mrs. Song swallowed her scruples about shopping on the black market, which did still have food, even rice at times, but the prices were prohibitively high. It cost 25 won to buy a kilo of rice that might cost less than one tenth of a won from the distribution center.

Mrs. Song still scoffed at the idea of trying to work on the market. What could she do there? She couldn't sell vegetables since she had no land. She had no business skills, other than the ability to count on an abacus. And with the four children, and her oldest daughter's wedding, they'd not been able to save money. She wondered if she should try to sell something from her home. In her mind she took inventory of her possessions. The Oriental painting. The television. Her husband's books. Maybe the sewing machine?

JUST AS MRS. SONG went through her mental calculus, thousands of others did the same. What did they have to sell? Where could they get something to eat?

Chongjin was basically a concrete jungle. Everything that wasn't the steep slope of a mountain had long since been paved over. It wasn't like you could go out to the woods and hunt birds or pick wild berries. The beach where Mrs. Song's family collected shellfish had slim pickings and the water was too deep to fish from shore. The only suitable farmland in the city was the vegetable plots and the rice paddies at the small inlets in Nanam.

People started going farther afield to get food. The orchards in Kyongsong county were a popular destination. On weekends, Chongjin families would hike down—the collective orchards were about three miles from the center of the city—often under the guise of a recreational excursion. Nobody wanted to admit they were doing it because they were hungry. The orchards were run by a collective farm, which raised the distinctive Korean pears that were exported to

Japan for hard currency. Korean pears are about the size and shape of a grapefruit, but have the russet color of Bosc pears and the crisp texture of apples. The perfectly round orbs of fruit would often fall from the trees and roll under the fence that surrounded the orchard, making for easy pickings. Many of the fruit pickers were children. As school lunches got smaller and finally disappeared, children started cutting school to look for food. They could easily slip under wire fences. A young man, who was ten years old in 1992, recalled with some pride that he climbed on the back bumper of a bus and rode down to the last stop in Nanam, then walked an hour. Alone and small, nobody noticed him. He slipped his tiny body through the fence and loaded as many pears as he could carry into a sack. "I plucked as many as I could and handed them out to all my friends," he said.

Other memories of this period were bitter. Kim Ji-eun, who was at the time a recent medical graduate doing her residency, went to the orchards one weekend with her parents, a married sister, the sister's husband, and two small children. Carrying the whiny toddlers most of the way, they didn't get to the orchards until midafternoon. Too many others had come before them. They found one slightly rotten pear on the ground. They took it home and boiled it, then cut it into five parts for the children, the elderly parents, and Kim Ji-eun's brother-in-law. Ji-eun and her sister didn't get any.

The date was September 9, 1993, and Kim Ji-eun would never forget it because it was the first time in her life that she would go an entire day without food. Few others could remember with such precision. The end of an era did not come in a single moment. It took years before people understood that their world was irreversibly altered.

CHAPTER 5

VICTORIAN ROMANCE

Kyongsong County Culture Hall.

MI-RAN WAS IN HIGH SCHOOL WHEN SHE FIRST NOTICED THAT city people were taking trips to the countryside to scavenge for food. When she would bicycle into Chongjin, she'd see them, looking like beggars with their burlap sacks, heading toward the orchards that lined both sides of the road. Some would even come farther down the road to the cornfields that stretched for miles south from her village toward the sea. The city people could also be found picking up firewood in the mountains near the kaolin mines where her father worked. It was surprising because she'd always figured that people who lived in Chongjin were way better off than anyone from Kyongsong. Chongjin had the universities, the big theaters, restaurants that were only for the Workers' Party members and their families, not for a girl like herself.

Kyongsong was essentially a cluster of villages around a small downtown that was like Chongjin in miniature—an overly wide main street with a large stone monument celebrating Kim Il-sung's victory over the Japanese in World War II. There were a couple of ceramic factories that processed the kaolin from the mine where Mi-ran's father worked, and a large manufacturer of electrical parts, the June 5 factory, named for a day in 1948 when Kim Il-sung visited and provided on-the-spot guidance. Her village wasn't exactly the countryside, but there was far more land available than in the city. Near the coast, the terrain was flat, sandy, and relatively fertile. Inland, as you climbed in elevation, the mountains were dense with pine thickets. The narrow strips between the harmonica houses were painstakingly cultivated with red peppers, radishes, cabbages, and even tobacco, because it was cheaper to roll your own than to buy cigarettes, and virtually all the men smoked. People whose roofs were flat would put pots up there to grow more vegetables. These private agricultural efforts were small enough that they didn't raise the ire of the Communist authorities. At least in the beginning, before the food shortage grew into a famine, they staved off hunger.

When the paycheck her father brought home from the mines grew smaller and smaller until it eventually disappeared, Mi-ran's mother stepped into the breach. She was never much of a housewife, but she was resourceful when it came to making money. She took in sewing, made homemade tofu, and for a time raised pigs—although there wasn't enough feed to sustain them. More successful was a recipe she invented for imitation ice cream. She bought a used freezer called a North Pole machine. Because it was almost impossible to buy milk or cream, she would use the water left over from the making of tofu and flavor it with red beans and sugar. She poured this strange concoction into ice cube trays and froze it. Koreans love to indulge their children and if there was a spare won in the house, they'd give it to their child for a treat. Sometimes Mi-ran's mother would hawk her wares on the back of a friend's truck. Workers' Party edicts forbade making private money, but she shrugged them off. It wasn't that she was a rebel so much as a pragmatist who didn't give much thought to ideology. The money she earned selling her ersatz ice cream allowed her to buy corn and sometimes rice on the black market.

—

MI-RAN'S SECRET ADMIRER was also insulated from the hunger. Jun-sang's paternal grandparents came to visit almost every year from Japan on the ferry. By the early 1990s, the boat no longer came to Chongjin, but to the port of Wonsan—farther down North Korea's east coast. Jun-sang's family would go to meet them at the dock, and the ritual involved much crying and hugging, during which Jun-sang's *harabogi,* or grandfather, could slip a fat envelope of cash into his son's pocket. It had to be done discreetly so that nobody with authority would see and demand a cut of the money. The envelope sometimes contained more than $2,000 worth of Japanese yen. The Koreans in Japan were well aware that their relatives in North Korea would go hungry without hard currency.

Jun-sang's family was also lucky to have a private yard. His father was a fastidious gardener, subdividing his modest walled domain into tidy vegetable plots. Hunched over, working in the garden, he showed his young seedlings a tenderness he'd rarely accorded his children. He recorded in a small notebook the seeds he planted, the depth of the furrows, the days it took for the seeds to germinate, and how long it would take for the vegetables to grow and ripen. Jun-sang's mother still had the fine kitchen equipment her family had brought from Japan. With a razor-sharp knife, she'd slice up carrots and radishes julienne-style, lay the crisp slivers of vegetables on top of freshly steamed rice, and roll them up in sheets of dried seaweed. They were the only family in the neighborhood to eat *kimbab,* a Korean interpretation of Japanese maki that is popular in South Korea, but virtually unknown in the North. With their home-grown vegetables and their black-market rice, they ate better than all but the most elite members of the Workers' Party.

The family's chief source of pride was Jun-sang himself. The years of drudgery, of studying until 1:00 A.M. and rising at dawn, the relentless nagging by his father, and his own wish to fulfill his family's ambitions for him, had all paid off. Jun-sang had been accepted to a university in Pyongyang. It wasn't Kim Il-sung University—the family's standing wasn't high enough for that—but it was a school that trained scientists and was more merit-based in its choice of students. North Korea, badly lagging in technology behind South Korea and Japan, could no longer afford to squander what talent it could find. Jun-sang would have preferred to study literature or philosophy, or, had there been such a program, filmmaking, but his father steered him into science, knowing it was the only way for a boy without good *songbun* to get to Pyongyang.

It was a tremendous achievement for a boy from North Hamgyong province to be accepted into the North Korean equivalent of MIT. It meant that Jun-sang wouldn't have to serve in the military. He would have a good chance of raising his family's *songbun*. It would be a path to Workers' Party membership. Notwithstanding some incipient doubts about the political system—he was beginning to wonder why the East Germans tore down the Berlin Wall if communism was so great—he knew that party membership and a Pyongyang education was his ticket to the core class.

Jun-sang was proud of himself. He was a modest boy, careful not to show off his brains or his money, but these days when he came home from Pyongyang he felt like a returning hero. Like soldiers, university students were supposed to wear their uniforms even when they were off campus. The ensemble consisted of a green double-breasted jacket and pants, a white shirt, and a tie. The green of his uniform was meant to allude to a quote from Kim Il-sung that described youth as being like "the green mountains." With his newly minted confidence, Jun-sang again began to think about asking Mi-ran out. Five years had passed since he first spotted her at the movie theater. Much to his amazement, he hadn't forgotten her. There were girls at his university in Pyongyang—smart girls, pretty girls—but none had captured his interest like she had.

Jun-sang had come to know Mi-ran somewhat. During high school, he had befriended her sister Mi-sook. Two years older than Mi-ran, she was the family's tomboy. She played on the women's volleyball team and was often around the gym where Jun-sang's friends practiced. He also had a friend from boxing class who lived in the same row of harmonica houses as Mi-ran. It gave Jun-sang an excuse to hang out in her neighborhood.

Mi-ran's family had managed to acquire a television, and like Mrs. Song, they too maintained an open-door policy. One day while visiting his friend, Jun-sang slipped into her house with some other neighbors. While everybody else watched the program, his eyes darted back and forth between the television set and Mi-ran. She had ripened into a beautiful teenager. He stared at her, trying to discern what it was about the particular alignment of eyes, nose, mouth, and hair that had so captivated him. He wondered whether it would be worth the risk to his reputation to ask her out. He decided that it was.

JUN-SANG PLANNED to make his move during a visit home from Pyongyang in the spring of 1991, his first year of university. He mooned around the center of Kyongsong, hoping that a "chance encounter" might provide the opportunity to speak to her. On the last day of his vacation, he spotted her at the market, but before he could get close enough to speak, he saw that her mother was a few paces behind her.

Soon after, Jun-sang confided his predicament to her sister Mi-sook, who agreed to act as a go-between. Jun-sang went to the house on his next vacation at a prearranged time. Mi-sook was hovering near the door. She called out to Mi-ran, "Little sister. Come out and talk to my friend."

Mi-ran stuck her head out the door. She let out a little yelp of embarrassment and ducked back in.

"Come, little sister, or I'll have to drag you out," Mi-sook persisted.

Finally she went outside to greet him. Face-to-face with her for the first time, he felt beads of sweat dampening the freshly ironed collar of his uniform. As he began to speak, he heard the telltale quiver in his voice. It was too late to turn back now so he pushed on. He couldn't think of small talk, so he just laid it out. He told her everything. Starting with spotting her at the movie theater. He ended by asking her if she would be his girlfriend.

"My studies. I'm supposed to be studying hard, but I can't concentrate because I think about you," he blurted out.

Mi-ran didn't say anything. She stood there, not averting her eyes as he might have expected, but not responding either. He felt like his head was going to explode. He tried harder to engage her in conversation.

"Didn't you notice me watching you all this time?" he asked.

"No, really, I didn't have a clue," she said.

He waited expectantly for her to say more.

"Well, it is not like I don't like you," she answered in a tangled syntax of double negatives, which in Korean are especially ambiguous. He wasn't really sure what she was saying, but he suspected it was a guardedly positive response. She promised to explain her feelings in a letter. For all her aloofness, Mi-ran was in fact thrilled. Her suitor was handsome, sweet, and frankly a great catch. She knew only a couple of boys who were going to college and none of them were in Pyongyang. Although she feigned surprise, she had noticed Jun-sang lurking around her neighborhood and had even dared to hope that perhaps it was because of her. The green uniform had not failed to impress her. He looked like a naval officer with the shiny double row of buttons. Although she had never dated, Mi-ran knew by instinct that she should play hard to get. She struggled to find the perfect way to say yes without appearing too eager. The end result was an awkwardly formal letter in her very best handwriting.

"Rather than create a situation where you cannot concentrate on your studies because of your unhappiness, I will for the moment accept your proposition," she wrote to him a few weeks later.

At least initially, the relationship took on a nineteenth-century epistolary quality. The only way they could stay in touch was by letter. In 1991, while South Korea was becoming the world's largest exporter of mobile telephones, few North Koreans had ever used a telephone. You had to go to a post office to make a phone call. But even writing a letter was not a simple undertaking. Writing paper was scarce. People would write in the margins of newspapers. The paper in the state stores was made of corn husk and would crumble easily if you scratched too hard. Mi-ran had to beg her mother for the money to buy a few sheets of imported paper. Rough drafts were out of the question; paper was too precious. The distance from Pyongyang to Chongjin was only 250 miles, but letters took up to a month to be delivered.

Mi-ran was in her last year of high school when the relationship began. She was intimidated by the relative sophistication of her college boy. In Pyongyang, Jun-sang could buy proper paper. He owned a ballpoint pen. His letters ran on for pages, long and eloquent. Their correspondence gradually evolved from stilted formalities to full-blown romance. Jun-sang had never seen a Hollywood romance, but his mind was fervid enough to conjure the clichés of modern love. His letters conjured up images of himself and Mi-ran running toward each other against the backdrop of a sky streaked orange and pink. He quoted to her from the novels he read in Pyongyang. He wrote love poems. On paper there was no trace of the reticence that had held him back for so long.

Jun-sang posted his letters to Mi-sook, who by then was working in an office where she could receive mail away from the scrutiny of her parents. She was the only person Mi-ran told about the relationship. Jun-sang told nobody. They never discussed the reasons for the secrecy, since sex and class background were not to be discussed openly in North Korea—in fact, complaining about your own *songbun* was tantamount to criticizing the regime. But the fact of Mi-ran's tainted blood hovered unspoken. They both knew if they were eventually to marry, it could hurt Jun-sang's career and his prospects of joining the Workers' Party. Certainly, if Jun-sang's father were to find out, he would forbid the romance. North Korean society demands that people stick to their own. Jun-sang knew he would be expected to marry somebody from the Korean-Japanese community. In any case, Jun-sang's father didn't approve of his son dating.

"Finish school first. Don't waste your time chasing girls," he lectured.

AN ASIDE HERE ABOUT sex in North Korea: the country doesn't have a dating culture. Many marriages are still arranged, either by families or by party secretaries or bosses. Couples are not supposed to make any public displays of affection—even holding hands in public is considered risqué. North Korean defectors insist that there is no premarital sex and no such thing as an unmarried student getting pregnant. "It would be unimaginably terrible. I couldn't even think of that happening," I was told by a North Korean woman who was herself no prude—she was working in the sex industry in Seoul at the time I met her. Certainly, North Korea doesn't have the love hotels of South Korea or Japan. You can't check into a regular hotel without a travel permit, and no hotel would ever admit an unmarried couple in any case. People from Chongjin have told me that unmarried couples who want to have sexual relations will go into the wilderness or even to a park by night, but I have never met anyone who has admitted to doing this.

The prudishness is part of traditional Korean culture. It is easy to forget when you're in Seoul and see schoolgirls wearing thigh-high tartan skirts that just a century ago respectable Korean women wore full-body coverings that would rival anything required by the Taliban. The nineteenth-century British travel writer Isabella Bird Bishop wrote of seeing women in a village north of Pyongyang in 1897 wearing burkalike contraptions that she described as "monstrous hats like our wicker garden sentry-boxes, but without bottoms. These extraordinary coverings are 7 feet long, 5 broad and 3 deep, and shroud the figure from head to toe." Women of the middle and upper classes were not permitted to leave the family compound except during specially designated times when the streets were cleared of men. Bishop had traveled extensively as well in the Islamic world, but she pronounced Korean women as being "very rigidly secluded, perhaps more absolutely so than women of any other nation."

The wicker baskets are long gone, but the old attitudes persist. After Kim Il-sung took over, he melded traditional Korean conservatism with the Communist instinct to repress sexuality. He closed not only brothels, but the more ambiguous *kisaeng* houses where women entertained wealthy men. Pornographers were executed. Notwithstanding his own excesses and those of Kim Jong-il, a playboy in his youth, party officials caught in adulterous affairs lost their jobs.

Kim Il-sung also discouraged early marriages, giving a "special instruction" in 1971 that men should marry at thirty and women should marry at twenty-eight. As a North Korean newspaper reported, "The Motherland and nation hope and believe that the youngsters will uphold the beautiful tradition of marrying only after they have done enough for the country and people." In fact

that was not Korean tradition at all—in the past women were expected to be married by the time they were fourteen. The regulation
was designed to keep up the morale of the soldiers, so they
wouldn't fear losing their girlfriends while completing their service;
it also kept down the birthrate. Although the ban on early marriage
was lifted in 1990, North Koreans still do not look kindly on young
couples, however innocent the relationship may be.

Propaganda campaigns advise women to adopt "traditional hair-
styles in accordance with the socialist way of life and the taste of the
epoch." For middle-aged women, that means hair cut short, and
permed; unmarried women can wear their hair longer if it is tied
back or braided. North Korean women are not permitted to wear
skirts above the knee, or sleeveless shirts. Interestingly, South Korea
had similar regulations about hair and dress in the 1970s under the
military dictator Park Chung-hee. It is a sign of how much North
Korea remains frozen in time and how much South Korea has
changed that the most radical differences between the two cultures
are manifested in sexuality and dress. A few years ago, while on a
trip to the pocket of North Korea that is frequented by South Korean tourists, I saw a North Korean hotel doorman look like he was
on the verge of fainting at the sight of a young South Korean
woman in low-cut jeans and a midriff-revealing top. Many North Korean defectors I have interviewed told me the thing that they found
most surprising about South Korea was that couples kiss in public.

SO IT WAS CONVENIENT that Jun-sang and Mi-ran's relationship
began just as the lights were going out. The darkness of North
Korea by night has an absoluteness that people from the electrified
world have never experienced. With no streetlights, no headlights,
no ambient light seeping from windows or under doors, the darkness is an all-encompassing shroud. You can tell somebody is walking down the street only when you see the glowing tip of his
cigarette.

After dinner, Jun-sang would come up with excuses to leave the
house. Though he was a university student, twenty years old and a
head taller, he was still terrified of his father.

"I'm off to see my friends," Jun-sang would call out, naming one or another of his high school buddies. He promised to be home by 9:00 P.M., fully knowing it would more likely be midnight. Then he would bolt before his father could ask questions.

The walk to Mi-ran's house took about thirty minutes. His steps were urgent, even though he knew he might have a long wait before she finished helping her mother clean up after dinner. He had no excuse now to hang out around her house, because his friend from boxing class—her neighbor—had moved away. So he stood in the shadows, keeping so still that he could feel the pounding of his heart.

By this time, the few places they might have gone on a date had closed. The Kyongsong County Culture Hall had no electricity to run the movie projector. The few restaurants that had operated years earlier were now closed. Along the waterfront in downtown Chongjin, next to the port, is the Chongjin Youth Park, on a lake, with rowboats and dilapidated amusement park rides, but travel regulations were so strict that a permit was required just to go from the suburbs into the city. They dared not enter the park in Kyongsong behind the train station where they might run into someone they knew.

Long walks were the best choice. There was only one road, running through town and heading up to the mountains. They walked as briskly as they could without appearing to be running away from something. They didn't speak as they walked past the billboard of a smiling Kim Il-sung, the signposts urging, "If the Party Decides, We Do" and "Let's Protect Kim Jong-il with Our Lives." A large colorful billboard of soldiers with bayonets was on one side of the street, where the road passed under a wide archway painted with blue flowers. Where the slogans petered out, the town ended and they could relax into the darkness. Their pupils dilated so they could take in the scenery without straining their eyes. Overgrown trees lined both sides of the road, leaning across to one another so that they formed a tangled canopy overhead. On clear nights the stars peeked through the branches. After a few minutes, the road began to climb so that a valley opened up on one side of the road as the hills rose steeper on the other. Thickets of pine clung to the rocky hillside, and between them, large unkempt mounds of purple wildflowers spilled over the rocks.

The road crossed over a small stream with sandy banks and turned sharply to the left, where it opened up into the Onpho hot springs resort, known as the only place in Korea where the alkaline waters gushed out from the sand, and at temperatures of 130 degrees (Fahrenheit) they were reputed to cure ills from indigestion to infertility. Up the road, blocked off by checkpoints, was a villa for Kim Il-sung—one of about thirty in scenic locations around the country maintained for his convenience. A sizable military presence kept people from straying onto the private road. Visible from the road, although also closed to the public, was a spa reserved for party officials. The spa for the public, barely operating because of the economic crisis, was a dilapidated cluster of stone and concrete buildings. The resort opened in 1946—its founding was celebrated in a mural of Kim Il-sung surrounded by doctors—and looked as though it hadn't been repaired since. The large overgrown grounds looked lush and wild by night. The young couple wasn't interested in the scenery. Their excitement at being together made them forget even their aching feet as they walked for miles into the night.

Walking and talking, that was all they did. The conversations were animated, consuming. When they were face-to-face, Jun-sang had none of the romantic bravado of his letters. He was polite, respectful, not daring even to hold Mi-ran's hand until they'd been dating for three years. He courted her with his stories. He described his friends, his dormitory. He told her how the students were organized into battalions and had to march in step, arms and legs swinging, as they reported for roll call in the courtyard. He regaled her with a travelogue about Pyongyang, where she had been only once, on a primary school field trip to see the monuments. Pyongyang was the epitome of modernity—as the propaganda claimed, a city offering the world's greatest achievements in architecture and technology. Jun-sang told her of the twin-towered Koryo Hotel with the revolving restaurant on top. He had never been inside, but gawked at the silhouette on the skyline—along with that of a 105-story pyramid under construction that was supposed to be the biggest in Asia. Jun-sang described the Pyongyang metro, a hundred yards underground, its stations adorned with chandeliers and gilded mosaics of Kim Il-sung.

Back in Pyongyang he visited a foreign-currency shop and with his Japanese yen bought Mi-ran a barrette shaped like a butterfly and studded with rows of square rhinestones. To Mi-ran it was most intricate and exotic—she had never owned anything so pretty in her life. She never wore it because she didn't want her mother to ask about it. She kept it hidden away, wrapped up in her underwear.

Jun-sang's experiences in Pyongyang gave Mi-ran a glimpse into a remote world of privilege. At the same time, it was hard to listen without a trace of jealousy. She was in her final year of high school and she feared it would be the end of her education. She had seen her sisters' disappointment as one by one they discovered that their father's background would thwart their ambitions. One even needed permission from the board of education to take the college entrance exam. Of her three sisters, only the eldest had gone on to college, and even then she was barred from the performing arts program despite an excellent singing voice. She ended up in a physical education program and dropped out halfway through to get married.

Mi-ran had a sudden insight into her own future. She saw it laid out before her like a straight, featureless highway—a job in a factory, marriage (most likely to a fellow factory worker), children, old age, death. As Jun-sang prattled on about his roommates at the university, she grew more and more miserable. He sensed her depression and probed more deeply until at last she told him how she felt.

"I feel I have no purpose in life," she blurted out.

He listened thoughtfully. A few weeks later, after he had returned to Pyongyang, he sent her a letter.

"Things can change," Jun-sang wrote. "If you want more in life, you must believe in yourself and you can achieve your dreams."

Mi-ran would later credit Jun-sang's words of encouragement with changing her life. Once a good student, she had let her grades drop in high school. What was the point in knocking herself out if her path would be blocked anyway? But now Jun-sang's ambition had rubbed off on her. She hit the books. She begged her mother to relieve her of her household chores so she could have more time to study. She asked her teacher to allow her to take the university qualifying exam. If she didn't make it to college, she wouldn't have herself to blame.

To her great surprise, she was accepted into a teachers' college. The Kim Jong-suk Teachers' College—named for Kim Jong-il's mother—was the best of the three teachers' colleges in Chongjin. How did she get so lucky when her sisters had failed? Mi-ran herself was rather mystified, as she was a very good student but not at the top of her class. She'd thought there were many young women from better families with grades at least as good as her own who would have sought the coveted places in the freshman class.

In the autumn of 1991, she moved out of her parents' house and into the college dormitory. The school was in the downtown Pohang district, across from the museum and behind the park at the back of the Kim Il-sung statue.

When she first arrived, Mi-ran was impressed. The dormitories were modern and each of the four girls who would share one room had her own bed rather than use the Korean bed mats laid out on a heated floor, the traditional way of keeping warm at night while expending little fuel. But as winter temperatures plunged Chongjin into a deep freeze, she realized why it was that the school had been able to give her a place in its freshman class. The dormitories had no heating. Mi-ran went to sleep each night in her coat, heavy socks, and mittens with a towel draped over her head. When she woke up, the towel would be crusted with frost from the moisture of her breath. In the bathroom, where the girls washed their menstrual rags (nobody had sanitary napkins, so the more affluent girls used gauze bandages while the poor girls used cheap synthetic cloths), it was so cold that the rags would freeze solid within minutes of being hung up to dry. Mi-ran hated the mornings. Just as in Jun-sang's school, they were roused by a military-style roll call at 6:00 A.M., but instead of marching off like proud soldiers, they shivered into the bathroom and splashed icy water on their faces, under a grotesque canopy of frozen menstrual rags.

The food in the cafeteria was even worse. North Korea was starting its "Let's Eat Two Meals a Day" campaign, but the school took it a step further and offered only one meal—a thin soup made of salt, water, and dried turnip leaves. The cafeteria would sometimes add in a spoon of rice and corn that had been cooked for hours to plump up the grains. The girls in the college began getting sick. One of Mi-ran's roommates was so malnourished that the skin was flaking off her face. She dropped out of school and others followed.

It was an awakening for Mi-ran, who had been largely sheltered from the economic crisis by her industrious mother. She begged her mother to send her extra food from home, but after a year, she couldn't take it any longer. Unwilling to forgo the education she had worked so hard for, she got permission from the school to live off campus. She slept on the floor of a relative's apartment nearby during the week and went home to her parents on weekends. Normally, it would not have been permitted, but the school administrators were happy to have one less mouth to feed.

JUN-SANG'S LIFE in Pyongyang was easier. The government put a high priority on the feeding and care of its most elite students—the scientists of tomorrow, whose achievements, it was hoped, would lift North Korea out of poverty. Jun-sang still marched off to the cafeteria with his battalion for three meals a day. Their dorm was heated at night and the electricity was kept on so that they could study after dark.

Jun-sang and Mi-ran saw each other when he came home from the university on the two vacations students got per year, summer and winter, as well as during the spring leave, when students would weed the fields in preparation for sowing. In the past, Pyongyang students performed this duty on the outskirts of the capital, but with the shortage of food, it was decided to send them to their hometowns, where their mothers could feed them. Jun-sang used to dread the "volunteer" duty in the fields, but now he counted the days until he was released from the university. This longing was a revelation for him, as he had spent his life with his books and studies. "I really wanted to abandon everything and go back home to see her. I realized for the first time in my life what human emotion is all about," he would later say of that period.

In the fall of 1993, Jun-sang's sister was getting married. Although his parents had told him not to disrupt his studies, Jun-sang saw it as a perfect excuse to surprise Mi-ran with a visit. He asked for a three-day leave to go home. By this time, the train service from Pyongyang to points north was sporadic at best, since the trains relied on electricity. Even if one managed to get a ticket, there was little chance of getting a seat unless the traveler was a high party official. The railroad stations were always full of waiting passengers. They would hang out in the dark, squatting and smoking until the train arrived. Then they would make a mad dash for it, scrambling in through broken windows, hanging on between the cars.

No train tickets were available, so Jun-sang waited at the station, looking for a train to hitch. After one day he spotted a cargo train on the northbound track. A gift of some cigarettes to an engineer elicited the information that it was heading toward Chongjin. He hoisted himself up into a carload of coal, a towel wrapped around his face to protect his eyes. It was the first time in his life—but not the last—that he would hitch a ride on a cargo train.

The last stop before Chongjin was Kyongsong—not far from Mi-ran's village. Jun-sang hopped off and ran straight to her home. It was morning, the sun high in the sky, not the time of day that they normally met, but he couldn't contain his impatience. He felt he would burst if he had to wait until dark to see her. It was a Sunday and he assumed she would be home from school. For the first time since they had started secretly dating, he went directly to the front door.

The door swung open. Mi-ran's mother gasped.

Jun-sang's face, like his clothing, was black with coal dust. Mi-ran's mother was acquainted with Jun-sang from the days that he used to mix with the neighborhood kids, but now she didn't recognize him. In any case, Mi-ran wasn't home.

"This very strange person came to see you," her mother told her later. "What peculiar friends you have."

They had other close calls. Jun-sang's father wasn't pleased at all that his son had interrupted his studies for his sister's wedding and questioned his motives. Jun-sang dared to enter Mi-ran's house one evening when her mother was out and her father was working the night shift at the mine. But when her father unexpectedly returned, Jun-sang had to hide until the coast was clear.

Later, Jun-sang and Mi-ran laughed for hours about these incidents. The truth was that they enjoyed deceiving their parents. The
secrecy was not merely necessary, it was fun. It injected a frisson of
the illicit and gave them a shared psychic space in a society where
privacy didn't exist. It was a relatively safe way to rebel against the
confines of their lives.

They laughed more. They talked more. Later, when they were
older and living in comfort and security, they would strangely look
back at those first years together as some of the happiest of their
lives. In their giddiness, they paid little attention to what was happening around them.

CHAPTER 6

TWILIGHT OF THE GOD

Kim Il-sung statue in Chongjin.

N JULY 1994, MI-RAN HAD JUST ONE EXAM TO GO BEFORE SHE would get her diploma from the teachers' college. She had been assigned to work as an apprentice teacher at a kindergarten in downtown Chongjin. At noon on July 9, the children had gone home for lunch and Mi-ran was tidying up the classroom. She was about to unpack her own lunch and join the other teachers in the lounge when suddenly she heard excited footsteps careening down the corridor. She stepped out of the room to see that one of the girls had just run back from home. Her ponytail was damp with sweat and she was out of breath, so agitated that the teachers couldn't make out what she was saying.

"He's dead, he's dead," the girl shouted, the words spilling out between gasps for breath.

"What are you talking about?" a teacher asked.

"The Great Marshal is dead!"

The term could refer only to Kim Il-sung. The teachers were shocked that anybody, even a child, could talk that way. By kindergarten, children were supposed to know not to jest about the leadership. They took the girl by the shoulders and tried to get her to calm down. She was hyperventilating.

"That's blasphemy against communism," a teacher scolded.

"No, no. I saw it on television at home," the girl insisted.

The teachers still didn't believe her. They knew well enough that five-year-olds could spin fanciful tales. Besides, the television news didn't even start until 5:00 P.M. But they were disquieted enough that they wanted to investigate even if it meant leaving their lunch uneaten. The school didn't have a radio or a television so they ran out into the street. The little girl excitedly steered them toward her apartment a few blocks away. They walked up the stairs and could see a crowd pushing its way toward the television set. Mi-ran tried to squeeze herself in. She couldn't hear, but she could see the faces around her were all swollen and pale. A low moan emanated from the crowd and rose to the rhythm of sobbing. From the open windows, the heaving sound rose from the streets, which were still wet from an extraordinarily violent electric storm the night before.

Mi-ran was numb. She couldn't understand it. She was a schoolteacher in training, an educated woman who knew that mortals were made of flesh and blood and lived finite lives. But Kim Il-sung, she thought, was something other. If the Great Marshal could die, then anything could happen.

ALL NORTH KOREANS can recall with extraordinary clarity where they were and what they were doing when they learned of Kim Il-sung's death. Over years of interviewing North Koreans, I've learned to pose the question "Where were you when you found out?" Invariably the interview subject, no matter how forgetful or recalcitrant, perks up. People who repressed so many of their traumatic memories of the 1990s can suddenly describe with great animation and detail their movements on that day. It was a moment when the ordinary laws of time and perception were frozen by shock.

The year leading up to Kim's death was one of the most tumultuous since the Korean War. Not only was the economy moribund, not only were China and Russia now cavorting with the enemy in Seoul, North Korea was fast cementing its reputation as a rogue state. The United Nations, egged on by an aggressive new U.S. president, Bill Clinton, was demanding that North Korea open its nuclear facilities to inspection. In March 1993, North Korea declared that it would pull out of the Nuclear Non-Proliferation Treaty in order to pursue the development of nuclear weapons, setting off the first post–Cold War nuclear panic. By the next year, as North Korea moved ahead to reprocess plutonium from its nuclear reactor at Yongbyon, a sprawling nuclear campus forty-five miles north of Pyongyang, the Pentagon was drawing up plans for a preemptive strike. The North Koreans in turn were warning of imminent war. At one point, Pyongyang's negotiator famously threatened to "turn Seoul into a sea of fire."

In June, the former U.S. president Jimmy Carter made a surprise three-day visit to Pyongyang. Carter elicited from Kim Il-sung a tentative agreement to freeze the nuclear program in exchange for energy assistance. Carter also conveyed an invitation to the South Korean president, Kim Young-sam, to visit Pyongyang. The landmark summit between the leaders of the estranged Koreas was set for July 25, 1994.

On July 6, Kim Il-sung went to inspect a guest villa in the mountains north of Pyongyang where he intended to host his South Korean counterpart. He also dispensed his famous "on-the-spot guidance" at a collective farm nearby. The day was scorching, nearly 100 degrees. After dinner, Kim Il-sung collapsed with a massive heart attack. He died a few hours later. The announcement of his death was delayed for thirty-four hours. Although Kim Jong-il had been designated the heir two decades before, Pyongyang needed to prepare the announcement of the first hereditary succession in the Communist world.

At the time of his death, Kim Il-sung was eighty-two years old, well beyond the life expectancy for Korean men of his generation. He had a glaringly visible goiter the size of a golf ball on his neck. It was obvious to everyone but the North Korean masses that he was nearing the end of his days, but there was no public discussion of Kim's deteriorating health. He wasn't merely the father of their country, their George Washington, their Mao, he was their God.

MRS. SONG WAS home making lunch for herself and her husband. Her factory had closed by then and Chang-bo had pared back his hours at the radio station because he seldom got a paycheck anymore. He was in the main room waiting for the television news to begin. They had heard there would be a special bulletin at noon, which they assumed was about the ongoing nuclear negotiations. The television news had done a special bulletin the month before, when North Korea announced it would no longer cooperate with the International Atomic Energy Agency. Chang-bo, the journalist, closely followed the twists and turns of diplomacy. Mrs. Song, on the other hand, was bored by all the talk of nuclear weapons. She had more immediate concerns—such as how to make yet another meal of corn porridge look appetizing. Suddenly, she heard her husband snap his fingers.

"Something's happened. Something big," he called out.

Mrs. Song poked her head through a pass-through that separated the kitchen from the main room of the apartment. She saw right away that something was amiss. The television anchorman wore clothes of mourning, a black suit and tie. She dried her hands on a towel and went into the living room to watch.

> The Central Committee of the Workers' Party of Korea, the Central Military Commission of the party, the National Defense Commission, the Central People's Committee and the Administration Council of the Democratic People's Republic of Korea report to the entire people of the country with deepest grief that the Great Leader Comrade Kim Il-sung, General Secretary of the Central Committee of the Workers'

Party of Korea and President of the Democratic People's Republic of Korea, passed away from a sudden attack of illness at 2:00 A.M.

Our respected fatherly leader who has devoted his whole life to the popular masses' cause of independence and engaged himself in tireless and energetic activities for the prosperity of the motherland and the happiness of the people, for the reunification of the country and independence of the world, till the last moments of his life, departed from us to our greatest sorrow.

Mrs. Song went blank. She felt an electric jolt shoot through her body as though the executioner had just pulled the lever. She'd felt this way only once before, a few years back when she'd been told her mother had died, but in that case the death was expected. She'd never once heard anything about Kim Il-sung having any kind of illness; only three weeks before they had seen him looking every bit the robust statesman greeting Jimmy Carter. This couldn't be true. She tried to concentrate on what the television broadcaster was saying. His lips were still moving, but the words were incomprehensible. Nothing made sense. She started to scream

"How are we going to live? What are we going to do without our marshal?" The words came tumbling out.

Her husband didn't react. He sat pale and motionless, staring into space. Mrs. Song couldn't keep still. She was pumped up with adrenaline. She rushed down the staircase and out into the courtyard of the building. Many of her neighbors had done the same. They were on their knees, banging their heads on the pavement. Their wails cut through the air like sirens.

AFTER HER MARRIAGE, Mrs. Song's oldest daughter, Oak-hee, had quit her job at the propaganda department of the construction company, but she was frequently called to volunteer for theater performances in the neighborhood. She had been trained as a broadcaster, exhorting workers to fulfill their quotas through the loudspeaker of a sound truck, and her crisp, authoritative voice was much in demand. Oak-hee couldn't exactly refuse when she was asked by the local police to narrate a play urging public cooperation. In all earnestness she had to recite lines such as "Let's catch more spies to protect the fatherland," and "Confess if you've committed a crime."

Trudging home from rehearsal, exhausted and looking forward to her lunch, Oak-hee noticed that the streets were deserted. She and her husband and their two children lived in an apartment kitty-corner to Chongjin's bustling train station.

When she got upstairs, she was also surprised to find the door locked, as she expected her husband to be at home. She heard the sounds of a television coming from another apartment. She nudged the door open to peer inside. Her husband was sitting alongside their neighbors, cross-legged on the floor. His eyes were rimmed in red, but this time he wasn't drunk.

"Hey, what's going on? Why is the news on at noon?" she asked.

"Shut up and watch," her husband barked. Mindful of his often-violent temper, Oak-hee obeyed.

Everyone in the room was in tears—everyone, that is, except for Oak-hee. She felt utterly blank inside, not sad, not happy, maybe just a little irritated. She was unable to think about anything except her growling stomach. *Kim Il-sung might be dead,* she thought, *but I'm not and I need to eat.* She sat as still as she possibly could to avoid bringing attention to herself and then after a respectable amount of time stood up to leave.

"Okay, I'm going home to make lunch," she told her husband.

He gave her a nasty look. Although his drinking and bad temper had kept him out of the Workers' Party, Yong-su fancied himself a senior official, taking it upon himself to offer guidance to everyone around him. He liked to instruct and scold. At home, he was the one who dusted the father-and-son portraits on their wall. Oak-hee refused. Now, Yong-su glared at his wife, who was so obviously unmoved by the death. He hissed at her as she left the room, "You're not human."

Oak-hee went back to the apartment and fixed her lunch. She turned on the radio to listen as she ate. The announcer was already talking about the succession.

The victory of our revolution is assured as long as our dear comrade Kim Jong-il, the only successor to the Great Leader, is with us.

As she sat alone in the apartment, the enormity of it all started to sink in. Any hope that the North Korean regime might change with the death of Kim Il-sung was quickly dashed. The power had passed to his son. Things weren't going to get any better. She heard her father's words replaying in her ears. "The son is even worse than the father."

"Now we're really fucked," she said to herself.

Only then did tears of self-pity fill her eyes.

KIM HYUCK, THE BOY who had stolen pears from the orchard, was twelve years old when Kim Il-sung died. He was in his first year at Chongjin's Malum Middle School, the equivalent of seventh grade. The morning the death was announced he was debating whether or not to go to school. He hated the place for many reasons, not the least of which being that there was rarely enough food for him at home to bring a lunch. He spent most of his time looking out the window, thinking that if he were outside he could go off and find something to eat. He'd either go back to Kyongsong county to the orchards or cornfields, or steal something from a vendor near the train station. He had played hooky the day before and the day before that. He dreaded going back today because his teacher was sure to beat him for all the days he'd missed school. He was already hours late and was dragging his feet ever slower, wondering whether to turn around.

When he saw his friends skipping away from the school Hyuck was delighted. They had been told to go home to listen to an urgent bulletin at noon.

"Hooray! No school," Hyuck shouted as he dashed away with his friends.

They headed to the market. They thought they might be able to beg or steal some food from one of the stalls. But when they got there, all the stalls were closed and the place was deserted. The few people they saw had their heads down, crying. Suddenly, Hyuck didn't feel like playing anymore.

IN PYONGYANG, JUN-SANG was enjoying a lazy Saturday morning. He was propped up in bed with a book on his knees, indulging in his favorite pastime at the university. At home, his father wouldn't permit him to read in bed, saying it would ruin his eyesight. Even early in the morning with the windows propped open, it was a stiflingly hot day, and he wore just a T-shirt and shorts. He was interrupted by one of his roommates, who came in to tell him that all the students were assembling in the courtyard at noon for an urgent announcement.

Jun-sang got up with annoyance and pulled on his pants. Like others, he assumed the bulletin was about the nuclear crisis. He had to admit he was nervous. Despite the Carter visit, Jun-sang was convinced his country was heading for a confrontation with the United States. A few months before, all the students at his university had been asked to nick their fingers in order to sign—in blood—a petition swearing they each would volunteer for the Korean People's Army in case of war. Of course everybody obliged, although some of the girls balked at cutting their own fingers. Now Jun-sang was bracing himself for the end of his university career, if not his life.

"This is it. We're definitely going to war," Jun-sang told himself as he marched out to the courtyard.

In the courtyard, nearly three thousand students and faculty were lined up in formation, ranked by their year, major, and dormitory affiliation. The sun beat down with full force, and they were sweating in their short-sleeved summer uniforms. At noon a disembodied female voice, tremulous and sorrowful, came booming through loudspeakers. The loudspeakers were old and produced scratchy sounds that Jun-sang could barely understand, but he picked up a few words—"passed away" and "illness"—and he grasped the meaning of it all from the murmur going through the crowd. There were gasps and moans. One student collapsed in a heap. Nobody knew quite what to do. So one by one each of the three thousand students sat down on the hot pavement, heads in hands.

Jun-sang sat down, too, unsure of what else to do. Keeping his head down so nobody could read the confusion on his face, he listened to the rhythm of the sobbing around him. He stole glances at his grief-stricken classmates. He found it curious that for once he wasn't the one crying. To his great embarrassment, he often felt tears welling in his eyes at the end of movies or novels, which provoked no end of teasing by his younger brother, as well as criticism from his father, who always told him he was "soft like a girl." He rubbed his eyes, just to make sure. They were dry. He wasn't crying. What was wrong with him? Why wasn't he sad that Kim Il-sung was dead? Didn't he love Kim Il-sung?

AS A TWENTY-ONE-YEAR-OLD university student, Jun-sang was naturally skeptical of all authority, including the North Korean government. He prided himself on his questioning intellect. But he didn't think of himself as seditious or in any way an enemy of the state. He believed in communism, or at least believed that whatever its faults, it was a more equitable and humane system than capitalism. He had imagined he would eventually join the Workers' Party and dedicate his life to the betterment of the fatherland. That was what was expected of all those who graduated from the top universities.

Now, surrounded by sobbing students, Jun-sang wondered: If everybody else felt such genuine love for Kim Il-sung and he did not, how would he possibly fit in? He had been contemplating his own reaction, or lack thereof, with an intellectual detachment, but suddenly he was gripped with fear. He was alone, completely alone in his indifference. He always thought he had close friends at the university, but now he realized he didn't know them at all. And certainly they didn't know him. If they did, he would be in trouble.

This revelation was quickly followed by another, equally momentous: his entire future depended on his ability to cry. Not just his career and his membership in the Workers' Party, his very survival was at stake. It was a matter of life and death. Jun-sang was terrified.

At first, he kept his head down so nobody could see his eyes. Then he figured out that if he kept his eyes open long enough, they would burn and tear up. It was like a staring contest. Stare. Cry. Stare. Cry. Eventually, it became mechanical. The body took over where the mind left off and suddenly he was really crying. He felt himself falling to his knees, rocking back and forth, sobbing just like everyone else. Nobody would be the wiser.

WITHIN A FEW HOURS of the noon announcement, people all around North Korea began converging on statues of Kim Il-sung to pay their respects. By one frequently cited figure there are 34,000 statues of the Great Leader in the country and at each of them loyal subjects prostrated themselves with grief. People didn't want to be alone with their grief. They burst out of their homes and ran toward the statues, which were in fact the spiritual centers of each city.

Chongjin is home to some 500,000 people, but has only one twenty-five-foot bronze statue, at Pohang Square. People filled the vast square, and spilled over into the front lawn of the Revolution-ary History Museum directly to the east. The crowds extended down the wide Road No. 1 all the way to the Provincial Theater and radiated out into the surrounding streets like spokes from a wheel. From above, the people looked like a line of ants streaming toward a common goal.

Hysteria and crowds make for a lethal combination. People started to surge forward, knocking down those in line, trampling people already prostrate on the ground, flattening the carefully trimmed hedges. From blocks away, the noise from the square car-ried through the humid air and sounded like the roar of a riot. The weather alternated between violent downpours and searing heat. No one was allowed to wear a hat or carry a parasol. The sun beat down on the bare heads and the wet sidewalks turned the streets into a roiling steambath. People looked like they were melting into a sea of tears and sweat. Many fainted. After the first day, the police tried to rope off the lines to keep the crowd under control.

The mourners were organized by their work units or their classes at school. Each group had to bring flowers—mostly chrysanthemums, the traditional flower of death in Asia—or if they couldn't afford them, wildflowers that they picked themselves. They lined up in rows ten to twenty-five people wide, waiting their turn, like waves to be swept forward. Those who were too overwrought to stand upright were supported by others by their elbows. Once in front, they approached within a few feet of the statue and fell to their knees, lowering their heads to the pavement and then looking up with awe. Kim Il-sung loomed overhead, filling the field of vision with his presence, his head rising above a tall grove of pine trees, as high as a three-story building, his bronze feet alone taller than any human being. To the supplicants at his feet, the statue was the man, and they addressed him directly in conversation.

"*Abogi, Abogi,*" the old women wailed, the Korean honorific used to address either one's father or God.

"How could you leave us so suddenly?" the men screamed in turn.

Those waiting in line would jump up and down, pound their heads, collapse into theatrical swoons, rip their clothes, and pound their fists at the air in futile rage. The men wept as copiously as the women.

The histrionics of grief took on a competitive quality. Who could weep the loudest? Who was the most distraught? The mourners were egged on by the TV news, which broadcast hours and hours of people wailing, grown men with tears rolling down their cheeks, banging their heads on trees, sailors banging their heads against the masts of their ships, pilots weeping in the cockpit, and so on. These scenes were interspersed with footage of lightning and pouring rain. It looked like Armageddon.

"Our country is enveloped in the deepest sorrow in the five-thousand-year history of the Korean nation," intoned an announcer on Pyongyang television.

The North Korean propaganda machine went into overdrive, concocting ever weirder stories about how Kim Il-sung wasn't really dead. Shortly after his death, the North Korean government began erecting 3,200 obelisks around the country that would be called "Towers of Eternal Life." Kim Il-sung would remain the president in title after death. A propaganda film released shortly after his death claimed that Kim Il-sung might come back to life if people grieved hard enough for him.

When the Great Marshal died, thousands of cranes descended from heaven to fetch him. The birds couldn't take him because they saw that North Koreans cried and screamed and pummeled their chests, pulled their hair and pounded the ground.

What had started as a spontaneous outpouring of grief became a patriotic obligation. Women weren't supposed to wear makeup or do their hair during a ten-day mourning period. Drinking, dancing, and music were banned. The *inminban* kept track of how often people went to the statue to show their respect. Everybody was being watched. They not only scrutinized actions, but facial expressions and tone of voice, gauging them for sincerity.

Mi-ran had to go twice a day for the ten-day mourning period, once with the children from the kindergarten and once just with her work unit of teachers. She began to dread it, not just the grief but the responsibility of making sure the fragile children didn't get trampled or work themselves into hysteria. There was one five-year-old girl in her class who cried so loudly and was so demonstrative in her grief that Mi-ran worried she would collapse. But then she noticed the girl was spitting in her hand to dampen her face with saliva. There were no actual tears.

"My mother told me if I don't cry, I'm a bad person," the girl confessed.

A well-known actress from Chongjin found herself in the uncomfortable position of being unable to force out her tears. This not only put her politically at risk, but professionally. "It's my job. I'm supposed to cry on demand," the actress, Kim Hye-young, recalled years later in Seoul.

Hyuck and his school friends went to the statue frequently because there were sticky rice cakes handed out after you bowed. They would pay their respects then get back in line for another rice cake.

Among the millions of North Koreans who took part in the mass display of grief for Kim Il-sung, how many were faking? Were they crying for the death of the Great Leader or for themselves? Or were they crying because everybody else was? If there is one lesson taught by scholars of mass behavior, from the historians of the

Salem witch hunts to Charles Mackay, author of the classic *Extraordinary Popular Delusions and the Madness of Crowds*, hysteria is infectious. In the middle of a crowd of crying people, the only natural human reaction is to cry oneself.

No doubt many people were sincerely overcome with grief at his passing. Whether it was due to shock or suffering, many older North Koreans suffered heart attacks and strokes during this period of mourning—so much so that there was a marked increase in the death rate in the immediate aftermath. Many others showed their distress by killing themselves. They jumped from the tops of buildings, a favorite method of suicide in North Korea since nobody had sleeping pills and only soldiers had guns with bullets. Others just starved themselves. One of these was the father of Dr. Kim Ji-eun, a pediatrician at the municipal hospital in Chongjin.

CHAPTER 7

TWO BEER BOTTLES
FOR YOUR IV

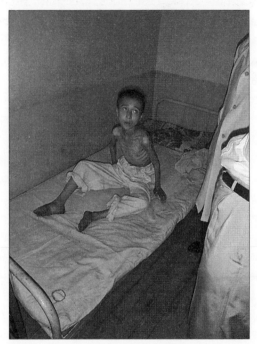

Boy in Hamhung hospital.

AT THE TIME OF KIM IL-SUNG'S DEATH THERE WAS NO GASO-
line for the few ambulances in Chongjin so patients had to be carried piggyback or wheeled on wooden carts to the hospital. Kim
Ji-eun worked at a small district hospital, but it was the closest to
Pohang Square—only a fifteen-minute walk away—so it received a
disproportionate share of the people who were injured or who collapsed in the commotions in front of the statue. Patients filled the

metal beds that were crammed five into small rooms while more waited their turn on wooden benches or sprawled on the floors of the dim corridors. Lights were rarely switched on during the day because the electrical supply was diverted to keep the Kim Il-sung statue illuminated around the clock. It had already been a busy summer because of an outbreak of typhoid. In pediatrics, parents carried in limp children who'd become dangerously dehydrated from crying in the hot sun. Some had even suffered convulsions. Dr. Kim's normal shift ran from 7:30 A.M. to 8:00 P.M., but these days she stayed at the hospital almost around the clock, except for the few times she ventured out to pay her respects at the statue. She never complained about the long hours, though. Dr. Kim took her medical oath seriously. Besides, hard work distracted her from the warning signs that her own life was falling apart.

At twenty-eight, Dr. Kim was one of the youngest doctors in the hospital and certainly the smallest. She was four foot eleven in heels, barely taller than some of her juvenile patients, and weighed less than a hundred pounds. Her pursed red-bow lips and heart-shaped face gave her a deceptively delicate appearance. Perhaps to compensate she adopted a no-nonsense personality and her colleagues, particularly the men, quickly learned not to patronize her. If they found her prickly, they also admired her dedication. She was always the first to volunteer for unpaid extra shifts. After hours, she worked in the secretariat of the Workers' Party. The hospital, like every North Korean institution, had a party secretary whose job it was to ensure the ideological health of the workplace and to choose the workers who would become party members. Though only one in four doctors at the hospital would be admitted to the party, Dr. Kim was certain she would be among the chosen. For one thing, women were often favored as party members because most didn't drink alcohol and were thought to be more rule-abiding. Then there was Dr. Kim's disciplined and somewhat unforgiving personality, which suited her profile as a committed future party member. No doubt her dedication to the North Korean system of government was sincere, having been nurtured by her father since childhood.

Manchuria has a large ethnic Korean population, the result of centuries of migration back and forth across the Tumen and Yalu Rivers, which form the boundary separating Korea from China. Dr. Kim's father was born in a Korean-speaking village just across the border. He moved to North Korea as a young man in the early 1960s to escape Mao's disastrous Great Leap Forward, which had resulted in millions of famine deaths. Dr. Kim's father viewed Kim Il-sung, not Mao, as the true inheritor of the Communist dream, the one who would be able to fulfill the promises of equality and justice made to workingmen like himself. He was a simple construction worker who had been schooled only through sixth grade, but his intelligence and devotion were recognized in North Korea and he had been admitted to the Workers' Party. He'd served as party secretary for his own construction team until a mild stroke a few years earlier had forced him to retire. Since he had no sons, it was his ambition that his daughter would continue his work for the party and contribute to the fatherland he embraced unreservedly.

The future Dr. Kim obliged with enthusiasm. She was thrilled when, at seven, she became a member of the Young Pioneers and tied around her neck their signature bright red scarf. At thirteen she graduated to the Socialist Youth League and wore her Kim Il-sung pin proudly. Admittance to the league is a standard rite of passage for North Koreans, but when a child is admitted—at thirteen, fourteen, or fifteen—depends upon conduct and grades. From her earliest days in elementary school, it was evident that Kim Ji-eun was a precocious student. She was the girl with the impeccable handwriting, the one who always raised her hand first to answer the teacher's questions, the student with the best grades. By midway through school, she had been plucked out of her class to attend medical school. No matter that she had dreamed of being a teacher or a journalist; it was an honor for the daughter of a construction worker to be chosen to become a doctor.

She entered Chongjin University Medical School at sixteen, two years younger than her peers, two thirds of whom were female. She still looked like a teenager when she finished the seven-year program and started her apprenticeship at Provincial People's Hospital No. 2, which was affiliated with the medical school and was the most prestigious hospital in North Hamgyong province. Locals called it the "Czech Hospital" because back in the 1960s, when it still meant something to be in the Communist family of nations, a team of doctors came from Czechoslovakia with X-ray machines and baby incubators. The hospital still enjoyed its European cachet though the Czechs were long gone and most of the equipment was held together with plastic tape. After her internship, Dr. Kim was sent out to be a general practitioner at one of the smaller hospitals, serving the Pohang district, where she lived.

Dr. Kim had to report to work by 7:30 A.M. Regulations required that she work a twelve-hour day and treat at least thirty-two patients. She usually spent the morning in the hospital, then was sent out in a team for the afternoons. She wore a white coat and a white cap that covered her hair and made her look a little like a short-order cook. She lugged with her a heavy bag that contained a stethoscope and syringes, bandages, digestive pills, and antibiotics. As part of a three-doctor team, she would visit schools and apartment compounds. Each block of homes had its own hygiene unit, which worked together with the *inminban*.

"The doctors are here! The doctors are here," the shouts would echo across the courtyards. People would start queuing up by the hygiene office, pushing crying toddlers forward in the line, ready to show off a sore hand or a rash they had been nursing for weeks in anticipation of the doctors' visit.

North Korean doctors are expected to serve the people selflessly. Because of a shortage of X-ray machines, they often must use crude fluoroscopy machines that expose them to high levels of radiation; many older North Korean doctors now suffer from cataracts as a result. They not only donate their own blood, but also small bits of skin to provide grafts for burn victims. Dr. Kim was excused from this last obligation only because her height and weight were far below average, but it didn't exempt her from the obligation of trekking out to the mountains to gather medicinal herbs.

Making one's own medicine is an integral part of being a doctor in North Korea. Those living in warmer climates often grow cotton as well to make their own bandages. Doctors are all required to collect the herbs themselves; Dr. Kim's work unit took off as much as a month in spring and autumn to gather herbs, during which time the doctors slept out in the open and washed only every few days. Each had a quota to fill. They had to bring their haul back to the hospital pharmacy, where it would be weighed, and if the amount was insufficient, they would be sent out again. Often, the doctors had to hike far into the mountains because the more accessible areas had already been scoured by ordinary citizens who sought to sell the herbs or use them for themselves. The most coveted was peony root, which was used as a muscle relaxant and to treat nervous disorders. Wild yam was thought to regulate menstrual cycles. Dandelion was used to stimulate digestion and ginger to prevent nausea. *Atractylodes,* which is also popular in Chinese medicine to strengthen immunity, was used when it was impossible to get antibiotics.

For years, North Korean hospitals had been using herbal remedies in combination with Western medicine. Instead of painkillers, the doctors used cupping, a technique in which a suction cup is applied to stimulate circulation to parts of the body. Another technique borrowed from the Chinese involved lighting sticks of mugwort next to the afflicted area. With anesthesia in short supply, acupuncture would be used for simpler surgeries, such as appendectomies.

"When it works, it works very well," Dr. Kim told me years later. And when it didn't? Patients would be strapped to the operating table to prevent them from flailing about. For the most part, North Koreans were stoical about enduring pain during medical treatment. "They weren't like South Koreans, who scream and holler about the slightest little thing," Dr. Kim said.

For all its shortcomings, North Korea's public health system provided the public with better care than they'd had in pre-Communist times. The right to "universal free medical service . . . to improve working people's health" was in fact written into the North Korean constitution. Dr. Kim was proud to be a part of the health-care system and gratified by the service she provided her patients. But by the early 1990s, the deficiencies in the system became more pronounced. Much of the medical equipment was obsolete and broken down, with spare parts impossible to obtain since the factories in the Communist-bloc countries where they were manufactured were by now privatized. The pharmaceutical factory in Chongjin curtailed its production due to a lack of supplies and electricity. There was little money to import pharmaceuticals from abroad. The bag that Dr. Kim carried on her rounds had gotten progressively lighter until she had nothing inside but her stethoscope. All she could do for patients was write prescriptions and hope that they had a connection in China or Japan, or a stash of money to buy the drugs on the black market.

Dr. Kim's frustration spilled out into the open in 1993 when she had her first serious clash with hospital management. She had been asked to treat a twenty-seven-year-old man who had been convicted of an economic crime—meaning he'd been engaged in private business. He had served three years of a seven-year term before he was transferred from prison to the hospital. He was bruised and badly malnourished, his ribs protruding. He suffered from acute bronchitis. She wanted to give him an antibiotic. Her boss overruled her.

"He's a convict. Let's save the antibiotic for someone else," he told Dr. Kim.

Dr. Kim was furious. "He's been admitted to the hospital. A patient is a patient. We can save him. He will die without it," she snapped back.

Her obsessive personality clicked in. Dr. Kim would not let the matter drop and she argued for days. The dying young man was discharged from the hospital untreated. Dr. Kim went to his home twice a day, but her patient grew sicker and more despondent, declaring, "I'm not fit to live." He committed suicide soon after. Dr. Kim was convinced that she and the hospital were responsible for his death. The tension with her boss lingered and she asked for a transfer into pediatrics, where she thought things would be less political.

At the same time, Dr. Kim's personal life was in tatters. Her love life had never kept pace with her professional success; her workaholic habits and perfectionism kept men at bay. A year after she started working full-time, a man she'd adored since college dumped her. She was devastated. She asked a friend to set her up with somebody else and got engaged to him on their second date. Her husband was the same age—twenty-six—but he was still in his freshman year of college because he had served in the military. Since she was already working, she figured they would survive on her salary until he graduated.

"You'll hurt his pride," Dr. Kim's mother warned. A female doctor marrying a college boy? "Men don't like it when their women earn more money."

On her wedding night, Dr. Kim knew she had made a terrible mistake, but she had gotten pregnant almost immediately and couldn't leave. A few months after she gave birth, having waited so she could breast-feed her infant son, she moved out of her husband's home and back in with her parents. The baby stayed with her in-laws in keeping with Korean tradition; custody goes to the father's family in the case of divorce.

If it was in fact her higher earnings that strained the marriage, the final indignity was that her salary disappeared. She had been earning 186 won per month, the equivalent of about $80 at the official exchange rate, triple that of an ordinary laborer. With that money, she had supported her husband and her retired parents and had helped out a married sister. As the paychecks vanished so did the food rations. It was in that period that she found herself stealing pears from the collective orchards and scouring the countryside for food. She sometimes accepted gifts from patients—a bag of noodles or a few ears of corn—which made her feel embarrassed and uncomfortable. Dr. Kim knew of other doctors who took bribes for medical care that was supposed to be free; she was determined not to be one of them. But then again, she was hungry.

By age twenty-eight, the promise of her early life had turned to disappointment. She was divorced, living with her parents. She had lost custody of her child. She was working harder than ever and receiving less compensation for her efforts than ever before. She was hungry and exhausted, poor and loveless.

These were the unhappy circumstances in which Dr. Kim was living the year leading up to Kim Il-sung's death.

LIKE MOST OTHER North Koreans, Dr. Kim learned of Kim Il-sung's death from the special broadcast at noon. She had just come back to the hospital after escorting a typhoid patient to a special clinic. When she entered the hospital lobby, she saw doctors, staff, and patients crying before the hospital's single television set.

She walked the forty minutes back to her apartment behind the city's main sports stadium, her eyes so blurred with tears she could barely see her feet slapping the pavement. Her father was at home sleeping. He sat up at the sound of her footsteps.

"What is wrong? Did one of your patients die?" he asked with alarm. He knew how emotional his daughter could be about her patients.

Dr. Kim collapsed into her father's arms. She had never cried so much, not when her boyfriend dumped her, not when her marriage broke up and her baby was taken away, not when her father had his stroke. Those were the setbacks that one had to expect in this life. Even though she was a doctor, educated in the frailties of the human body and only too aware of its mortality, Dr. Kim had never considered that such things could apply to Kim Il-sung himself.

Her colleagues felt similarly. As they worked through the night in the hospital's dim corridors, they traded conspiracy theories. One theory had it that Kim Il-sung had been assassinated by the American warmongers who wanted to sabotage his upcoming summit with the South Korean president, Kim Young-sam—one of the perennials of North Korean propaganda being that the United States kept the Korean peninsula divided.

Those first days after Kim Il-sung's death went by in a blur. Between the shock and the sleep deprivation, it took a while for Dr. Kim to notice the crisis brewing in her own home. Her father had been depressed ever since his illness had forced him to retire. The Great Leader's death was more than he could handle. He stayed in bed and refused to eat.

"If a great man like Kim Il-sung can die, why should a good-for-nothing like me go on living and consume food?" he cried.

Dr. Kim tried reasoning. She cajoled, she screamed, she threatened.

"If you don't eat, I won't eat either. We'll all die together," she told him. Her mother also threatened a hunger strike. Dr. Kim brought the Workers' Party secretary in from the hospital to persuade him. She tried to keep up her father's strength by administering intravenous nourishment.

Her father grew delirious. He alternately praised Kim Il-sung and railed against him. One day he would say his love for the marshal was such that he couldn't live without him, the next he whispered that Kim Il-sung's mortality was proof positive that the whole North Korean system had failed. He asked his daughter to bring paper home from the hospital. He mustered the strength to prop himself up and scribbled a note:

As my last task as a member of the Workers' Party, I dedicate my oldest daughter to continue my work. Please make her into a good and loyal worker for the party.

He gave the letter to Dr. Kim and asked her to take it to the hospital's party secretary. Then he took another sheet of paper. On it he scrawled what looked like an intricate pyramid, the steps labeled with names and numbers. They appeared to be the scribblings of a madman. Dr. Kim thought her father had lost his mind.

He gestured for her to sit by his side. He couldn't raise his voice beyond a whisper.

"These are our relatives in China. They will help you," he said.

It was a family tree. Dr. Kim was shocked. Could it be that her father was telling her to leave the fatherland for China? Her loyal father who had fled China himself and then schooled her at his knee in the love of Kim Il-sung? Could he be a traitor? Dr. Kim's first instinct was to tear it up, but she couldn't destroy her father's last words. So she took out a small metal keepsake box with a lock and key, one of the last vestiges of her girlhood.

She folded up her father's chart and locked it in the box.

KIM IL-SUNG WAS LAID to rest in an underground mausoleum, his body embalmed and put on display according to the Communist tradition that began with the death of Vladimir Lenin in 1924. The North Korean government staged an elaborate funeral that took place over two days, July 19 and 20. Radio Pyongyang reported that two million people attended the procession as Kim Il-sung's coffin cruised through the city on the roof of a Cadillac, followed by goose-stepping soldiers, brass bands, and a fleet of limousines carrying huge portraits of the leader and sprays of flowers. The hundred-vehicle procession started at Kim Il-sung Square, passed through Kim Il-sung University and past the city center's hundred-foot-tall statue of Kim Il-sung, the largest in the country, and ended at the Revolutionary Arch, a replica of Paris's Arc de Triomphe, only bigger. The following day, there was a memorial service. At the stroke of noon, around the country, sirens wailed, trains and ships blew their horns, and people stood at attention for three minutes. The mourning period had come to an end. It was time for the nation to get back to work.

Dr. Kim had plenty of opportunity to bury her misery in her job. Her father died just a week after Kim Il-sung's funeral, so she had little desire to go home at night and worked even longer hours. The heat wave had not broken and the typhoid outbreak that had begun earlier in the summer had turned into a full-fledged epidemic. Chongjin was always prone to epidemics because its sewage system, hastily rebuilt after the Korean War, spilled untreated feces into the streams where women often did the laundry. With the electricity blinking on and off, running water became unreliable. Usually electricity and water worked for one hour in the morning and one hour in the evening. People stored water in big vats at home (few had bathtubs), which turned into breeding grounds for bacteria. Nobody had soap. Typhoid is easily treated by antibiotics, which by 1994 were almost entirely unavailable.

After the hot summer of 1994 came an unusually cold winter, with temperatures in the mountains plunging to 35 degrees below zero. That was followed by torrential rains the following summer, flooding the rice paddies. This gave the North Korean government a face-saving excuse to admit publicly for the first time that it did indeed have a food shortage. A U.N. relief team that was permitted to visit in September 1995 was told that the floods had caused $15 billion worth of damage that affected 5.2 million people; that 96,348 homes had been damaged, displacing 500,000 people; and 1.9 million tons of crops had been lost.

In the pediatric ward, Dr. Kim noticed that her patients were exhibiting peculiar symptoms. The children she treated, born in the late 1980s and early 1990s, were surprisingly smaller, even smaller than she'd been as the tiniest kid in her elementary school class. Now their upper arms were so skinny she could encircle them with her thumb and forefinger. Their muscle tone was weak. It was a syndrome known as wasting, where the starved body eats away at its own muscle tissue. Children came in for constipation that was so acute they were doubled over in pain, screaming.

The problem was with the food. Housewives had started to pick weeds and wild grasses to add to their soups to create the illusion of vegetables. Corn was increasingly the staple again instead of rice, but people were adding leaves, husks, stems, and cobs to make it go further. That was okay for adults, but it couldn't be digested by the tender stomachs of children. In the hospital the doctors discussed this problem among themselves, and gave the mothers what amounted to cooking advice. "If you use grass or bark, you have to grind it up very fine, then cook it a very long time so it is soft and easy to eat," Dr. Kim told them.

Among older children and adults, there was another strange new affliction. The patients had shiny rashes on their hands, around their collarbones as though they were wearing necklaces, or around their eyes so that it looked like they had glasses. It was sometimes called the "eyeglass disease." In fact, it was pellagra, which is caused by a lack of niacin in the diet and often is seen in people who eat only corn.

Often children came in with minor colds or coughs or diarrhea and then suddenly, they were dead. The poor diet lowered their resistance. Even if the hospital had antibiotics, their bodies were too weak. The babies were in the worst shape. Their mothers, themselves undernourished, didn't produce enough breast milk. Baby formula was nonexistent and milk rare. In the past, mothers who couldn't produce enough breast milk would feed their babies a watered-down congee made from cooked rice; now most of them couldn't afford the rice either.

Then there were children who had no diagnosable symptoms at all, just a vague malaise. They would appear pale or slightly bluish, their skin papery and lacking in elasticity. Sometimes they had swollen bellies, but sometimes nothing at all.

"I can't figure out what it is. I just can't get my child to stop crying," the mothers would tell Dr. Kim.

She nodded sympathetically because she recognized the condition, but she was at a loss for words. How do you tell a mother her child needs more food when there is nothing more to give?

Dr. Kim would write out a slip admitting the child to the hospital, knowing she had no cure for this condition. The hospital didn't have any food either. As she did her rounds, walking through the pediatric ward, the children would follow her with their eyes. Even when her back was turned, she could feel their eyes staring at her white gown, wondering if she could relieve their pain and soon realizing that she could not.

"They would look at me with accusing eyes. Even four-year-olds knew they were dying and that I wasn't doing anything to help them," Dr. Kim told me years later. "All I was capable of doing was to cry with their mothers over their bodies afterward."

Dr. Kim hadn't been a doctor long enough to have erected the protective wall that would insulate her from the suffering around her. The children's pain was her pain. Years later, when I asked her if she remembered any of the children who had died on her watch, she answered sharply, "I remember all of them."

Over the years the hospital provided less and less. The furnace in the basement went out after it ran out of coal, so the hospital had no heat. When the running water went off, nobody could properly mop the floors. Even during the day it was so dark in the interior of the building that doctors had to stand by windows to write up their reports. Patients brought their own food, their own blankets. Since bandages were scarce, they would cut up bedding to make them. The hospital was still able to manufacture intravenous fluid, but they didn't have bottles for it. The patients had to bring their own, which were often empty bottles of Chongjin's most popular beer, Rakwon, or "Paradise."

"If they brought in one beer bottle, they'd get one IV. If they brought in two bottles, they would get two IVs," Dr. Kim said. "It sounds too embarrassing to admit, but that's just the way it is."

Eventually the hospital emptied out. People stopped bringing their sick loved ones. Why bother?

—

KIM IL-SUNG'S DEATH had, in fact, not changed much in the country. Kim Jong-il had gradually been assuming power over the decade preceding his father's death. The economy's inevitable collapse had been set in motion years before under the weight of its own inefficiencies. But North Korea's Great Leader picked a convenient time to die, one that would prevent his legacy from being tarnished by the catastrophic events of the coming years. Had he lived a moment longer, North Koreans today would not be able to look back with nostalgia at the relative plenty they had enjoyed during his lifetime. His passing coincided with the last gasps of his Communist dream.

By 1995, North Korea's economy was as stone-cold dead as the Great Leader's body. Per capita income was plummeting, from $2,460 in 1991 to $719 in 1995. North Korea's merchandise exports dropped from $2 billion to about $800 million. The collapse of the economy had an organic quality to it, as though a living being were slowly shutting down and dying.

In Chongjin, the hulking factories along the waterfront looked like a wall of rust, their smokestacks lined up like the bars of a prison. The smokestacks were the most reliable indicators. On most days, only a few spat out smoke from their furnaces. You could count the distinct puffs of smoke—one, two, at most three—and see that the heartbeat of the city was fading. The main gates of the factories were now coiled shut with chains and padlocks—that is, if the locks hadn't been spirited away by the thieves who had already dismantled and removed the machinery.

Just north of the industrial district the waves lapped quietly against the empty piers of the port. The Japanese and Soviet freighters that used to make regular calls to pick up steel plates from the mills were gone. Now there was only North Korea's fleet of rusting fishing vessels. Perched on a cliff above the port, giant letters proclaimed KIM JONG-IL, SUN OF THE 21ST CENTURY, but even they appeared to be crumbling into the landscape. The red lettering on the propaganda signs along the road hadn't been repainted for years and had faded to a dull pink.

One of the most polluted cities in North Korea, Chongjin now took on a new beauty, stark and quiet. In autumn and winter, the dry seasons in northeast Asia, the sky was crisp and blue. The sharp odor of sulfur from the steelworks had lifted, allowing people once more to smell the sea. In summer, hollyhocks crept up the sides of concrete walls. Even the garbage was gone. Not that North Korea ever had much litter—there was never enough of anything to go to waste—but with economic life at a standstill, the detritus of civilization was disappearing. There were no plastic bags or candy wrappers wafting in the breeze, no soda cans floating in the harbor. If somebody stamped out a cigarette on the pavement, somebody else would pick it up to extract a few flecks of tobacco to roll again with newspaper.

THE ACCORDION AND
THE BLACKBOARD

Accordion lessons in Pyongyang, 2005.

K IM IL-SUNG'S DEATH CAUSED MI-RAN'S FINAL EXAM IN MUSIC
to be postponed, so she was not able to graduate until the fall of
1994. It was an inauspicious time to be launching a teaching career—or anything else, for that matter. Mi-ran was eager to move
back home with her parents, as food distribution in Chongjin had
stopped entirely. She requested a teaching assignment close to home
and was fortunate to be sent to a kindergarten near the Saenggir-

yong mines, where her father had worked. The mines were carved into hills the color of milky coffee two miles north of Kyongsong on the main road to Chongjin. Mi-ran's parents were relieved to have her back home where they could make sure she ate properly. It was common in Korea for unmarried adults, especially girls, to live with their parents. She could help around the house and keep her father company, since he hardly went to work these days. The two rooms of their harmonica house felt empty now that her two older sisters had married, and her brother was in teachers' college.

The kindergarten was about a forty-five-minute walk from home and looked almost identical to the one in Chongjin where she had apprenticed. It was housed in a single-story concrete building that might have looked grim if not for the iron fence with colorfully painted sunflowers that encircled it and formed an archway over the entrance with the slogan "We are happy." In the courtyard out front were a few old pieces of playground equipment—a swing set with broken wooden seats, a slide, and monkey bars. The classrooms were standard issue with matching father-and-son portraits of Kim Il-sung and Kim Jong-il presiding above the blackboard. The squat double desks were made of worn wooden planks on metal frames. On one side of the room under the windows were folded stacks of mats to be used at nap time. The other side had a large bookcase with only a few books, now barely legible because they'd been photocopied long ago from the originals and were now in varying shades of gray. Books and paper were always scarce, and ambitious mothers had to hand-copy textbooks if they wanted their children to study at home.

The difference between the schools was evident in the pupils themselves. The village children were visibly poorer than their city counterparts. Kindergartners did not yet wear uniforms, so they came to school in a motley assortment of hand-me-downs, often swathed in many layers since there was little heating in the school. Mi-ran was surprised by how ragged the children looked. As she helped them off with their outerwear, she peeled layer after layer until the tiny body inside was revealed. When she held their hands in her own, their baby fingers squeezed into fists as tiny as walnuts. These children, five- and six-year-olds, looked to her no bigger than three- and four-year-olds. In Chongjin, her pupils had been the children of factory workers and bureaucrats; these were the children of miners. Mi-ran realized that for all the problems with the food supply in the city, it was even worse for the miners. In the past, miners got extra rations—900 grams daily as opposed to the 700 grams for the average worker—to reward them for their hard physical labor. Now that both the kaolin and coal mines around Saenggiryong were closed most of the year, food rations for the miners had been cut. Mi-ran wondered if some of the children were coming to school mainly for the free lunch the cafeteria served, a thin soup made of salt and dry leaves like she'd had in the college dorm.

Still, Mi-ran approached her new job with enthusiasm. To be a teacher, a member of the educated and respectable class, was a big step up for the daughter of a miner, not to mention one from a family from the lowest rungs of society. She couldn't wait to get up in the morning and put on the crisp white blouse that she kept pressed under her bed mat at night.

The school day started at 8:00 A.M. Mi-ran put on her perkiest smile to greet the children as they filed into the classroom. As soon as she got them into their assigned seats, she brought out her accordion. All teachers were required to play the accordion—it had been her final test before graduation. It was often called the "people's instrument" since it was portable enough to carry along on a march to a construction site or for a day of voluntary hard labor in the fields—nothing like a rousing march played on accordion to motivate workers in the field or on the construction site. In the classroom teachers often sang "We Have Nothing to Envy in the World," which had a singsongy tune as familiar to North Korean children as "Twinkle, Twinkle, Little Star."

Mi-ran had sung it as a schoolgirl and knew the words by heart:

Our father, we have nothing to envy in the world.
Our house is within the embrace of the Workers' Party.
We are all brothers and sisters.
Even if a sea of fire comes toward us, sweet children
do not need to be afraid,
Our father is here.
We have nothing to envy in this world.

Mi-ran wasn't blessed with her sister Mi-hee's musical talent—as smitten as Jun-sang was with her, he would wince whenever she sang. Her little students were less fussy. Their faces tilted up at her, bright with animation, when she sang. They adored her and responded to her enthusiasm in kind. Mi-ran always regretted that her brother was so close to her in age that he was a rival rather than a little brother she could instruct and boss around. She loved her job. As far as the content of what she was teaching, she didn't pause to contemplate whether it was right or wrong. She didn't know education could be any different.

In his 1977 *Theses on Socialist Education*, Kim Il-sung wrote, "Only on the basis of sound political and ideological education will the people's scientific and technological education and physical culture be successful." Since Mi-ran's pupils could not yet read from the Great Leader's copious works (his name was affixed to more than a dozen books, Kim Jong-il's to another dozen), she would read excerpts aloud. The children were encouraged to repeat key phrases after her in unison. A cute little girl or boy reciting the sayings of Kim Il-sung in a childish, high-pitched voice would always inspire a chuckle and a broad smile from the adults. After the ideological training, the lessons moved on to more familiar subjects, but the Great Leader was never far from the children's minds. Whether they were studying math, science, reading, music, or art, the children were taught to revere the leadership and hate the enemy. For example, a first-grade math book contained the following questions:

"Eight boys and nine girls are singing anthems in praise of Kim Il-sung. How many children are singing in total?"

"A girl is acting as a messenger to our patriotic troops during the war against the Japanese occupation. She carries messages in a basket containing five apples, but is stopped by a Japanese soldier at a checkpoint. He steals two of her apples. How many are left?"

"Three soldiers from the Korean People's Army killed thirty American soldiers. How many American soldiers were killed by each of them if they all killed an equal number of enemy soldiers?"

A first-grade reading primer published in 2003 included the following poem, entitled "Where Are We Going?":

Where have we gone?
We have gone to the forest.
Where are we going?
We are going over the hills.
What are we going to do?
We are going to kill the Japanese soldiers.

One of the songs taught in music class was "Shoot the Yankee Bastards":

Our enemies are the American bastards
Who are trying to take over our beautiful fatherland.
With guns that I make with my own hands
I will shoot them. BANG, BANG, BANG.

Reading primers told stories of children who were beaten, bayoneted, burned, splashed with acid, or thrown into wells by villains who were invariably Christian missionaries, Japanese bastards, or American imperialist bastards. In a popular reader, a young boy was kicked to death by GIs when he refused to shine their shoes. American soldiers were drawn with beakish noses like the Jews in the anti-Semitic cartoons of Nazi Germany.

Mi-ran had heard a lot about U.S. atrocities during the Korean War, but she wasn't sure what to believe. Her own mother remembered the American GIs who drove through her town as tall and handsome.

"We used to run after them," her mother recalled.

"Run *after* them? You didn't run away?"

"No, they gave us chewing gum," her mother had told her.

"You mean they didn't try to kill you?" Mi-ran was incredulous when she heard her mother's story.

For history class, the children went on an excursion. All of the larger elementary schools had one room set aside for the purpose of teaching about the Great Leader, called the Kim Il-sung Research Institute. The children from the mining kindergarten walked to Kyongsong's main elementary school to visit this special room, which was

housed in a new wing and was clean, bright, and better heated than
the rest of the school. The Workers' Party conducted periodic spot
checks to make sure the school janitors were keeping the place im-
maculate. The room was like a shrine. Even the kindergartners knew
they were not permitted to giggle, push, or whisper when in the special Kim Il-sung room. They took off their shoes and lined up quietly.
They approached the portrait of Kim Il-sung, bowed deeply three
times, and said, "Thank you, Father."

The centerpiece of the room was a model of Kim Il-sung's birthplace in Mangyongdae, a village on the outskirts of Pyongyang, in a
glass-topped case. The children peered through the glass at a miniature thatched-roof cottage, and learned that this was where the
Great Leader was born, in humble circumstances, and that he hailed
from a family of patriots and revolutionaries. The children were told
how he shouted anti-Japanese slogans during the March 1 Movement, a 1919 uprising against the occupation—no matter that Kim
Il-sung was only seven years old at the time—and how he used to
scold wealthy landlords, having been a Communist in spirit at an
early age. They heard how he left home as a thirteen-year-old to lib-
erate his nation. Oil paintings lining the walls of the room depicted
Kim Il-sung's exploits in the anti-Japanese struggle. From the North
Korean perspective, he almost single-handedly defeated the Japanese. The official history omitted his time spent in the Soviet Union
and Stalin's role in installing him into the North Korean leadership.

If anything, Kim Il-sung appeared greater in death even than life.
Pyongyang ordered that the calendars be changed. Instead of marking time from the birth and death of Christ, the modern era for
North Koreans would now begin in 1912 with the birth of Kim
Il-sung so that the year 1996 would now be known as Juche 84. Kim
Il-sung was later named "eternal president," ruling the country in
spirit from the confines of his climate-controlled mausoleum beneath the Tower of Eternal Life. Kim Jong-il assumed the titles of
general secretary of the Workers' Party and chairman of the National Defense Commission, the latter being the highest office in the
nation. Although there was no doubt that Kim Jong-il was the head
of state, his deferral of the presidential title to his father demon-
strated his filial loyalty while allowing him to wield power in the

name of a father who was genuinely revered and far more popular than himself. Prior to 1996 he banned statues of himself, discouraged portraits, and avoided public appearances, but after his father's death he began to assume a higher profile. That year, the Ministry of Education issued orders for schools around the country to set up Kim Jong-il Research Institutes. They would be just like the special rooms for his father, except in place of the humble village of Mangyongdae, the room would have a model of Mount Paektu, the volcanic mountain straddling the Chinese–North Korean border where the younger Kim's birth was claimed to have been heralded by a double rainbow. Mount Paektu was a good choice: Koreans have long revered it as the birthplace of the mythological figure Tangun, the son of a god and a she-bear who was said to have established the first Korean kingdom in 2333 B.C. No matter that Soviet records showed Kim Jong-il was actually born near Khabarovsk, in the Russian Far East, while his father was fighting with the Red Army.

Reinventing history and erecting myths was easy enough in North Korea; much more difficult in 1996 was actually putting up a building. The Kim Jong-il room had to be of comparable quality with his father's room, but with the factories out of commission, bricks, cement, glass, and even lumber were in scarce supply. The material most difficult to procure was glass for the windows, as the glass factory in Chongjin had closed. These days, when windows broke, they were covered with boards or plastic. The only place that still manufactured glass was a factory in Nampo, a Yellow Sea port, but schools had no money to purchase the glass. The school in Kyongsong devised a plan. Students and teachers would collect some of the area's famous pottery—produced from the kaolin of the mines—and take it to Nampo, which was home to famous salt flats. The group would trade their pottery for salt, sell the salt at a profit, and use the proceeds to pay for the glass. It was a rather convoluted plan, but nobody had a better idea. They had been instructed to build the Kim Jong-il room with their own resources as part of a nationwide campaign. The principal was asking teachers and parents to join the trip. As Mi-ran was known to be energetic and resourceful, and most of all trustworthy, she was asked to go to Nampo.

MI-RAN STARTED PLOTTING the minute she heard about the trip. She furtively consulted a map of the railroad lines. As she suspected, Nampo was on the other side of the Korean peninsula, to the southwest of Pyongyang. Whichever train they took would have to go through Pyongyang and would most likely stop at the big terminus on the outskirts where the universities were concentrated. She would be within a few miles of Jun-sang's campus!

Since Kim Il-sung's death, it had become harder than ever for them to stay in touch. They had long passed the awkward stage in which being together brought about as much discomfort as pleasure; now they were relaxed in each other's company, and enjoyed the simple friendship. But lately the letters that once took weeks to arrive now took months or would not arrive at all. People suspected that railroad employees burned mail to keep warm during the bitingly cold winter.

The intervals between Jun-sang's visits home also grew longer. Mi-ran hated being the one stuck at home waiting, hoping for a knock on the door, a surprise visit, even a letter, any sign that he was thinking of her. She wasn't a passive person by nature and would have liked to take the initiative herself to visit him, but travel permits to Pyongyang were notoriously hard to get. In order to keep Pyongyang as a showcase city, the North Korean government restricted visitors. Mi-ran knew of a family in her neighborhood who had been forced to move from Pyongyang because one of the sons suffered from dwarfism. Ordinary people from the countryside would visit Pyongyang only on a group trip, with their work unit or their school. Mi-ran had been to her nation's capital only once before, on a field trip. She would have no chance of getting a permit on her own. But who would stop her from hopping out at the train station?

There were five of them traveling together—two parents, the principal, another teacher, and Mi-ran. The trip to Nampo took three days because of the poor track conditions. As the train stopped and started, jostling over the rails, Mi-ran stared out the window, lost in thought, trying to figure out how to make her break from the group. It didn't take long for her traveling companions to wonder why the young teacher, usually the most vivacious of the bunch, was incommunicative and withdrawn.

"Oh, you know. Family problems," she told them. The fib gave her an idea, and one lie gave birth to another. On the return trip she would get off the train near Pyongyang to meet a relative at the station. She would catch the next train back to Chongjin on her own. They shouldn't question her too closely as this was an urgent, personal matter.

Mi-ran's traveling companions nodded knowingly, averting their eyes with embarrassment as she got off the train. They assumed that she was stopping in Pyongyang to beg money from a wealthier relative. They could relate. Everybody in Chongjin was broke, especially the teachers. They hadn't been paid in over a year.

As the train disappeared down the tracks carrying her colleagues back to Chongjin, Mi-ran stood frozen on the platform. It was a cavernous station, barely illuminated, the exhaust from the train engines blotting out what little light seeped through the roof. Mi-ran had never traveled alone before. She had almost no money and no proper documentation. The travel papers she carried stated very clearly that she was allowed only transit through Pyongyang. She looked at the crowd of passengers that had disembarked from the train being funneled into a line that led to a single exit, flanked by police. It was much stricter than the control system in Chongjin. She hadn't thought through this part of the plan at all. If she were caught trying to sneak out with the wrong papers, she would most certainly be arrested. She could be sent to a labor camp. At best, she would lose her teaching job—yet another black mark for a family already plagued by their low class rank.

Mi-ran walked slowly down the platform, trying to find another exit through the haze. She turned and noticed that a man in uniform was watching her. She kept walking and then glanced back again. He was still watching. Then she realized that he was following her. Not until the man came close enough to speak to her did she understand that he'd been staring because he found her attractive. Nor did she realize that his uniform was that of a railroad mechanic, not the police. The man was about her own age and had a kind, trusting face. She explained her predicament, more or less, just omitting the part about the boyfriend.

"My older brother lives near the station," she blurted out, genuine in her distress although lying. "I wanted to visit him but I forgot my papers. Is the control here very strict?"

The railroad mechanic fell for the damsel-in-distress act. He escorted her past crates of cargo to a freight exit that was unguarded. Then he asked if he might see her again. She scribbled down a fake name and address. She felt guilty. In just one day, she'd committed a lifetime's worth of duplicity.

AT THE FRONT GATE of the university, the student guarding the entrance eyed Mi-ran suspiciously. He then went off to look for Jun-sang. He directed her to sit down in the guardhouse, which she did reluctantly. She tried to compose herself, even as she felt curious eyes on her from the university's courtyard beyond the gate. She didn't want to look as if she was primping so she stifled the impulse to smooth her hair or to resettle her blouse, which was sticking to her skin in the heat. It was late summer and the day was still hot even though the sun had just dropped behind the row of university buildings. She watched the young men crisscrossing through the shadows on their way to dinner. The science academy was nominally coeducational, but the female students lived at another end of campus and were sufficiently few in number to be a novelty. One of the students poked his head into the guardhouse and started ribbing her. "So is he *really* your brother? Not your boyfriend?"

It was almost dark by the time she spied Jun-sang emerging from the courtyard. He was pushing a bicycle and was dressed in a T-shirt and gym pants—he clearly was not expecting a visitor. A security light in the courtyard behind him had been switched on, obscuring the expression on his face. All Mi-ran could see as he approached were the contours of his cheekbones pushing out into a startled grin that she saw stretched across his face when he turned toward her. He kept his hands on the handlebars—it was out of the question to hug her—but she had no doubt that he was thrilled to see her.

He laughed. "No, no, no. It can't be."

She stifled her own smile. "I just happened to be in the neighborhood."

Mi-ran and Jun-sang walked off campus with the same measured gait they used to demonstrate their nonchalance when they went out back home. Behind them, Mi-ran heard a few of the male students whistling and making catcalls, but she and Jun-sang didn't flinch or look back; it was better to act cool. Gossip about them that started at the university could eventually filter back to Jun-sang's parents, perhaps even to Mi-ran's. He wheeled the bicycle so that it formed a barrier between them, but once they were out of sight, Mi-ran hopped on the luggage rack, sitting sideways for modesty's sake, as Jun-sang pedaled. Only her bare upper arm grazed Jun-sang's back as they rode into the dark. It was as much physical intimacy as had ever passed between them.

Jun-sang marveled at her audacity. His relatives hadn't even managed to get a travel permit to visit him in Pyongyang. When the student had come to tell him an hour earlier that his "younger sister" was waiting for him at the front gate, he assumed it was a mistake. He had never dared to imagine, not in his wildest fantasies, that Mi-ran would come. Jun-sang was always trying to figure out what exactly it was about her that kept him so hooked, and now he remembered—she was full of surprises. On the one hand, she seemed so girlish, so naïve, so much less capable than he, but on the other hand she had the nerve to pull off a stunt like this. He reminded himself that he should never underestimate her. He was surprised again that evening when, sitting together on a bench under a tree with drooping branches, she did not protest when he put his arm around her shoulders. The night carried the first hint of autumn's chill, and he offered his arm for warmth. He was sure she would brush him away, but they sat there, comfortably nestled together.

The night passed quickly that way. They talked until the conversation would without warning run out, and then they would walk some more until their legs grew tired and they looked for another place to sit. Even in Pyongyang street lamps by now weren't working and no ambient light leaked from the buildings. Just like at home, they could hide in the darkness. Once the eyes adjusted, you could discern the outline of the person immediately next to you, but everybody else was invisible, their presence marked only by the shuffling of footsteps and the babble of other conversations. Mi-ran and Jun-sang were wrapped in a cocoon with life streaming by them, never intruding.

After midnight, Mi-ran's exhaustion began to show. She hadn't slept much during the journey. Jun-sang reached into his pocket to see if he had enough money from his allowance to pay for a room in the hotel next to the railroad station. With a small gratuity, he assured her, the proprietor would overlook her lack of travel papers so that she could have a decent night's sleep before heading home. He had no other intentions; in all innocence it hadn't occurred to him that a hotel room could be used for anything else.

"No, no, I must go home," she protested. She had already violated enough rules and customs and was not about to break the taboo against a young woman sleeping in a hotel.

They walked together to the railroad station, the bicycle again between them. Although it was well past midnight, it was lively around the station. People had acquired the habit of waiting all night for trains, since they didn't run on fixed schedules anymore. Near the station, a woman had set up a small wood-burning stove on which she stirred a big cauldron of *doenjang jigae,* a spicy soybean soup. They ate side by side on a low wooden plank. Mi-ran accepted Jun-sang's gift of some biscuits and a bottle of water for the journey. By the time the train left, it was 5:00 A.M., and she quickly fell asleep in the first light of morning.

MI-RAN'S ELATION AFTER the trip soon evaporated. As the adrenaline rush of the adventure left her, she felt drained and uneasy. The difficulty of getting to and from Pyongyang underscored the hopelessness of the romance. She didn't know when she would see Jun-sang again. He was ensconced in university life, while she lived with her family back home. How was it that, in a country as small as North Korea, Pyongyang could feel as far away as the moon?

She was also nagged by some of what she'd seen on her journey. It had been the first time in years that she'd traveled outside

Chongjin, and even in her distracted state, she couldn't help noticing how shabby everything looked along the way. She saw children barely older than her own pupils dressed in rags, begging food at the train stations.

Their last night in Nampo, after buying the glass, she and her companions were sleeping outside the train station since they didn't have money for a hotel and the weather was mild. In front of the station, there was a small park, really more like a traffic rotary with a tree in the center and a grassy lawn on which people had spread out cardboard boxes and vinyl mats to sleep. Mi-ran had dropped into a fitful sleep, turning this way and that trying to get comfortable, when she saw that a group of people had stood up. They were talking quietly among themselves and pointing to one of the people near them, curled up under the tree, soundly asleep. Except he wasn't. He was dead.

After a while, a wooden ox cart pulled up. The people who were standing around grabbed the body by the arms and ankles and hoisted it up. Just before the body dropped with a thud onto the wooden planks, Mi-ran caught a glimpse of it. The dead man looked young, maybe even a teenager, judging from the smooth skin around his chin. His shirt fell open as the legs were lifted, revealing the bare skin of his chest. The ridges of his ribs glowed luminescently out of the darkness. He was emaciated, skinnier than any human being she'd ever seen, but then again, she'd never seen a dead body before. She shuddered and drifted back off to sleep.

Afterward she wondered what had happened to the man. Could he have died of hunger? Despite the fact that nobody had quite enough food these days and even the government had acknowledged a food crisis after the floods of the previous summer, Mi-ran had never heard of anybody starving to death in North Korea. That happened in Africa or in China. Indeed, the older people talked of all the Chinese who died during the 1950s and 1960s because of Mao's disastrous economic policies. "We're so lucky to have Kim Il-sung," they would say.

Mi-ran regretted that she hadn't asked Jun-sang what was going on—she hadn't mentioned it because she didn't want to ruin their few hours together—but now, back at home, she started noticing things she hadn't before. She had remarked when she first came to the kindergarten on the small size of her pupils; now they looked like they were growing younger, time turning backward, like a movie reel run in reverse. Each child was supposed to bring from home a bundle of firewood for the furnace in the school basement but many had trouble carrying it. Their big heads lolled on top of scrawny necks; their delicate rib cages protruded over waists so small that she could encircle them with her hands. Some of them were starting to swell in the stomach. It was all becoming clear to her. Mi-ran remembered seeing a photograph of a famine victim in Somalia with a protruding stomach; although she didn't know the medical terminology, she remembered from her teachers' college course on nutrition that it was caused by severe protein deficiency. Mi-ran also noticed that the children's black hair was getting lighter, more copper-toned.

The school cafeteria had closed for lack of food. The students were instructed to bring a lunch box from home, but many came empty-handed. When it was only one or two who didn't have lunch, Mi-ran would take one spoon each from those with to give to those without. But soon the parents who sent lunch came in to complain.

"We don't have enough at home to share," pleaded one mother.

Mi-ran heard a rumor that the school might get some biscuits and powdered milk from a foreign humanitarian aid agency. A delegation was visiting another school in the area and the children with the best clothing were brought out, the road leading to the school repaired, the building and courtyards swept immaculately clean. But no foreign aid arrived. Instead, the teachers were given a small plot of land nearby on which they were ordered to grow corn. The corn was later scraped off the cob and boiled until it puffed up like popcorn. It was a snack to ease the children's hunger pangs, but it didn't provide enough calories to make a difference.

The teachers weren't supposed to play favorites, but Mi-ran definitely had one. The girl was named Hye-ryung (Shining Benevolence), and even at the age of six she was the class beauty. She had the longest eyelashes Mi-ran had ever seen on a child and they surrounded bright round eyes. In the beginning, she was a lively, attentive student, one of the ones who delighted Mi-ran by the way she stared adoringly at her teacher as though trying to capture every word. Now she was lethargic and sometimes fell asleep in class.

"Wake up. Wake up," Mi-ran called out to her one day when she saw the girl slumped over her desk, her head turned so that her cheek pressed against the wooden desk.

Mi-ran cupped her hands under the girl's chin and held up her face. Her eyes had narrowed to slits sunken beneath swollen lids. She was unfocused. The hair spilling out around Mi-ran's hands was brittle and unpleasant to the touch.

A few days later, the girl stopped coming to school. Since Mi-ran knew her family from the neighborhood, she thought she should stop by the home to ask after her. But somehow she held back. What was the point? She knew exactly what was wrong with Hye-ryung. She had no way of fixing it.

Too many others in her class were in the same situation. They'd flop over their desks during lessons. At recess, when others went scampering out to the monkey bars and swings, they stayed put, either sleeping at their desks or stretched out on the nap-time mats.

Always the same progression: first, the family wouldn't be able to send the quota of firewood; then the lunch bag would disappear; then the child would stop participating in class and would sleep through recess; then, without explanation, the child would stop coming to school. Over three years, enrollment in the kindergarten dropped from fifty students to fifteen.

What happened to those children? Mi-ran didn't pry too deeply for fear of the answer she didn't want to hear.

THE NEXT TIME MI-RAN saw Jun-sang it was winter. It was his turn to surprise her. He had come home from school early for vacation. Rather than dropping by her house and risking an encounter with her parents, he came to the kindergarten. School had let out for the day, but she was still there, cleaning the classroom.

The classroom had no adult chairs, so Mi-ran folded herself into the little chair behind the wooden desk where her favorite pupil was so easily able to wedge her tiny body. She told Jun-sang what was happening to her students. He tried to reassure her.

"What can *you* do?" he said. "Even a king couldn't help these people. Don't take it all on your shoulders."

The conversation was awkward, as they talked around the embarrassing truth. Neither was suffering for lack of food. What Jun-sang's father couldn't grow in his vegetable patch next to the house, they bought on the black market with their stash of Japanese yen. Oddly enough, Mi-ran was eating better than she had in years, a result of having left the college dormitory for her parents' home. In the midst of the economic crisis, somehow the family's poor class standing didn't matter so much. Mi-ran's gorgeous eldest sister had married surprisingly well, her good looks trumping the troubled family background. Her husband was in the military and used his connections to help the rest of the family. Mi-ran's mother continued to find new ways to make money. After the electricity went out, she couldn't operate the freezer she used for her soy-milk ice cream, but she started a few other businesses—raising pigs, making tofu, grinding corn.

A DECADE LATER, when Mi-ran was a mother herself, trying to lose her postpregnancy weight through aerobics, this period of her life weighed like a stone on her conscience. She often felt sick over what she did and didn't do to help her young students. How could she have eaten so well herself when they were starving?

It is axiomatic that one death is a tragedy, a thousand is a statistic. So it was for Mi-ran. What she didn't realize is that her indifference was an acquired survival skill. In order to get through the 1990s alive, one had to suppress any impulse to share food. To avoid going insane, one had to learn to stop caring. In time, Mi-ran would learn how to walk around a dead body on the street without paying much notice. She could pass a five-year-old on the verge of death without feeling obliged to help. If she wasn't going to share her food with her favorite pupil, she certainly wasn't going to help a perfect stranger.

CHAPTER 9

THE GOOD DIE FIRST

Propaganda poster for the Arduous March.

IT HAS BEEN SAID THAT PEOPLE REARED IN COMMUNIST COUN-
tries cannot fend for themselves because they expect the government to take care of them. This was not true of many of the victims
of the North Korean famine. People did not go passively to their
deaths. When the public distribution system was cut off, they were
forced to tap their deepest wells of creativity to feed themselves.
They devised traps out of buckets and string to catch small animals
in the field, draped nets over their balconies to snare sparrows. They
educated themselves in the nutritive properties of plants. They
reached back into their collective memory of famines past and recalled the survival tricks of their forefathers. They stripped the
sweet inner bark of pine trees to grind into a fine powder that could

be used in place of flour. They pounded acorns into a gelatinous paste that could be molded into cubes that practically melted in your mouth.

North Koreans learned to swallow their pride and hold their noses. They picked kernels of undigested corn out of the excrement of farm animals. Shipyard workers developed a technique by which they scraped the bottoms of the cargo holds where food had been stored, then spread the foul-smelling gunk on the pavement to dry so that they could collect from it tiny grains of uncooked rice and other edibles.

On the beaches, people dug out shellfish from the sand and filled buckets with seaweed. When the authorities in 1995 erected fences along the beach (ostensibly to keep out spies, but more likely to prevent people from catching fish the state companies wanted to control), people went out to the unguarded cliffs over the sea and with long rakes tied together hoisted up seaweed.

Nobody told people what to do—the North Korean government didn't want to admit to the extent of the food shortage—so they fended for themselves. Women exchanged recipe tips. When making cornmeal, don't throw out the husk, cob, leaves, and stem of the corn—throw it all into the grinder. Even if it isn't nutritious, it is filling. Boil noodles for at least an hour to make them appear bigger. Add a few leaves of grass to soup to make it look as if it contains vegetables. Powder pine bark to make cakes.

All ingenuity was devoted to the gathering and production of food. You woke up early to find your breakfast and as soon as it was finished, you thought about what to find for dinner. Lunch was a luxury of the past. You slept during what used to be lunchtime to preserve your calories.

Ultimately it was not enough.

AFTER THE GARMENT FACTORY CLOSED, Mrs. Song floundered, wondering what to do with herself. She was still a good Communist with a natural dislike of anything that reeked of capitalism. Her beloved marshal, Kim Il-sung, had warned repeatedly that socialists must "guard against the poisonous ideas of capitalism and revision-ism." She liked to quote that particular saying.

Then again, nobody in the family had gotten paid since the Great Leader's death—not even her husband, with his party membership and prestigious job at the radio station. Chang-bo wasn't even get-ting the free wine and tobacco that were the customary perks of a journalist. Mrs. Song knew it was time to put aside her scruples and make money. But how?

She was about as unlikely an entrepreneur as one could imagine. She was fifty years old and had no business skills other than the abil-ity to tally numbers on the abacus. When she mulled this predica-ment with her family, however, they reminded her of her talents in the kitchen. Back in the days when you could get ingredients, Mrs. Song enjoyed cooking, and Chang-bo liked to eat. Her repertoire was naturally limited in that North Koreans had no exposure to for-eign cuisines, but their own was surprisingly sophisticated for a country whose name is now synonymous with famine. (In fact, many restaurateurs in South Korea come from north of the border.) North Korean cooks are creative, using natural ingredients such as pine mushrooms and seaweed. Whatever happens to be fresh and seasonal is mixed with rice, barley, or corn, and seasoned with red bean paste or chilies. The signature dish is Pyongyang *naengmyon,* cold buckwheat noodles served in a vinegary broth with myriad re-gional variations, adding hard-boiled eggs, cucumbers, or pears. If she was busy, Mrs. Song bought noodles from a shop; if not, she made them from scratch. Using the limited range of ingredients from the public distribution system, she could make *twigim,* batter-fried vegetables that were light and crisp. For her husband's birthday, she turned rice into a sweet glutinous cake called *deok.* She knew how to make her own corn liquor. Her daughters boasted that her kimchi was the best in the neighborhood.

Her family urged her to make her first stab at business in the kitchen and that the best product would be tofu, a good source of protein in difficult times. Tofu is widely used in Korean cooking, in soups or stews, fried crispy or fermented. Mrs. Song would use it in place of fish, sautéing it with oil and red pepper. In order to raise the money to buy soybeans, the family started selling their possessions. The first to go was their prized television—the Japanese model they'd gotten thanks to Chang-bo's father's intelligence service during the Korean War.

Making tofu is relatively easy, if labor-intensive. Soybeans are ground, then boiled, and a coagulating agent is added. Then, like cheese, it is squeezed through a cloth. Afterward, you are left with a watery milk and the husks of the soybeans. Mrs. Song thought it might be a good idea to complement her tofu business by raising pigs, which she could feed with the residue from the tofu. Behind their apartment building was a row of sheds used for storage. Mrs. Song bought a litter of piglets at the market and installed them in one of the sheds, securing the door with a big padlock.

For a few months, the business plan was a success. Mrs. Song converted her tiny kitchen into a tofu factory, boiling big vats of soybeans on the *ondol* stove in the apartment. Chang-bo tasted her recipes and approved. The piglets grew fatter on the bean husks and soy milk and whatever grass Mrs. Song could clip for them each morning, but it was becoming increasingly difficult to get wood and coal to fuel the stove. The electricity was working only a few hours a week, and even then its use was restricted to a single 60-watt lightbulb, a television, or a radio.

Without fuel to cook the soybeans, Mrs. Song couldn't make tofu. Without the tofu, she had nothing to feed the hungry pigs. It took hours for her to pick enough grass to satisfy them.

"Listen, we might as well eat the grass ourselves," she told Chang-bo, mostly in jest. Then she thought about it a bit and added, "If it doesn't poison the pigs, it won't poison us."

So they began their grim new regimen, quite a fall from grace for a couple who had fancied themselves gourmets. Mrs. Song would hike north and west from the city center to where the landscape hadn't yet been paved, carrying a kitchen knife and a basket to collect edible weeds and grass. If you got out to the mountains, you could maybe find dandelion or other weeds so tasty that people ate them even in good times. Occasionally, Mrs. Song would find rotten cabbage leaves that had been discarded by a farmer. She would take the day's pickings home and mix it with whatever food she had enough money to buy. Usually, it was ground cornmeal—the cheap kind made from the husks and cobs. If she couldn't afford that, she would buy a still cheaper powder made out of the ground inner bark of the pine, sometimes extended with a little sawdust.

No talent in the kitchen could disguise the god-awful taste. She had to pound away and chop endlessly to get the grasses and the barks into a soft-enough pulp to be digestible. They didn't have enough substance to be molded into a recognizable shape like a noodle or cake that might fool a person into thinking he was eating real food. All she could make was a porridge that was flavorless and textureless. The only seasoning she had was salt. A little garlic or red pepper might have disguised the terrible taste of the food, but they were too expensive. Oils were unavailable at any price and their complete absence made cooking difficult. Once while visiting her sister's sister-in-law for lunch, Mrs. Song was served a porridge made out of bean and corn stalks. Hungry as she was, she couldn't swallow it. The stalks were bitter and dry, and stuck in her throat like the twigs of a bird's nest. She gagged, turned beet red, and spat it out. She was mortified.

In the year after Kim Il-sung's death the only animal product she consumed was frog. Her brothers had caught some in the countryside. Mrs. Song's sister-in-law stir-fried the frogs in soy sauce, chopped them into small pieces, and served them over noodles. Mrs. Song pronounced it delicious. Frog wasn't typically part of Korean cuisine; Mrs. Song had never tried it before. Unfortunately, it would be her last opportunity. North Korea's frog population would soon be wiped out by overhunting.

By the middle of 1995, Mrs. Song and her husband had sold most of their valuable possessions for food. After the television went the used Japanese bicycle that was their main means of transportation, and then the sewing machine with which Mrs. Song had made their clothes. Chang-bo's watch was gone, as was an Oriental painting given to them as a wedding present. They sold most of their clothes and then the wooden wardrobe in which they stored them. The two-room apartment that had always seemed too small to contain the family and its clutter was now empty, the walls entirely bare except for the portraits of Kim Il-sung and Kim Jong-il. The only thing left to sell was the apartment itself.

This was an odd concept. In North Korea, you don't own your own home; you are merely awarded the right to live there. But an illegal real estate market had cropped up as people quietly swapped homes, paying off bureaucrats to look the other way. Mrs. Song was introduced to a woman whose husband was one of a number of North Korean workers who had been sent to work in the lumberyards in Russia and who therefore had some disposable income to spend on a better apartment.

Mrs. Song's apartment was in an excellent location in the heart of the city, which was ever more important now that the trolleys weren't working. Mrs. Song and Chang-bo had lived there for twenty years and had many friends—it was indeed a tribute to Mrs. Song's good nature that she had run the *inminban* for so many years without making enemies. She and Chang-bo agreed they didn't need so much space anymore. It was just the two of them and Chang-bo's mother. The girls were all married. Their son had moved in with his girlfriend, the older woman of whom Mrs. Song disapproved. It was a disgrace, she thought, but at least it was one less mouth to feed.

The apartment fetched 10,000 won—the equivalent of about $3,000. They moved to a single room. Mrs. Song decided she would use the money for another business venture: trading rice.

Rice is the staple of the Korean diet—in fact, the same word, *bap*, means rice or a meal. After 1995, Chongjin residents could get rice only if they had cash to buy it on the black market. North Hamgyong province was too cold and mountainous for rice paddies. With the exception of a small marshy inlet near Nanam, all the rice consumed in the city had to be transported in by train or truck, which jacked up the price since the road and rail lines were in such bad shape. Mrs. Song figured she could buy rice down the coast where it was cheaper, and carry it up by train. Trading rice—or any staple grain, for that matter—was highly illegal (sales of vegetables and meat were more tolerable to the government), but since everybody was doing it, Mrs. Song decided it would be okay to join in. She'd make a small profit and keep some rice for herself and Chang-bo. Her mouth watered at the thought. They hadn't had a proper bowl of rice since 1994. Corn was half the price.

Mrs. Song set out with 10,000 won stashed in her underwear, layers of winter clothing disguising the bulges. She took the train to South Pyongan province and bought 200 kilos of rice. On the morning of November 25, 1995, she was on her way home, less than a day's journey away, with the sacks of rice stuffed under her seat. Chang-bo's connections as a journalist had allowed her to get a choice sleeping berth in the third car of the train—the first two being for Workers' Party officials and military officers. It was at times like these that she appreciated the privileges of her rank. The train was long, and each time it rounded a curve, the back cars would come into view just long enough for her to see that the people without connections were all standing. They were packed in so tightly that they appeared to be one dark mass of humanity. Still more people clung to the roof. She had just climbed down from her berth at about 8:30 A.M. and was chatting with the other passengers in her sleeper—a soldier, a young woman, and a grandmother— about the poor condition of the tracks. The train had stopped and started throughout the night and was lurching so violently that they couldn't eat their breakfast. Their words came out in short bursts of staccato, each new jolt punctuating the conversation, until there was one bounce that lifted Mrs. Song right out of her seat and dumped her rudely on what seemed to be the floor. She was lying on her side, her left cheek pressed against something cold that turned out to be the metal frame of the window. The carriage was on its side.

She heard screams from behind. The train was a cage of twisted metal. The crowded back carriages had been almost entirely destroyed and most passengers killed. The elite front cars somehow were spared. The final death toll from the accident, which took place near Sinpo, 150 miles down the coast from Chongjin, was rumored to be about 700, although like most North Korean disasters, it was not reported.

Mrs. Song emerged from the wreckage with a gash in her cheek, the skin ripped off her leg, and a sprained back. The contents of the sleeper had fallen on top of her, but the fact that it was a closed compartment probably saved her life. She returned to Chongjin four days after the accident. She had always thought of herself as a lucky person—for being born under the loving care of Kim Il-sung, for her wonderful family—and now felt especially so, for having survived the train wreck. She was so clenched in pain that she had to be carried off the train upon her return to Chongjin, but when she glimpsed her husband and even her son, with whom she hadn't spoken for months, on the platform, she again counted her blessings. She got back most of her rice.

Mrs. Song's injuries proved more debilitating than she had thought. Once the euphoria wore off, she realized that she was badly hurt. She saw a doctor who gave her painkillers and warned her not to get out of bed for three months. She ignored the advice. Somebody needed to gather food for the family.

IN A FAMINE, people don't necessarily starve to death. Often some other ailment gets them first. Chronic malnutrition impairs the body's ability to battle infection and the hungry become increasingly susceptible to tuberculosis and typhoid. The starved body is too weak to metabolize antibiotics, even if they are available, and normally curable illnesses suddenly become fatal. Wild fluctuations of body chemistry can trigger strokes and heart attacks. People die from eating substitute foods that their bodies can't digest. Starvation can be a sneaky killer that disguises itself under bland statistics of increased child mortality or decreased life expectancy. It leaves behind only circumstantial evidence of "excess mortality"—statistics that show higher than normal deaths during a certain period.

The killer has a natural progression. It goes first for the most vulnerable—children under five. They come down with a cold and it turns into pneumonia; diarrhea turns into dysentery. Before the parents even think about getting help, the child is dead. Next the killer turns to the aged, starting with those over seventy, then working its way down the decades to people in their sixties and fifties. These people might have died anyway, but so soon? Then starvation makes its way through people in the prime of their lives. Men, because they have less body fat, usually perish before women. The strong and athletic are especially vulnerable because their metabolisms burn more calories.

Yet another gratuitous cruelty: the killer targets the most innocent, the people who would never steal food, lie, cheat, break the law, or betray a friend. It was a phenomenon that the Italian writer Primo Levi identified after emerging from Auschwitz, when he wrote that he and his fellow survivors never wanted to see one another again after the war because they had all done something of which they were ashamed.

As Mrs. Song would observe a decade later, when she thought back on all the people she knew who died during those years in Chongjin, it was the "simple and kindhearted people who did what they were told—they were the first to die."

In her own family, Mrs. Song's mother-in-law was the first to go. Chang-bo's mother had come to live with them shortly after their marriage in keeping with a tradition that confers on the oldest son responsibility for his parents. It is of course the daughter-in-law who carries the burden, so the relationship between a Korean wife and her mother-in-law is often fraught with resentment. Mrs. Song's mother-in-law had been a merciless critic in the early years of the marriage, especially after the birth of the three girls. She mellowed only a little after her grandson was born, but Mrs. Song took her filial duties seriously and worked hard to please.

Spring is always the leanest season in Korea because the autumn harvest is running out and the fields are being tilled for the next crop. This year, it was especially hard for Mrs. Song, who was recuperating from her train accident six months earlier. Her mother-in-law was seventy-three years old, a very ripe old age given North Korean life expectancy, and it would have been easy enough to dismiss her death as "her time to go," but Mrs. Song had no doubt that the tough old lady would have lived many more years if fed properly. Unable to work or hike into the mountains, she threw whatever weeds and grass she could find near her home into the soup. Her mother-in-law turned into a brittle sack of bones, with the telltale signs of pellagra around her eyes. In May 1996, she took ill with violent stomach cramps and dysentery. She was dead in a few days.

Mrs. Song had failed in the worst possible way a Korean woman could fail her family. Her despair at the death of her mother-in-law was heightened by the propaganda campaign that autumn that urged all citizens to work harder through the hard times. Posters showed a man with a bullhorn exhorting people to "charge forward into the new century in the spirit of victory in the Arduous March," followed by a helmeted soldier, a miner with a pickax, an intellectual wearing eyeglasses and carrying a blueprint, a farmer with a kerchief, and a general carrying a red flag. Even Kim Jong-il was reported by the official news service to be eating simple meals made of potatoes.

Now that it was just the two of them, Mrs. Song and Chang-bo decided to move again, to an even smaller place. This one was little more than a shack, its floor bare concrete and its walls crumbling plaster so fragile that Mrs. Song couldn't even hang the obligatory father-and-son portraits. She wrapped them carefully and left them in a corner. They had few possessions left. She had sold all of Chang-bo's books, except for the works by Kim Il-sung and Kim Jong-il, which one was not permitted to sell. She had sold her beloved kimchi urns. All they needed now were two pairs of chopsticks, two spoons, a few bowls and pans.

Chang-bo had quit the provincial radio station and took a new job with a broadcasting operation run by the railroad. The railroad had no money to pay him—just a promise that he would have a higher priority for the next distribution of food. But the food never arrived. After a few months, Mrs. Song and her husband had run through all the money they'd made selling the last apartment. Their oldest daughter, Oak-hee, would occasionally sneak a sack of corn from her own home, but she had to be careful not to be caught by her ill-tempered husband, who would beat her for "stealing food." His family had money, but didn't care to share with the in-laws.

Mrs. Song still couldn't hike into the mountains, so she got up ever earlier, at 6:00 A.M., then 5:00, in the hope of getting the overnight growth of sprouted weeds, which might be more tender and easier to digest. She would cook her weeds and bark until they were soft, adding salt to make a porridge and then mixing in a few spoons of cornmeal.

Mrs. Song didn't feel hungry so much as depleted. After she finished eating, the spoon would drop from her hand with a clang into the metal dish. She would collapse into a heap on the floor without bothering to change clothes, falling into a deep sleep until somehow her instinct for survival told her that, although it was still dark, she had to resume the search for food. She had lost her will to do anything else. She stopped combing the curly hair of which she used to be so proud; she didn't bother washing her clothes. Her weight dropped so much she couldn't get the single pair of trousers she owned to stay up over her hips. She had the sensation that she was already dead, floating above the empty receptacle of what once had been her body.

It was Chang-bo, though, whose health suffered the most. He had been an uncommonly large North Korean, weighing nearly 200 pounds in his prime. He was so heavy that his doctor some years back advised him to take up smoking as a way to lose weight. Now the protuberant belly of which he had been so proud—fat being something of a status symbol in North Korea—had turned into a hollow pouch. His skin became flaky, as though he was suffering from a bad case of eczema. His jowls sagged and his speech slurred. Mrs. Song took him to a doctor at the Railroad Management Bureau Hospital who diagnosed a mild stroke. After that episode, Chang-bo found it difficult to work. He couldn't focus. He complained of blurry eyesight. He couldn't lift the fountain pen he used for writing.

Chang-bo took to his bed, or rather to the quilts on the floor that was all they had left. His legs swelled up like balloons with what Mrs. Song had come to recognize as edema—fluid retention brought on by starvation. He talked incessantly about food. He spoke of the tofu soups his mother made him as a child and an unusually delicious meal of steamed crab with ginger that Mrs. Song had cooked for him when they were newlyweds. He had an uncanny ability to remember details of dishes she had cooked decades earlier. He was sweetly sentimental, even romantic, when he spoke about their meals together. He would take her hand in his own, his eyes wet and cloudy with the mist of his memories.

"Come, darling. Let's go to a good restaurant and order a nice bottle of rice wine," he told his wife one morning when they were stirring on the blankets. They hadn't eaten in three days. Mrs. Song looked at her husband with alarm, worried that he was hallucinating.

She ran out the door to the market, moving fast and forgetting all about the pain in her back. She was determined to steal, beg— whatever it took—to get some food for her husband. She spotted her older sister selling noodles. Her sister wasn't faring well—her skin was flaked just like Chang-bo's from malnutrition—so Mrs. Song had resisted asking her for help, but now she was desperate, and of course, her sister couldn't refuse.

"I'll pay you back," Mrs. Song promised as she ran back home, the adrenaline pumping her legs.

Chang-bo was curled up on his side under the blanket. Mrs. Song called his name. When he didn't respond, she went to turn him over—it wasn't difficult now that he had lost so much weight, but his legs and arms were stiff and got in the way.

Mrs. Song pounded and pounded on his chest, screaming for help even as she knew it was too late.

AFTER CHANG-BO'S DEATH, their son, Nam-oak, came to live with Mrs. Song. They had been estranged ever since he'd taken up with his older girlfriend. In truth, Mrs. Song's relationship with her only son had been uneasy since he was a teenager. It was not that he was outwardly rebellious, it was that she had a hard time breaking through his silence. Now, in the face of so much tragedy, the fact that he was living out of wedlock with an older woman seemed trivial. And the truth of the matter was that they needed each other. Mrs. Song was alone. Nam-oak's girlfriend's family was even worse off than his own and they had nothing at all to eat in the house.

Nam-oak had spent his entire youth training to be a boxer, but conditions were so bad at the athletic school that he came home one winter with his ear damaged from frostbite. He returned to Chongjin and got a job at the railroad station through family connections that dated to the Korean War, when Mrs. Song's father had been killed in the U.S. bombing. Just as they did with his father, the Railroad Management Bureau couldn't pay Nam-oak a salary, but there was the expectation that he would get priority for food when the distribution system resumed.

Mrs. Song's son was a strong, fit young man, the spitting image of his father but more athletic, more muscular, and at five foot nine, taller. He needed a lot of fuel to survive. When at first his body fat disappeared, he looked as lean and taut as a marathon runner, but eventually the muscle, too, was consumed, turning him into a cadaver. In the cold winter of 1997–98 when the temperatures dropped below freezing, he caught a bad cold that turned into pneumonia. Even with his weight loss, Nam-oak was too heavy for Mrs. Song to carry to the hospital—there were no ambulances working by now—so she went herself and explained his condition. A doctor wrote her a prescription for penicillin, but when she got to the market she found it cost 50 won—the same price as a kilo of corn.

She chose the corn.

Nam-oak died in March 1998, alone in the shack. Mrs. Song was at the market again scrounging for food. He was buried on a hill above town, next to his father's grave, close enough that it was visible from her home. The Railroad Management Bureau was able to provide a coffin, as it had for Chang-bo.

BY 1998, AN ESTIMATED 600,000 to 2 million North Koreans had died as a result of the famine, as much as 10 percent of the population. In Chongjin, where food supplies were cut off earlier than the rest of North Korea, the toll might have been as high as 20 percent. Exact figures would be nearly impossible to tally since North Korean hospitals could not report starvation as a cause of death.

Between 1996 and 2005, North Korea would receive $2.4 billion worth of food aid, much of it from the United States. But as much as the North Korean regime was willing to accept foreign food, it rejected the foreigners who came along with it. Aid agencies trying to help were initially restricted to Pyongyang and other carefully groomed locations. When they were allowed out of their offices and hotels, shabbily dressed people were ordered off the streets; during visits to schools and orphanages, only the best-dressed and best-fed could be seen. The government was asking for more aid and at the same time concealing those most in need. Aid agency staff living in Pyongyang weren't even permitted to study the Korean language.

In 1997 a few aid officials were allowed entry to Chongjin, with even greater restrictions than in Pyongyang. An aid worker for the French agency Action Contre la Faim (Action Against Hunger) wrote in a journal that she was not allowed to leave the Chonmason Hotel, located near the Chongjin port, on the grounds that she might be hit by a car. The agency pulled out soon afterward, reporting that it could not verify that aid was getting to the intended recipients. Doctors Without Borders also withdrew from the country. While big ships laden with donated grains from the U.N. World Food Programme started docking at Chongjin's port in 1998, the relief was off-loaded into trucks by the military and driven away. Some food reached orphanages and kindergartens, but much of it ended up in military stockpiles or sold on the black market. It took nearly a decade working inside North Korea before the U.N. agency was able to set up a satisfactory monitoring system. By the end of 1998, the worst of the famine was over, not necessarily because anything had improved but, as Mrs. Song later surmised, because there were fewer mouths to feed.

"Everybody who was going to die was already dead."

CHAPTER 10

MOTHERS OF INVENTION

A makeshift restaurant in Chongjin.

Mrs. Song did not attend her son's funeral. Grief, hunger, and the accumulated stress of the past few years had taken hold of her mind and body. She couldn't bring herself to return to the shack where her son had died. "I left him to die alone, I left him," she moaned repeatedly. She refused to eat. She wandered the streets until she collapsed.

Her daughters went out to look for her and found her lying in the weeds near their house, delirious with hunger and hypothermia. It was late March, but the temperatures at night were low enough to kill a seriously malnourished person. The daughters were shocked at their mother's appearance. Mrs. Song had been vain about her thick, curly hair; now it was matted and filthy. Her clothes were caked with mud. They carried her back to the home of the second daughter, stripped her, and bathed her as though she were a child. In fact, at fifty-two, Mrs. Song was so emaciated that she barely weighed more than Oak-hee's eight-year-old son. The women pooled their money to buy a bag of noodles for her. After fifteen days of consuming proper food, Mrs. Song was coherent enough to remember exactly what had happened and to plunge again into despair over the enormity of her loss.

Three deaths in three years—her mother-in-law in 1996, her husband in 1997, and her son in 1998. Mrs. Song had lost everything, including her Dear Marshal, whose loss she still grieved as much as that of her husband and son.

She finally worked up the courage to return home, to the shack that she considered the scene of the crime; she alone was responsible for the deaths in her family. As she walked, she looked up at the bald hills and saw simple wooden stakes that marked the graves of the recently deceased; her second son-in-law had made markers like that for both her husband and her son, who were buried on the hill. When she reached the shack she found the door ajar. She'd nailed it shut before she left because she didn't have a padlock, but somebody had clearly pried it open. She pushed the door open and stuck her head in to make sure nobody was lurking inside. The shack was empty. No people. No stuff. The dented aluminum pot she'd used for cooking porridge, the cheap metal bowls in which they ate it, the pair of chopsticks, the blanket in which her son was wrapped when he died—it was all gone. The thief had even removed the glass from the portraits of Kim Il-sung and Kim Jong-il, leaving the portraits behind.

Mrs. Song left, not even bothering to close the door behind her. She had nothing more that could be taken away, only her own life, which didn't matter much anymore. She couldn't understand why she was still alive. She thought she would just keep walking until she could collapse in the grass. She wanted to lie down and die. But somehow, she didn't. She started another business instead.

THIS WAS A STRANGE side effect of the famine: Just when things were hitting bottom, with deaths reaching the hundreds of thousands, a new spirit of enterprise was born. The collapse of the socialist food distribution system presented an opportunity for private businesses. It wasn't as though everybody could trek out to the mountains to pick leaves and berries and scrape pine bark; people had to buy their food somewhere and somebody had to supply it to them. North Koreans needed vendors: fishmongers, butchers, and bakers to fill the gap left by the collapse of the public system.

All of it was highly illegal. Kim Jong-il had taken an even harder line against individual enterprise than his father. "In a socialist society, even the food problem should be solved in a socialist way . . . Telling people to solve the food problems on their own creates egoism among people," he said in a December 1996 speech, one of the few in which he acknowledged the food crisis. Other than vegetables grown at home, food was not supposed to be sold on the market. To sell rice or any other grain was strictly forbidden; North Koreans considered it illegal and immoral, a stab in the heart of Communist ideology. Any private endeavor fell under the rubric of an "economic crime" and the penalties could include deportation to a labor camp and, if corruption was alleged, possible execution.

Then again, death was a virtual certainty for people who didn't show some private initiative. A human being needs at least 500 calories per day on average to survive; a person subsisting on a diet made up of what could be foraged in the woods would not survive more than three months. The imminence of death gave reluctant capitalists like Mrs. Song new courage.

After the debacle of trading rice, Mrs. Song knew she had to stick to the simplest possible business that didn't require travel or a big initial investment. Her most marketable skill, her only marketable skill, was cooking. But cooking was getting more and more difficult, as the supply of firewood grew ever more scarce. The hills nearby had turned brown and the tree line receded farther out of reach.

After some deliberation, Mrs. Song decided her future lay in cookies. Cookies needed only ten minutes in the oven; a modest bundle of firewood could bake four or five batches. They were easier to bake than bread and they made a quick meal for hungry people on the move.

Mrs. Song was joined in the cookie business by her youngest

daughter, Yong-hee, who was newly divorced—her marriage having broken up after only three months when Yong-hee discovered that her husband was a compulsive gambler. Yong-hee borrowed some money to buy scrap metal and found an unemployed welder from the steel mill to make it into an oven. It was basically a square box, divided in two so that charcoal could burn in the lower compartment while cookies could bake in the upper one. He also made a cookie sheet. Mrs. Song and Yong-hee walked through the markets of the city, taking note of the other vendors. There were many women who'd had the same idea, and for a while Mrs. Song took a job with one of them to watch and learn. She bought samples from other vendors to taste and compare. When she found one she liked, she tried to replicate the recipe.

Their trial efforts were dismal. The first batches were not suitable to sell to the public, not even by desperate North Korean standards. Mrs. Song and her daughter ate their failures rather than waste the precious ingredients. Eventually she figured out that she had to use more sugar and leavening. She added milk to the recipe. The dough was cut in five different shapes and it looked more like biscuits—a not-too-sweet and easy-to-digest snack food.

Mrs. Song got up at 5:00 A.M. to do the baking. The competition was stiff and her cookies needed to be fresh. She didn't have a cart or even a crate from which to sell her product, so she put the cookies in a plastic basin that she would carry wrapped on her back like a baby until she got to a main street with a lot of pedestrians and not too many competitors. She hung around markets and the big square in front of the train station. With her back still aching, she'd painfully ease herself into a cross-legged position on the ground with the cookies on her knees.

Her back still hurt from the accident, so she called out to passersby with the same enthusiasm she'd deployed as head of the *inminban* to get her neighbors to recycle garbage and collect night soil for the good of the fatherland.

"*Gwaja sassayo.*" The words had a singsongy rhythm in Korean. "Buy cookies."

Mrs. Song was a natural saleswoman. People were drawn to her warmth; if they were going to buy cookies, they would just as soon buy from her as from one of the dozens of other women doing the same. At the end of a fourteen-hour workday, she had about 100 won—50 cents—in her pocket, and a few bags of other goods, sometimes red peppers or a few lumps of coal, that she took in exchange for cookies. It was just enough for her to buy food for dinner and the ingredients for the next batch of cookies. She would trudge home exhausted and drop off to sleep, only to wake in a few hours to start all over again. Only now, she wasn't going to bed hungry.

THOUSANDS OF MIDDLE-AGED women were doing much the same thing as Mrs. Song. They were self-employed. They ran no workshops or stores; they didn't dare to set up the kiosks that were so ubiquitous in Russia during the time of perestroika. They knew nothing of business other than what they had been taught—all private endeavor was egoistic. But out of hunger and desperation, they were reinventing the concept of a free-market economy, which required *unlearning* a lifetime of propaganda. They had figured out that there was value in bartering skills; young people with more endurance could make the hike into the distant mountains to get the firewood that Mrs. Song couldn't reach and trade it for her cookies. If you owned a ladder, you could collect copper wire from the electric lines (no danger of electrocution anymore) and sell it for food. If you had the key to an abandoned factory, you could dismantle the machines, the windows, and the flooring to put to new use.

Whether a baking sheet or a wheelbarrow, it had to be made individually, by hand, because virtually no factories were operating. Women cut up scraps of canvas, melted discarded pieces of rubber, and stamped out crude sneakers. Old tires, wooden doors, and wires made a cart for transporting merchandise from market to home.

People educated themselves. A coal miner, an uneducated man, found a book on Oriental medicine and pored over it to recognize medicinal herbs that could be found in the mountains around Chongjin. He became as good as the doctors in identifying the herbs, but much better at getting out to the remote areas because he was used to physical labor.

Doctors, too, found other ways of making money. They didn't

have drugs themselves, but they could perform simple procedures in the hospital or at home. The most lucrative were abortions, which were technically illegal without special permission but were nonetheless a common form of birth control. To the extent that women were still getting pregnant—hunger impaired both libido and fertility—families didn't want to have children that they couldn't afford to feed. When Oak-hee took a friend to get an abortion years earlier, it cost 400 won, the equivalent of 17 pounds (8 kilos) of rice, but these days the price could be as low as a bucket of coal.

Dr. Kim wasn't trained to perform operations. She survived with her pen, writing doctor's notes stating that patients were required to stay home from work on medical grounds. Absenteeism in North Korea was punishable by a thirty-day stay in a detention center, even though jobs were no longer providing salaries. But people needed to take time off to hunt for food and fuel. In return, they gave Dr. Kim small gifts of whatever they found that day to eat. She cringed at writing the false notes—it violated every oath she had ever made to her profession and her country—but she knew she was helping her patients and herself to survive.

Mi-ran's resourceful mother stumbled into another business that thrived on adversity. Through the connection of the oldest daughter, she got permission to operate a mill. Unlike her ice cream and tofu businesses, which failed once the electricity went out, the mill was a traditional one, operated by hand. Tae-woo, who had built beams inside the mines, made a wooden shed for the mill. Neighbors were enlisted to help raise the roof. Even Jun-sang, who happened to be home for vacation, came by to help. Once the mill was finished, people came from miles around carrying sacks of corn. It was cheaper for them to buy whole corn and then decide how much of the corn to throw in the grinder, whether to include the stems, leaves, cobs, and husks—or even whether to throw in some sawdust. It was indigestible unless it was finely pulverized, so mills were an important business.

IF YOU COULDN'T come up with anything to sell, you sold yourself. Even though Kim Il-sung had closed down the *kisaeng* houses, prostitution had never been completely stamped out, but it took place with the utmost of discretion, through private arrangements inside people's homes. The famine not only put prostitution back onto the street, it brought out a new class of prostitute—often young married women desperate to get food for their children. They often asked for nothing more than a bag of noodles or a few sweet potatoes as payment. Their gathering point was the square outside the main Chongjin train station. Given the long waits for trains, there were invariably hundreds of people loitering in the plaza. The women worked the crowd as though they were mingling at a cocktail party. Their clothing was drab and modest since the Public Standards Police would arrest any woman who wore a skirt that was too short, a shirt that was too low-cut or tight, blue jeans, or showy jewelry, so the prostitutes signaled their intent with a swipe of red lipstick and a beckoning glance at a passing man.

Oak-hee lived directly across from the train station, where her husband worked. Whenever she saw the women, she'd lower her eyes in embarrassment, resisting the impulse to stare. There was one woman, however, who managed to make eye contact and some-times appeared to be giving Oak-hee a little smile. She was a little better dressed than the others, more confident, and somehow more professional.

One day as she was leaving her apartment building, Oak-hee found this woman just a few feet from her front door, almost as though she was waiting for her.

"Listen, sister," she said familiarly. "My brother just came from out of town and we have something to discuss in private. Think you could loan us a room?"

She nodded toward a man who stood shuffling his feet behind them, his face averted. Oak-hee was a little squeamish about sex, but she could recognize a good deal when she saw one. Her husband was at work. Her children were at school. The prostitute paid her 50 won to use the room for one hour. She became a regular after that, not only paying for the room, but bringing candies for Oak-hee's children.

Of course, it was all illegal, but then again, so much was these days. It was a crime to accept remuneration for any service—be it sex or bicycle repair. But who cared anymore? Everybody needed a scam to survive.

MOST BUSINESS TOOK place at the old farmers' markets. Even in the glory days of communism, Kim Il-sung had grudgingly permitted the markets to operate with the restriction that they could sell only supplementary foods that people raised at home in their "kitchen gardens." When her children were young, Mrs. Song used to go to an empty lot near her apartment to buy eggs, which, if she had the money, made a nutritious treat for breakfast. Depending on the season, she might find hot red peppers drying in the sun, dried fish or cabbage. People often brought in used clothing, shoes, and dishes, but it was forbidden to sell anything newly manufactured, which had to be sold at a state store.

During the 1990s, even as the death grip of famine tightened around Chongjin, strangely, more and more food appeared at the markets. Cabbages, radishes, lettuce, tomatoes, scallions, and potatoes were for sale. The vegetables came from secret gardens that dotted the mountains in the countryside. Farmers had discovered their best chance of survival was to dig their own plot into the slopes, even on land that in the past they had thought too steep to cultivate. Attention was lavished on the private plots, the vegetables in rows as perfectly even as typewriter keys, the beans and squash tied to stakes and trellises, while the collective farms were slovenly with neglect.

There was also suddenly white rice, lots of it, in big 40-kilo burlap sacks imprinted with Roman letters (USA, WFP, EU) and the interlocking olive branches of the United Nations symbol and the U.S. flag, which every North Korean recognized from the propaganda posters where it was invariably shown dripping with blood or pierced with bayonets.

Why was there rice in sacks with the flag of North Korea's most dreaded enemy? Somebody told Mrs. Song that the North Korean army had captured rice from the American warmongers. One day Mrs. Song spotted a convoy of trucks driving away from the port with similar burlap sacks stacked in the back. Although the trucks had civilian license plates, Mrs. Song knew they had to belong to the military—nobody else had gasoline—and she finally figured out that this was humanitarian aid that somebody in the military was selling for profit at the market.

No matter where it was from, people in Chongjin were happy to see white rice, which hadn't been available at the public distribution center for years.

Every time she went to the market, Mrs. Song saw something that astonished her. Peaches. Grapes. Bananas. She couldn't remember the last time she'd seen a banana—maybe twenty years ago, when Chang-bo brought some home as a treat for the children. One day she saw oranges, real oranges! Mrs. Song had never tasted an orange—she only recognized it from pictures. Another day, she saw a mottled yellow-brown fruit with green spikes growing from the top.

"What is *that* thing?" she asked a friend, who told her it was a pineapple.

For the first time, the markets stocked household goods so cheap even North Koreans could buy them. The results of Deng Xiao-ping's economic reforms of the 1970s and 1980s were seeping into North Korea. From China came writing paper, pens and pencils, fra-grant shampoos, hairbrushes, nail clippers, razor blades, batteries, cigarette lighters, umbrellas, toy cars, socks. It had been so long since North Korea could manufacture anything that the ordinary had become extraordinary.

The clothing was also a revelation, an invasion of alien colors from another world. Pink, yellow, tangerine, and turquoise—colors as luscious as the tropical fruits now on the market, in fabrics much softer and shinier than anything made in North Korea. Occasionally you'd see some better-quality clothes at the market with the labels ripped out. The vendors would whisper that these came from *areh dongae*, "the village below," a euphemism for South Korea. People would pay more for clothing from the enemy state.

Every time Mrs. Song went to the market it seemed bigger and bigger. It was no longer just the old ladies squatting over tarpaulins in the dirt; there were hundreds of people laying out merchandise on wooden crates or carts. Vendors brought in tables and display cases and umbrellas to protect their wares from the sun.

The biggest market in Chongjin sprang up in an industrial waste-land near the Sunam River, which cut inland from the port through the center of the city. Behind the pitiful wreckage of the Chemical Textile factory, the Sunam Market would eventually become the largest market in North Korea. It was organized much like markets elsewhere in Asia—several aisles devoted to food, others to hard-ware, pots and pans, cosmetics, shoes, and clothing. It wasn't until 2002 that Kim Jong-il belatedly legalized the markets. The Chongjin authorities, however, had recognized their de facto reality years ear-lier and begun to regulate them. The market authorities charged the vendors 70 won a day rent—about the price of a kilo of rice. The vendors who couldn't afford the rent set up outside the gates, and so the market expanded further, spilling onto the sloping banks of the river. Mrs. Song's cookie business never rose to the level where she would get her own booth. She didn't want to pay the rent. But she did become part of a community of vendors who worked around the edges of a market in Songpyeon, a district west of the port where she moved once she made a little money.

The markets were magnets for all sorts of other businesses. Out-side Sunam, along a whitewashed wall crawling with hollyhocks, was a line of crude wooden carts. Their owners usually slept on top, waiting for customers who needed merchandise transported. Chongjin had no taxis, not even the rickshaws or pedicabs of China (the North Korean government thought them demeaning), but peo-ple had decided to fill a void by setting themselves up as porters. Hairdressers and barbers trained by the government's Convenience Bureau, the agency that was supposed to provide all services, set up mobile haircutting services. All they needed was a pair of scissors and a mirror. They worked near the food market, often getting into quarrels with the other vendors, who didn't want hair wafting into their food. The hairdressers clipped quickly, one eye making sure a razor didn't nick an ear, the other looking out for the police, who would confiscate their equipment if they were caught engaging in private business. Still, it was lucrative. Women with stomachs growl-ing from hunger would shell out their last won for a perm.

By a market at the train tracks, people set up makeshift restau-rants with planks of wood laid across bricks for tables, overturned buckets for chairs. The customers ate quickly, their spoons scraping small metal bowls of steaming soup or noodles. The cooks sweated over cylindrical metal stoves no bigger than paint cans, cranking old-fashioned bellows to fan the fires. It was not unusual to see a woman squatting over the fire with a baby strapped onto her back.

The vast majority of the vendors were women. Koreans accorded a low status to markets, so traditionally they were frequented only by women. This remained the case in the 1990s even as the markets expanded. Men had to stay with their work units, around which all life in North Korea revolved, but women were sufficiently expendable that they could wriggle out of their day jobs. Joo Sung-ha, a North Korean defector from Chongjin who became a journalist in Seoul, told me he believed that Kim Jong-il had tacitly agreed to let women work privately to relieve the pressure on families. "If the *ajummas* [married women] hadn't been allowed to work, there would have been a revolution," he said.

The result was that the face of the new economy was increasingly female. The men were stuck in the unpaying state jobs; women were making the money. "Men aren't worth as much as the dog that guards the house," some of the *ajummas* would whisper among themselves. Women's superior earnings couldn't trump thousands of years of patriarchal culture, but they did confer a certain independence.

From the outside, Chongjin looked unchanged. The same gray facades of the Stalinist office buildings stared out at empty stretches of asphalt. The roads were still marked by the faded red propaganda signs extolling the achievements of Kim Jong-il and the Workers' Party. Indeed, the place looked frozen in time, as if the clocks of world history had stopped in 1970. But Mrs. Song knew better. It was a topsy-turvy world in which she was living. Up was down, wrong was right. The women had the money instead of the men. The markets were bursting with food, more food than most North Koreans had seen in their lifetime, and yet people were still dying from hunger. Workers' Party members had starved to death; those who never gave a damn about the fatherland were making money.

"*Donbulrae*," Mrs. Song muttered under her breath. Money insects.

In the past, she took comfort in knowing that she and everyone else she knew were more or less equally poor. Now she saw the rich getting richer; the poor getting poorer. People who would have been branded economic criminals a decade earlier strutted around in leather shoes and new clothes. Others were starving even though they were working full-time. Inflation was out of control. The black-market price of rice would hit 200 won per kilo by the end of 1998. Even after salaries were restored, an ordinary office worker or teacher couldn't afford to buy his family even two or three days' worth of food each month. The children scrounged through the dirt on their hands and knees, picking out grains of rice or corn that spilled from the split seams of the burlap sacks.

She knew a boy, Song-chol, nine years old. He used to come to the market with his father, a gruff man the other vendors nick-named "Uncle Pear" because that was what he sold. But the pear business wasn't so good, and Uncle Pear had difficulty feeding his family.

"Why don't you go and snatch yourself something to eat like the other boys?" Uncle Pear told his son one day at the market.

Song-chol was an obedient boy. He marched off to a stand where men were drinking alcohol and eating crab. Back by his father's side, he complained of a stomachache. He had picked up fish entrails from the ground that had spoiled. He died of acute food poisoning, before Uncle Pear could spend his last won to pay a porter to take him to the hospital.

Hardly a day went by that Mrs. Song didn't stumble across the dead and dying. For all she had been through with her own family, she could not get used to the constant presence of death. Late one day on her way home from the market, she took a detour to the train station, hoping to find customers for some unsold cookies. Workers were sweeping up the station's plaza. A couple of men walked by, pulling a heavy wooden cart. Mrs. Song looked to see what they were transporting. It was a heap of bodies, maybe six of them, people who had died at the station overnight. A few bony limbs flopped out of the cart. A head lolled as the cart jostled over the pavement. Mrs. Song stared; the head belonged to a man about forty years old. His eyes blinked faintly. Not quite dead yet, but close enough to be carted away.

Mrs. Song couldn't help thinking of her own dear husband and son. How fortunate she was that at least they died at home in their beds, and she was able to give them a proper burial.

CHAPTER 11

WANDERING SWALLOWS

Boys at a North Korean market.

IN HER FREQUENT VISITS TO THE CHONGJIN TRAIN STATION, Mrs. Song probably crossed paths with a boy wearing an indigo factory uniform so big that the crotch hung down to his knees. His matted hair was crawling with lice. He wore vinyl bags on his feet instead of shoes. His age was indeterminate; at fourteen, he was barely the size of an American eight-year-old.

If Mrs. Song had a leftover cookie, she might give him one. Otherwise she would have walked by without paying much attention. There was nothing about the boy to distinguish him from hundreds of other children hanging around the train station. North Koreans called them *kochebi*, "wandering swallows"—children whose parents had died or gone off to find food. Left to fend for themselves, they tended to flock like pigeons scavenging for crumbs at the train station. They were a strange migratory phenomenon in a country that previously had never heard of homelessness.

Kim Hyuck was tiny, but strong and wily. If you bought a snack to eat at the station, he could snatch it from your hand before it reached your mouth and swallow it in a single gulp. Vendors covered buckets of food with tightly woven nets to keep out sticky fingers, but at the precise moment that the net was lifted, he could topple the bucket and grab something from the pavement. These were skills acquired at an early age and perfected over the course of a childhood marked by food deprivation. Without them, he wouldn't have survived for very long.

How Hyuck ended up homeless at the train station is a case study in the decline of North Korea's core class. Hyuck was a child of privilege, born in 1982 into a family with solid Communist bona fides. His father had served in an elite military unit that was trained to infiltrate South Korea. He was later rewarded with membership in the Workers' Party and a job in a military-run company that raised foreign currency by exporting fish and pine mushrooms. Hyuck's family lived in Sunam near the Chemical Textile factory, where his mother worked. Hyuck was sent at the age of two months to the factory's day-care center along with the children of other working mothers.

Hyuck's life began to derail when his mother died suddenly of a heart attack when he was three years old. He was left with only the dimmest recollection of her face—the earliest memory he could recount was the smell of incense burning at her funeral. Hyuck's father remarried soon after. Hyuck and his brother, Cheol, who was three years older, clashed with their stepmother, often about food.

The boys were mischievous, wild—and constantly hungry. They believed that their stepmother was giving more food to her own daughter, their stepsister. They stole corncobs from their kitchen and traded them for cooked noodles at the market. When their stepmother locked up the food, they swiped her blanket to barter for food.

The first time Hyuck stole from a stranger he was ten years old.

He took a sticky rice cake with red bean filling from a vendor's cart and ran for it. His little legs pumped faster than the vendor's and he should have gotten away with it. His undoing was that the rice cake was so sweet and delicious that he came back for a second helping.

Hyuck's father picked him up at the police station. Hyuck kept his head bowed in shame as the tears welled in his eyes. At home, his father whipped him with a leather belt, raising red welts on his calves.

"No boy of mine will be a thief," his father raged. "Better to starve than to steal."

Hyuck didn't agree. He kept stealing, each time ranging farther from home in search of food. Just south of Chongjin, in Kyongsong county, were the coal mines. Beyond the coal mines were the orchards. Hyuck and his friends used to hitch themselves to the back bumpers of buses to get there. By the 1990s, he was making the trip regularly. When the pears ran out, they started stealing corn. Once he got caught, but he was young enough that the guards let him off with only a warning. Hyuck was shameless in his thievery. Even in the mourning period after Kim Il-sung's death, he tried to swipe extra rice cakes that had been put out for people paying their respects at the big bronze statue.

Hyuck's father was outraged by his sons' conduct, but he had nothing to offer as a deterrent. The family had so little food at home that Hyuck's stepmother had taken his stepsister and moved back to live with her parents. Hyuck's father had switched jobs, becoming party secretary at a nursing home for the mentally ill. He installed his sons in a room where the caretaker had previously lived. Hyuck enjoyed living at the nursing home and talking to the patients. They were lonely like he was and they made conversation with him as though he was a real person, not just a kid. But the nursing home was also short of food. Although his father's position as party secretary was more powerful than the director's, it didn't earn him extra rations. What it did get him were connections to get his sons into an orphanage.

As in many Communist countries, North Korea's orphanages weren't strictly for orphans, but for children whose parents could no longer care for them. Like boarding schools, the orphanages were supposed to provide education, room, and board. It was a privilege to be accepted.

The Donsong No. 24 orphanage was in Onsong, a county seat in the northernmost reaches of the province, near the Chinese border. Their father took his boys by train the first week of September, so that they could be enrolled in time for the start of the school year. Hyuck was eleven years old and about to begin his last year of primary school; his brother fourteen and in middle school. The ride took six hours and was so crowded that the boys and their father had no seats. They stood in glum silence the whole way.

"You two are brothers. You'll have each other. Don't let anybody push you around," their father said just after signing the papers that relinquished them to the care of the orphanage.

When his father turned to walk away, Hyuck noticed for the first time how much his father had aged. The man who once appeared so tall and handsome was now gaunt, his posture stooped, his hair streaked with gray.

AT LEAST INITIALLY, the orphanage's cafeteria kept the boys' hunger at bay. It was autumn, the harvest season, and food was abundant. The boys were delighted to get a daily bowl of rice. Even though it was mixed with corn, barley, and cheaper grains, it was the best food they had had in years. In the spring, they discovered that the wooded grounds of the orphanage were planted with apricot trees. They could pick and eat their fill.

But by winter, their rations were cut. Instead of rice, the children got corn noodles floating in a bowl of salted soup. In the first three months of 1996, twenty-seven children died at the orphanage. Hyuck and his brother cut classes and walked to town to look for food. They discovered the situation wasn't much better there. Hyuck met a boy his own age who was living with his six-year-old sister because their parents had died. Neighbors came in periodically with bowls of porridge, but otherwise the children were fending for themselves.

Hyuck and his brother, along with their new friend, went out together to forage for food. Hyuck was a good climber, with long, muscular arms that compensated for his short, stubby legs. He could scale pine trees and with a sharp knife peel away the outer bark to get to the tender bark underneath. It was yellow, chewy, and sweet, and sometimes he would eat it while clinging to the tree. Others were trying to do the same, but Hyuck could get higher, where the bark was untouched.

"You're a little monkey," his friend told him with admiration.

Hyuck became a hunter. He killed rats, mice, and frogs and tadpoles. When the frogs disappeared, he went for grasshoppers and cicadas. As a small boy in Chongjin, he used to watch his friends catch and eat cicadas at the Sunam River, but he'd always found it disgusting. Now he was not so fussy. He took some netting and devised traps for sparrows, dangling a kernel of corn on a string as bait. They plucked the birds' feathers and barbecued them on a spit. He also tried to catch pigeons with a basin and string, but discovered the pigeons were too smart.

Not so the dogs. Hyuck found a small and friendly stray, wagging its tail as it followed him into his friend's yard. Hyuck shut the gate behind them. He and his friend grabbed the animal and shoved it into a bucket of water, holding down the lid. The drowning dog struggled for ten minutes before dying. They skinned it and barbecued it. Dog meat was part of the traditional Korean diet, but Hyuck liked animals and felt bad, though not so bad that he didn't try it again—although by mid-1996 dogs too were scarce.

Hyuck continued to steal. He and his brother climbed walls and dug up clay kimchi pots that had been buried in private gardens. They shoveled the kimchi straight out of the pots into their mouths.

All the while, Hyuck remembered his father's admonition: "It's better to starve than to steal."

In the imaginary dialogue that Hyuck kept up with his father, he retorted, "You're no hero if you're dead."

HYUCK WAS HOMESICK. He missed his father as well as Cheol, who had been discharged from the orphanage when he turned sixteen, the legal age of adulthood. Hyuck had always relied on his brother to be his bodyguard, protecting him during the many scrapes of his wild and unruly childhood. Cheol had inherited their father's imposing height. Without him, Hyuck was regularly beaten up. One day he was out chopping wood when he encountered a gang of boys from Onsong who were doing the same. The town kids often picked fights with the orphanage kids, whom they accused (rightfully) of stealing their food. At first, Hyuck thought the boys had thrown a bucket of water at him. Then he realized his feet were drenched in blood. They had gashed his thigh with an ax. As soon as his wound healed, he decided to sneak onto a train heading back to Chongjin.

When he arrived Hyuck barely recognized his hometown. Chongjin looked like a dead city. Everything was dilapidated, broken, cheerless. Stores were closed. There were no trolleys near the train station. He walked home along Road No. 1 parallel to the ocean. As he crossed the Sunam River, he could see clear out to the smokestacks along the waterfront. Not a puff of smoke was in the air. After the bridge, he turned off the main road toward the Chemical Textile factory, where his mother had worked. The front gate was padlocked shut, the building itself gutted. Thieves had looted all the machinery inside. It was growing dark, and by the time Hyuck reached his own neighborhood he was beginning to lose his bearings. He felt as though he was standing in the middle of a field on a moonless night. The landmarks of his childhood had rearranged themselves in his absence and disappeared in the shadows.

Hyuck finally located his own apartment building. Pushing open the unlocked front door, he walked into a dark stairwell and groped his way up the steps, counting floor by floor. It was so quiet it seemed that the building was abandoned except for the sound of a crying baby that grew louder as he climbed. He was beginning to wonder if he had made a mistake. His apartment was on the eighth floor—second from the top. When he got upstairs, he saw a crack of light from under the door—an oil lamp, perhaps—and his heart raced with hope.

He knocked. A young, pretty woman opened the door with a baby in her arms. She invited Hyuck inside and explained that she and her husband had bought the apartment almost a year earlier from Hyuck's father. He hadn't left a forwarding address, but he did leave a message: "If my sons come home, tell them to look for me at the train station."

CHONGJIN STATION. That was where people went when they had nothing left and no place else to go. It wasn't quite like giving up and lying down by the side of the road. The movement of the trains created an illusion of purpose that kept hope alive against all odds. It allowed one to fantasize that a train would pull into the station with something to eat or that a train might be going someplace better and you could hop aboard. Chongjin is a major terminus in the rail-road network—the north-south lines that run up the coast connect with the lines running west to the Chinese border. People showed up in Chongjin hoping to find food because other cities—Hamhung, Kilju, Kimchaek—had it even worse. People kept moving. They hadn't given up yet.

The station was an enormous granite building with a row of tall, narrow windows, two stories high. Up high was an oversized por-trait of Kim Il-sung, the dimensions commensurate with the size of the building. Below the portrait was a stone-faced clock that occa-sionally told the correct time. Inside, the air was thick with the ex-haust of the trains and cigarette smoke.

People sat on their haunches, waiting. If they were too weak, they sprawled on the floor of the waiting room and lined the dim corridors. Hyuck wandered among the crowds looking for a man with his father's loping, long-limbed gait. He bent down to stare into the faces, hoping to make eye contact with somebody familiar. Many of his former neighbors were living in squalor in the station, but nobody could provide Hyuck with information about his father or brother. With nowhere else to go, Hyuck found a slot into which a heavy iron gate was meant to retract. He sucked in his chest, slipped into the alcove, curled up, and fell into a fitful sleep. In the morning, he found a working faucet, so he could splash water on his face, but he couldn't get rid of the lice on his scalp.

It is worth noting here how extraordinary it was for anyone to be homeless in North Korea. This was, after all, the country that had developed the most painstaking systems to keep track of its citizens. Everybody had a fixed address and a work unit and both were tied to food rations—if you left home, you couldn't get fed. People didn't dare visit a relative in the next town without a travel permit. Even overnight visitors were supposed to be registered with the *inminban*, which in turn had to report to the police the name, gender, registration number, travel permit number, and the purpose of the visit. Police conducted regular spot checks around midnight to make sure nobody had unauthorized visitors. One had to carry at all times a "citizen's certificate," a twelve-page passport-size booklet that contained a wealth of information about the bearer. It was modeled on the old Soviet ID.

All that changed with the famine. Without food distribution, there was no reason to stay at your fixed address. If sitting still meant you starved to death, no threat the regime levied could keep people home. For the first time, North Koreans were wandering around their own country with impunity.

Among the homeless population, a disproportionate number were children or teenagers. In some cases, their parents had gone off in search of jobs or food. But there was another, even stranger, explanation. Facing a food shortage, many North Korean families conducted a brutal triage of their own households—they denied themselves and often elderly grandparents food in order to keep the younger generation alive. That strategy produced an unusual number of orphans, as the children were often the last ones left of entire families that had perished.

The *kochebi*, the wandering swallows, stood out among the crowds in the station. Just like Hyuck, they wore adult-sized indigo factory uniforms that hung from their bodies. There were surplus uniforms now that the factories had closed, so the authorities sometimes handed them out for free. They called them "social outfits." Few of the children had shoes. If they did, they would soon swap them for food and instead use plastic bags to cover their feet. They often suffered frostbite.

In the first years of the food shortage, the children at the train station survived by begging food, but before long there were simply too many of them and too few people with food to spare. "Charity begins with a full stomach," the North Koreans like to say; you can't feed somebody else's kids if your own are starving.

When begging failed, the children picked up anything on the ground that was vaguely edible. If they couldn't find food, they would pick up cigarette butts and reroll whatever tobacco remained with discarded paper. Almost all the children smoked to dampen their hunger.

Hyuck sometimes joined up with children who formed themselves into gangs to steal together. Chongjin always had a nasty reputation due to its street gangs, but their activities took on new urgency in hard times. There was a natural division of labor between the bigger kids—who were faster and stronger—and the little ones, who were less likely to get beaten up or arrested if caught. The big ones would rush at a food stand, toppling everything onto the ground. As they sprinted off with the angry vendor in hot pursuit, the little kids would scoop up the food.

Another trick was to find a slow-moving train or a truck carrying grain and slit the sacks with a sharp stick. Whatever spilled out was fair game for the children. Eventually, the railroad company hired armed guards with shoot-to-kill orders to prevent such thefts.

It was a dangerous life. The children couldn't sleep without worrying that somebody, perhaps another gang member, would steal what little they had. There were strange stories going around about adults who preyed on children. Not just for sex, but for food. Hyuck was told about people who would drug children, kill them, and butcher them for meat. Behind the station near the railroad tracks were vendors who cooked soup and noodles over small burners, and it was said that the gray chunks of meat floating in the broth were human flesh.

Whether urban legend or not, tales of cannibalism swept through the markets. Mrs. Song heard the stories from a gossipy *ajumma* she had met there.

"Don't buy any meat if you don't know where it comes from," she warned darkly. The woman claimed she knew somebody who had actually eaten human flesh and proclaimed it delicious.

"If you didn't know, you'd swear it was pork or beef," she whispered to a horrified Mrs. Song.

The stories got more and more horrific. Supposedly, one father went so insane with hunger that he ate his own baby. A market woman was said to have been arrested for selling soup made from human bones. From my interviews with defectors, it does appear that there were at least two cases—one in Chongjin and the other in Sinuiju—in which people were arrested and executed for cannibalism. It does not seem, though, that the practice was widespread or even occurred to the degree that was chronicled in China during the 1958–62 famine, which killed as many as 30 million people.

Even without cannibals or other predators in their midst, the children couldn't survive long on the streets. The younger ones rarely lived more than a few months. Mrs. Song's oldest daughter, Oak-hee, who lived in a second-floor apartment across from the station, used to pass the children every day on her way home.

"Those little ones will be dead by morning," Oak-hee would tell herself, in part justifying her own decision to walk by without helping.

Most of the people I met from Chongjin spoke of the large number of bodies scattered around the station and on the trains. A factory worker told me she was riding a train from Kilju to Chongjin in 1997 and realized that a man seated in her carriage was dead. He was a retired army officer and clutched in his rigid fingers his Workers' Party membership papers. She said the other passengers were completely blasé about the corpse. She presumed that the body was removed when the train reached Chongjin Station.

At the station, employees from the cleaning staff regularly made rounds through the public areas, loading bodies onto a wooden handcart. They would walk through the waiting rooms and plaza out front, trying to figure out which of the huddled figures on the floor hadn't moved since the day before. Hyuck says that some days they removed as many as thirty bodies from the station. It was difficult to identify them because often their documents, along with better clothing and shoes, had been stolen. Since it was likely that the family was dead or dispersed, the bodies would be buried in mass graves. This was a disgrace in a Confucian society, where it is widely believed that the location of an ancestor's grave is critical to present-day fortunes.

Several such burials near the Chinese border were witnessed by the South Korean Buddhist organization Good Friends, and one by an American aid official, Andrew S. Natsios. He saw what appeared to be bodies wrapped in white vinyl sheets being loaded into a large pit near a graveyard. Afterward, the workers stood around the pit with their heads bowed in what appeared to be a silent meditation or service.

Hyuck believes his father was probably buried in one of those graves. An acquaintance he met years later told him that his father had lived at the train station for a while in the winter of 1994 and in 1995 he'd entered a hospital. The proud man who vowed he would never steal was likely one of the first to die of starvation.

ONCE HE GAVE UP hope of finding his father, Hyuck had no reason to stay in Chongjin. He started to sneak onto trains. It was easy. The trains lurched slowly along rutted tracks, making frequent unscheduled stops. Hyuck would run after a train and grab on to the railing between the carriages and hoist himself up with his monkeylike arms. The cars were so crowded the police could barely get through the aisles to check travel permits and tickets. Hyuck didn't like closed spaces anyway, so he would scramble up to the roof. The trains were slightly rounded on top, like bread loaves. He would find a level spot in the middle where he would flatten himself to avoid the electric lines overhead. With his pack as a pillow, he would lie on his back that way for hours, rocked by the motion of the train, staring up at the clouds moving overhead.

At first, Hyuck went no farther than the outskirts of the city. He returned to Kyongsong, where he had swiped pears and corn as a boy. It was harder now to steal—the farms were patrolled by armed guards—so Hyuck ventured farther afield. He went back to the orphanage in Onsong. By now, Onsong didn't look any better than Chongjin. The lush woods he remembered from the orphanage grounds were similarly stripped bare. He knew that only a few miles away from the orphanage, just on the other side of a ridge of squat hills visible from his dormitory window, was a slender gray ribbon of water—the Tumen River—that ran as far as you could see. And on the other side of the river, there was a place where the trees still had bark and the cornfields weren't guarded by guns.

The place was called China.

THE BORDER BETWEEN China and North Korea extends for 850 miles along two rivers, both originating at the dormant volcano known as Mount Paektu to the Koreans and Mount Changbai to the Chinese. To the south, the Yalu River is the famous line where Chinese troops pushed back U.S. forces during the Korean War. Much of the official business between China and North Korea today takes place across the Yalu, mostly at its mouth near the Yellow Sea. Compared with the Yalu, the Tumen is barely more than a piddling stream, shallow with gentle currents. To the north, it runs a meandering course that delineates the northeastern border of North Korea before spilling out southwest of Vladivostok. It is narrow enough that even during the rainy season, when the waters are high, a swimmer could easily make it across.

The boys at the orphanage weren't allowed to play near the Tumen. The entire shoreline was a closed military area. If they got too close while swimming in one of the tributaries they would get chased away by the border police. The riverbanks were flat and sandy with nothing growing tall enough to provide cover. But an hour or two's hike south of Onsong was a sparsely inhabited area with bushes and tall grass along the banks. The border guards were spaced far enough apart that one could sneak through after dark. The guards worked two to a post so that one could sleep while the other watched, but after 1:00 A.M., often both fell asleep.

The first time Hyuck crossed the Tumen, it was late 1997. This was the dry season and the river level was low, the sandy banks on either side of the border reaching toward each other like extended fingertips. But the water was icy, and when Hyuck stepped into it the cold hit him like a knockout punch. Though it came up no higher than his chest, the currents kept sweeping him off his feet. He was dragged downstream, so that he ended up crossing on a diagonal. When he finally clambered out on the other side into the cold air, his clothes froze like a suit of armor.

Hyuck never before had much interest in China—another Communist country as poor as his own, he thought. It didn't look much different at first glance, but as he ventured farther from the river he could see fields stretching for miles where the corn had been harvested. Little redbrick houses had cribs of husked corn filled as high as the tile roofs and trellises with curling stalks of pumpkins and beans. He wandered into a small town. It was livelier than he'd imagined, with taxis, motor scooters, and bicycle pedicabs. The signs were in both Chinese and Korean. He was happy to learn that many of the residents, although Chinese citizens, were of Korean origin and spoke his language. They immediately picked him out as a North Korean, and not just from his shabby clothing. At fifteen, he was just four foot seven, but his head was large for his body, a telltale sign of chronic malnutrition. When children are poorly nourished over a long period, their heads develop to a normal size, but their limbs are stunted.

At a market, Hyuck met a man who was selling used dishes, jewelry, and bric-a-brac. He asked Hyuck if he could bring over some irons from North Korea—the old-fashioned kind that would heat up over hot coals. Almost all North Korean families had these irons at home, but people barely bothered to use them anymore—especially since their clothing was all synthetic. Hyuck was able to buy the irons in North Korea for almost nothing and resell them in China for the equivalent of ten dollars each. It was more money than he'd ever seen in his life. With his profits, he went back to North Korea and bought more items to sell. Pottery, jewelry, paintings, jade. He bought a *podegi*, a cloth that Korean women traditionally use to carry babies. By strapping the merchandise to his back with the cloth, he could carry more than he could in a knapsack.

Hyuck started making regular border crossings. He learned the spots where the border guards were inattentive, lazy, or corrupt. He learned that it was best to strip off all your clothing before getting into the river. He became adept at keeping his balance as he walked through the water with his clothing and merchandise held high over his head (wrapped tightly in plastic in case he stumbled). He never stayed too long in China because he'd been warned that the Chinese police would hand over any North Koreans they found on the wrong side of the river.

He stopped stealing. If he wanted a bowl of noodles, he bought it with his own money. He bought trousers, a T-shirt, a blue parka, and sneakers so that he wouldn't look like a refugee. He was trying to go straight and take control of his life. Buying merchandise privately and selling it for a profit was illegal, and crossing an international border without a travel permit compounded the crime. At sixteen, Hyuck was legally considered an adult, and his misdeeds from here on would be taken seriously.

CHAPTER 12

SWEET DISORDER

North Korean guards stand at attention in Pyongyang.

NORTH KOREANS HAVE MULTIPLE WORDS FOR PRISON IN MUCH the same way the Inuit do for snow. Somebody who commits a minor offense—such as skipping work—might be sent to a *jibkyulso*, a detention center operated by the People's Safety Agency, a low-level police unit, or maybe a *rodong danryeondae*, a labor camp, where the offender would be sentenced to a month or two of hard labor, such as paving a road.

The most notorious prisons are the *kwanliso*—which translates as "control and management places." These are in fact a colony of labor camps that stretch for miles in the northernmost mountains of the country. Satellite intelligence suggests they house up to 200,000 people. Emulating the Soviet gulag, Kim Il-sung set up the camps shortly after taking power to sweep aside anybody who might challenge his authority. Rival politicians, descendants of landlords or Japanese collaborators, Christian clergymen. Somebody caught reading foreign newspapers. A man who, after too many drinks, cracked a joke about Kim Jong-il's height. "Insulting the authority of the leadership" is the most serious of what are called "antistate crimes." A woman at Mrs. Song's factory was sent away for writing something politically incorrect in a diary. The North Koreans I know whisper of somebody they knew—or knew of—who disappeared in the middle of the night and was never heard from again. Sentences for the *kwanliso* are for life. Children and parents and siblings are often taken away as well to get rid of the "tainted blood" that carries over for three generations. Since they are not blood relatives, spouses are usually left behind and forced to divorce. Little is known about what happens inside the *kwanliso* and few emerge to tell their tales.

Another type of labor camp is called the *kyohwaso*, which means "enlightenment center," reflecting the camp's purported goal to rehabilitate the wayward. These were for the nonpolitical prisoners, people who had illegally crossed borders, smuggled, or simply conducted business. These camps were less terrifying than political camps because in theory a prisoner could be released—if he or she managed to survive.

KIM HYUCK WAS arrested shortly after his sixteenth birthday. He was staying in the home of a friend in Onsong, not far from the orphanage, which was the closest thing to a home that he'd known, and he always found himself drawn back to it. He had just returned from one of his many jaunts to China—one trip too many, as it turned out, because his travels had attracted the attention of the police.

Hyuck was waiting for the August heat to die down so he could chop some wood. Around four P.M. he went out to the yard in back of the house. He spotted a man, then another, watching him. He could see just enough of them to note that they weren't wearing uniforms, but there was something in the intensity of their gaze that made him realize they were looking for him. He took his ax and walked slowly around to the front of the house, thinking he could quickly scale the wall and run. But he could see there were more men in front. Maybe eight in total. So he stayed put and started chopping the wood, as though the crack of the splitting wood could chase away his own anxiety and still his pounding pulse.

The undercover police dragged Hyuck to an office building in the center of Onsong. They turned out to be from the Bowibu, the national security agency that investigates political crimes. It was more serious than he'd thought. While in China, Hyuck had sketched a map for some Chinese traders who wanted to sneak into North Korea. This was tantamount to treason under the North Korean criminal code's Article 52, Betrayal of the Fatherland: "Any citizen of the Republic who flees to a foreign country or to the side of an enemy, including the seeking of asylum in a foreign embassy . . . (or) assists an agency or citizens of a hostile country, by serving as a travel guide or interpreter, or by providing moral or material support . . . shall be subject to the death penalty."

The police quickly extracted a confession with the help of a square wooden stick. They pounded Hyuck on the back, shoulders, legs, feet, and arms, actually everywhere but his head since they wanted to keep him conscious. He curled himself into a fetal position to ward off the blows. They didn't have their own jail, just an office. They kept him locked in a room so small he couldn't lie down and even leaning his bruised body against the walls was excruciating. He couldn't sleep at night and yet by day he felt himself drifting off into sleep or some other oblivion even as he was being beaten. Hyuck had no idea what to expect. For all his misadventures, he'd been arrested only once before—when he'd stolen rice cakes as a ten-year-old. He'd always been the kind of kid who was able to wriggle out of any jam. Now he was being treated as a serious criminal, as an adult. He felt trapped, defeated, without dignity. During interrogation, he babbled away. He would have told his tormentors whatever it was they wanted to know, but all they wanted was to find the Chinese traders and Hyuck simply didn't know where they were.

After a few months, they transferred him to an ordinary county jail where the beatings started all over again.

Hyuck didn't have a trial, but the national security police eventually dropped the charges of treason against him because they'd been unable to find the Chinese traders and didn't want to be held accountable. Hyuck was charged instead with illegal crossing of the national frontier. That in itself was a serious crime, punishable by three years in a labor camp.

KYOHWASO NO. 12 IS LOCATED on the outskirts of Hoeryong, another border town, about forty miles south of Onsong. Hyuck was taken there by train in handcuffs. At the station, he met up with other incoming prisoners. Tied together with thick ropes, they marched through the town and into the mountains to the camp. An engine growled and the heavy iron gate slowly creaked open to admit the new arrivals. Above the gate were quotations of Kim Il-sung. Hyuck was too intimidated to lift his eyes to read them.

Hyuck was first taken to a clinic, where he was measured and weighed. The camp had no uniforms, so prisoners wore their own clothing. If a shirt had a collar, it was cut off because collars were a status symbol, not befitting inmates of a labor camp. Any brightly colored clothing was taken away. The blue jacket that Hyuck had bought in China was confiscated by the guards. A fellow prisoner took his sneakers.

The labor camp held about fifteen hundred prisoners, as best Hyuck could tell, all of them older men. Hyuck was by far the smallest, but not the weakest. He had been surprisingly well fed by the national security agents—they had only a few prisoners, so they'd bought noodles for them at the market. With his first dinner in prison Hyuck understood why the older men looked so knobby and thin, why their shoulders protruded from their shirts like clothes hangers. A guard gave out what was called a rice ball, although actually it was mostly corn, cobs, husks, and leaves. No bigger than a tennis ball, it fit easily into Hyuck's palm. That was dinner. Some days they would get a few beans in addition to the rice ball.

Prisoners were expected to work from 7:00 A.M. to sunset. The camp was a veritable hive of industry, containing lumberyards, a brick factory, a mine, and farmlands. The labor camps produced everything from furniture to bicycles. Hyuck was assigned to a work crew that chopped wood. Because he was so short, he kept the register of how much wood the others gathered. He was also supposed to keep a log of the time prisoners took to rest. Hyuck didn't consider himself lucky to get this job. How was he supposed to exercise authority over men who were ten years his senior?

"Any punishment they get, you'll get, too," growled the guard who assigned Hyuck his job. "If any of those guys tries to run away, they'll be shot. And you, too."

Somebody did try to run away, although not on Hyuck's watch. The man slipped out of his work crew and ran through the woods, looking for an escape route. But the camp's fences were nearly ten feet high and topped with coils of razor-sharp concertina wire. The man ran through the woods all night, then ended up back at the front gate pleading for mercy. In fact, they spared his life, citing the "generosity of the fatherly leader."

The only time prisoners were permitted to stop working was for meals, sleep, and ideology sessions. During the New Year's holiday they had to repeat Kim Jong-il's New Year's message until they had it memorized word for word. "Our people should accelerate the general advance this year, firmly adhering to the policies placing great importance on our ideology, arms, science, and technology."

At night the men slept on a bare concrete floor, fifty to a room. Since they had only a few blankets, the men huddled together for warmth. Sometimes ten men slept under one blanket. At night the men were so exhausted they were unable to talk, but would scratch each other's backs or give each other foot rubs to relax and fall asleep. To fit more people under the blanket, they often slept alternating head to foot, in which case they could give each other foot rubs.

When he first arrived, Hyuck was as frightened of the prisoners as the guards. He expected hardened criminals, scary, violent men, sexual predators. In fact, one side effect of starvation was a loss of libido. There was almost no sexual activity at the camp and little fighting. Aside from the man who stole Hyuck's shoes, the prisoners weren't nearly as fierce as the children he used to hang out with at the train station. Mostly they were "economic criminals" who'd gotten in trouble at the border or the market. The actual thieves among them had stolen nothing more than food. One of them was a forty-year-old rancher who had worked on a collective farm raising cattle. His crime was that he had failed to report the birth of a dead calf, instead taking the stillborn home to feed his wife and two young children. By the time Hyuck met him, he had served five years of a ten-year term. Hyuck often slept under a blanket with the rancher, his head nestled on the man's arm. The rancher was gentle and soft-spoken, but one of the senior guards took a strong dislike to him. His wife and children came twice to visit, but were not allowed in to see him or to send gifts of food, privileges allowed some of the more favored prisoners.

The rancher died of starvation. It happened quietly; he went to sleep and didn't wake up. It was a common occurrence that somebody would die in the night. Often it was obvious in the close sleeping quarters, because the dying man would evacuate his bladder and tiny bubbles would appear on his lips as fluid seeped out of the body. Usually nobody bothered to remove the body until morning.

"Oh, so-and-so is dead," one of the men would remark matter-of-factly before notifying a guard.

The bodies were taken for cremation on the same mountain where the men chopped wood. Families weren't notified until they came to visit. In Hyuck's room alone, two or three men died each week.

"Nobody ever thinks they are going to die. They all think they will survive and see their families again, but then it just happens," Hyuck told me years later when he was living in Seoul. He had returned not long before from a human rights conference in Warsaw where he testified. Afterward he toured Auschwitz and noted the parallels with his own experience. In his labor camp, nobody was gassed—if they were too weak to work they were sent to another prison. Although some were executed and some were beaten, the primary means of inflicting punishment was withholding food. Starvation was the way the regime preferred to eliminate its opponents.

It is hard to confirm Hyuck's account of life in Kyohwaso No. 12, but impossible to refute. The details he described are much in keeping with testimony of other North Korean defectors, both former prisoners and guards.

Hyuck was released from Kyohwaso No. 12 in July 2000. Combined with the time he had spent in police custody, he'd served twenty months of his three-year sentence. He was told his pardon was in celebration of an upcoming anniversary of the founding of the Workers' Party. Hyuck was convinced he was released to make room for a flood of incoming prisoners. The North Korean regime had more important enemies than Kim Hyuck.

"THE FOOD PROBLEM is creating anarchy," Kim Jong-il complained in a December 1996 speech delivered at Kim Il-sung University. He warned that the rise of private markets and trading would cause the Workers' Party to "collapse and dissolve . . . [as] illustrated by past incidents in Poland and Czechoslovakia." As well as any of the world's strongmen, he understood perfectly the cliché that an absolutist regime needs absolute power. Everything good in life was to be bequeathed by the government. He couldn't tolerate people going off to gather their own food or buying rice with their own money. "Telling people to solve the food problem on their own only increases the number of farmers' markets and peddlers. In addition, this creates egoism among people, and the base of the party's class may come to collapse. This has been well illustrated by past incidents in Poland and Czechoslovakia."

As the food shortage stabilized, Kim Jong-il felt he had been too tolerant during the crisis and that he had to reverse the tide of liberalization. The prisons burst at the seams with newly minted criminals—vendors, traders, smugglers, and scientists and technicians who'd been trained in the Soviet Union or Eastern Europe—once-Communist countries that had betrayed Communist ideals. The regime was striking back at anybody who could possibly be a threat to the old status quo.

At the same time, Kim Jong-il sent reinforcements to patrol the 850-mile-long border with China. Additional border police were stationed along the shallow stretches of the Tumen River where Hyuck had first started crossing. The North Koreans also called on the Chinese government to hunt down and repatriate defectors. Chinese undercover police started patrolling markets and other places where

North Korean escapees might be scavenging food. They allowed North Korea to send its own undercover agents into China, who would sometimes pose as defectors.

If they'd done nothing more than wade across to search for food, escapees might get only a couple of months in prison, but anyone caught trading over the border or having contact with South Koreans or missionaries was sent to a labor camp.

Not even the homeless children were spared in the crackdown. Kim Jong-il recognized that his system could not survive if citizens, no matter their age, rode trains without travel permits and waded across the river into China. He set up what came to be known as 927 centers, named after September 27, 1997, when he ordered the creation of shelters for the homeless. The centers had no heat and little food and sanitation. The homeless immediately recognized them as prisons and made every effort to avoid getting caught by the police.

Chongjin bore the brunt of it. As the capital city of a region that had been home to exiles, dissidents, and misfits since the times of the Chosun emperor, Chongjin was once again at odds with the political center. North Hamgyong province had lost its food supply earlier than other parts of North Korea. Some suggested that Kim Jong-il had deliberately cut off the province because he believed it was less loyal. With the possible exception of Hamhung, malnutrition rates in Chongjin appeared to be the highest in the country. But the effect of this was that the city's underground economy had developed faster.

"Why doesn't the government just leave us alone to live our lives?" the women at the market would grumble among themselves.

"Nobody listens to the government anymore," a young man from Chongjin told me a few years ago.

As much as any city in North Korea, Chongjin had strayed from the party line. By 2005, Chongjin's Sunam was the biggest market in North Korea, with more variety of merchandise than anything in Pyongyang. You could buy pineapples, kiwis, oranges, bananas, German beer, and Russian vodka. Right in the market, you could buy illegal DVDs of Hollywood films, although the vendors kept them under the counter. Sacks of rice and corn obviously intended as humanitarian aid were sold out in the open. Sex was sold just as blatantly. The prostitutes soliciting in front of Chongjin's train station didn't bother to disguise intent. Compared with straitlaced Pyongyang, Chongjin was the Wild West.

Kim Jong-il couldn't let North Korea's third-largest city deviate from the hard line of the Workers' Party. Although now idled for lack of fuel, its steel and iron works, chemical textile plants, and machine works were a vital part of the industrial engine he hoped to rebuild. From a military standpoint, Chongjin was crucial given its proximity to Japan, North Korea's greatest enemy, after the United States. The coastline south of Chongjin was dotted with military installations directed at Japan, including the Musudan-ri missile base from which a long-range missile was test-fired in 1998.

The year after his father's death, Kim began a purge of the 6th Army corps stationed in Chongjin. The 6th Army was one of twenty corps of ground troops in North Korea's million-man army. Its headquarters were in the center of Nanam, a district south of the city center, just north of the coal mines. Late one night, people heard the dull engine roar of dozens of trucks and tanks and smelled the acrid fumes of exhaust. The entire corps of three thousand men, their tanks, trucks, and armored vehicles was pulling out of town. The convoys first gathered around Nanam Station, then moved slowly over the rutted roads, producing terrible thunder. Residents shuddered but dared not rise from their bed mats to peek out the door.

Not a word appeared in *Rodong Sinmun* or on the broadcast news. It was impossible to get firsthand information because the North Korean People's Army typically conscripted soldiers for ten years, assigning them far from their hometowns without any means of contacting their families.

In the absence of hard news, there was rumor. Was the army preparing for the long-awaited war with the American bastards? An invasion by the South Koreans? A coup d'état? The story spread quickly that the 6th Army officers had been foiled in their plans to seize control of Chongjin's port and military installations while fellow plotters in Pyongyang planned to assassinate Kim Jong-il.

At the hospital, Dr. Kim heard from a patient that the coup plotters were bankrolled by wealthy Chinese businessmen.

At the kindergarten, the teachers gathered in the cafeteria to listen intently to a cook who claimed to have firsthand information from a relative who was one of the plotters. He said that the plot was funded by the South Korean president, Kim Young-sam.

A teacher at the school claimed that she saw one of her neighbors, who was related to one of the plotters, being taken away along with his three-month-old baby, because of their tainted blood. It was late at night when the truck came for them.

"They tossed the baby into the back of the truck like a piece of furniture," the teacher whispered. The image of the baby rolling around the back of the truck struck a chord of terror in Mi-ran and for years that terrifying scene would recur both in her waking mind and in her dreams.

In the end, the entire 6th Army was dissolved, replaced eventually by units from the 9th Army from Wonsan. The process dragged on for many months. To this day, the exact reasons remain a mystery.

Intelligence analysts tend to dismiss the story of the attempted coup. Over the years many reports of attempted putsches, rebellions, and assassination attempts have emerged from North Korea— as yet, none of them confirmed. The most plausible explanation about the 6th Army is that it was disbanded because Kim Jong-il wanted more control over its financial activities. The North Korean military ran various trading companies that exported everything from pine mushrooms and dried squid to amphetamines and heroin—illicit drugs being a large source of hard currency for the regime. It was assumed the military had its finger in the theft of humanitarian-aid rice sold on the black market in Chongjin and elsewhere. Supposedly, corruption was rampant within the 6th Army and its officers were skimming off the profits for themselves and, like capos in the Mafia, were punished by the big boss. A military officer who defected to South Korea in 1998 told investigators there that the 6th Army officers had taken profits from the sale of opium poppies grown on collective farms on the outskirts of Chongjin.

Not long after the army purge, there were more strange happenings in Chongjin. Special teams of prosecutors called *groupa* started coming up from Pyongyang to crack down on corruption in the factories. A particular target was Kimchaek Iron and Steel, the largest steelworks in North Korea, which had been largely idle through the 1990s; only two of its ten smokestacks were operating at any given time. Some of the managers had organized employees to collect scrap metal to trade across the Chinese border for food. When that proved insufficient, they dismantled the machines themselves, selling off the parts at the border. The cash raised from the equipment was used at least in part to buy food for factory employees.

The steelworks' managers—about ten in total—were executed by a firing squad. The People's Safety Agency carried out the executions on a muddy lawn that sloped down from Sunam Market to the Suseon stream.

Afterward, the prosecutors went after smaller targets. They executed people who had stolen copper wire from telephone poles to swap for food, goat thieves, corn thieves, cattle thieves, and black marketers of rice. In 1997, notices went up around Chongjin and other cities warning that people who stole, hoarded, or even sold grains were "stifling our style of socialism" and could be subject to execution.

North Korea's criminal code limited the death penalty to premeditated murder, treason, terrorism, "antistate activities," and "antipeople activities," but these definitions were loose enough to include any activity that might offend the Workers' Party. North Korean defectors in South Korea told of executions in the 1990s for adultery, prostitution, resisting arrest, disorderly conduct. In Onsong, the border town where Hyuck lived in the orphanage, four students were reportedly executed for streaking naked after a bout of drinking.

In the past, North Korea was an orderly, austere, and predictable place. If somebody was murdered, it was usually the result of a gang fight or a romantic jealousy. There was little theft because nobody had much more than anyone else. People knew what the rules were and which lines not to cross. Now the rules were in play—and life became disorderly and frightening.

CHAPTER 13

FROGS IN THE WELL

A student in the Grand People's Study House
in Pyongyang, the largest library in North Korea.

JUN-SANG WITNESSED A PUBLIC EXECUTION ONE SUMMER WHEN
he was home for summer vacation. For days, sound trucks had been
driving by announcing the time and date. The head of the *inminban*
had knocked on doors telling people their attendance was expected.
Jun-sang didn't care for this sort of spectacle. He hated blood and
couldn't stand to see a person or an animal suffer. When he was
twelve years old, his father had forced him to slaughter a chicken.
Jun-sang's hands trembled as he grasped the bird by the neck. "How
can you be a man if you can't do this?" his father berated him. Jun-
sang dutifully brought down the hatchet, more afraid of his father's
ridicule than of a headless chicken, but refused to eat that night's
dinner. Watching the death of a human being was unthinkable to
him. He vowed to stay away. But when the day arrived and all the

neighbors headed out to watch, he found himself falling in step with the crowd.

The execution was to take place on a sandy embankment of a stream not far from the hot springs resort where he and Mi-ran went on their nighttime walks. About three hundred people had already gathered, the children pushing forward to the front. Schoolboys competed to collect spent bullet cartridges from public executions. Jun-sang elbowed his way through the crowd to get a better look.

The state security had converted the clearing by the stream into a makeshift courtroom, with tables set up for the prosecutors and a sound system with two enormous speakers. The man was accused of climbing electric poles and cutting copper wire to sell.

"The theft caused extensive damage to the nation's property and was done with the intention to damage our social system. It was an act of treason that aided the enemies of the socialist state," the prosecutor read, his voice bellowing through the scratchy speakers. Then a man acting as a sort of lawyer for the accused spoke, although he offered no defense: "I have determined that what the prosecutor says is true."

"The accused is hereby sentenced to death and the sentence will be carried out immediately," decreed a third man.

The condemned man was bound to a wooden stake at the eyes, the chest, and the legs. The firing squad would aim to sever the ropes in order, three bullets in each location—nine in total, top to bottom. First the lifeless head would slump over so that the body would crumple in an orderly heap at the foot of the stake. Neat and efficient. It would look like the condemned was bowing in death as if to apologize.

A murmur went through the crowd. It seemed Jun-sang was not the only one who thought execution was excessive punishment for a minor theft. The electric lines weren't working anyway. The few meters of copper wiring the man had stolen probably had gotten him no more than a few bags of rice.

"A pity. He has a younger sister," Jun-sang heard somebody say.

"Two sisters," said another.

Jun-sang figured the man's parents must be dead. Clearly he

knew nobody with influence to intervene on his behalf. He probably had a poor class background as well. Maybe he was the son of a miner, like the kids Mi-ran taught.

As Jun-sang contemplated these possibilities, the shots rang out.

Head. Chest. Legs.

The head burst open like a water balloon. Blood spurted out over the dirt, almost spilling onto the feet of the crowd. Jun-sang felt as if he was going to vomit. He turned and elbowed his way back out of the crowd and headed home.

FOR JUN-SANG, VISITS to Chongjin often yielded unpleasant discoveries about his own country. At the university, Jun-sang was insulated from the worst of the deprivations. He had enough to eat and electricity most nights. Students at Pyongyang's top universities were among the most privileged citizens in a privileged city. But once he left the academic cocoon, reality slapped him in the face.

The places he associated with happy memories were all closed—the restaurants where he'd eaten as a boy, the movie theater where he'd first spotted Mi-ran. There was no electricity except on the occasional public holiday, such as the birthdays of Kim Il-sung and Kim Jong-il.

Evenings at home were spent in darkness, listening to his parents complain. His wealthy grandfather in Tokyo had passed away and the surviving relatives were not as generous about sending money to their poor relations. His mother's rheumatism had gotten so bad she couldn't walk to the market or use the precious sewing machine she'd brought from Japan.

It was the same every night. His father sat smoking, the ember of his cigarette glowing red in the dark. He would exhale a cloud of smoke and sigh loudly, the preface to some bad news he was about to convey.

"You know who died? Do you remember . . ."

His father named teachers from Jun-sang's high school. His math teacher. His Chinese teacher. The literature teacher who was a fellow cinema buff and used to lend Jun-sang copies of a magazine called *Film Literature*, about Eastern European cinema and the role of film in anti-imperialism. The teachers were all intellectuals in their fifties, who discovered they had no marketable skills after the school system stopped paying their salaries. Jun-sang used to drop in on his old high school teachers on his trips home from Pyongyang; the teachers were always happy to see this student who had done so well for himself. Now Jun-sang avoided seeing anybody from his high school. He didn't want to hear who else had died.

The deaths weren't confined to the older people. Jun-sang's mother told him about classmates who had died of starvation, guys who hadn't passed their university exams and had to join the army instead. Jun-sang had lost touch with them, but he had taken comfort in the assumption that they'd done okay during the tough times because soldiers were supposed get the first provisions of food. After all, it was Kim Jong-il himself who proclaimed the *songun* idea, or "military first." Schoolchildren were made to sacrifice so that a strong army could protect them from the bombs of the American bastards.

Jun-sang could see now that it wasn't true. The soldiers around Chongjin were a ragtag bunch with fake leather belts cinching tight the uniforms that no longer fit their skinny frames. Their complexions were sallow from malnutrition and many of them were only five feet tall. (The North Korean army had to lower its height requirement from five feet three in the early 1990s because of the stunting of the younger generation.) At night they abandoned their posts and clambered into private gardens, digging up kimchi pots and pulling up vegetables.

Most of the families in his neighborhood had raised the walls around their houses, ignoring a regulation that restricted the height to 1.5 meters so that police could look in. Still, three times burglars managed to climb the wall and ransack Jun-sang's yard. They yanked out garlic, potatoes, cabbage. Jun-sang's father had kept careful notations in his gardening journal, writing down the types of seeds he used and the time it took them to germinate.

"Why couldn't they at least have waited until it was fully grown?" he wailed.

Jun-sang's mother fell into a deep depression when somebody stole one of their dogs. She had been raising jindo puppies since Jun-sang was a boy. She doted on her dogs, cooking their food herself. Her letters to him at school were filled with news of the puppies. She couldn't bear the thought that in all likelihood the dog had been eaten.

In truth, they were lucky it was only the dog that was killed. Everybody knew that the families who'd come from Japan had money, so they were frequently targets for thieves. An entire family in their village had been murdered in a botched robbery. Jun-sang and his family had to be more careful than ever before. They quickly ate their dinner behind the high walls of their house, hoping their neighbors wouldn't see that they had enough to eat.

EVER SINCE HE FAILED to muster genuine tears over Kim Il-sung's death, Jun-sang had come to recognize his growing disenchantment with the system. Everything he saw, everything he heard or read pushed him further from politically correct thinking. His experiences at the university were also changing him. For the first time in his life he was exposed to new ideas.

As a child, Jun-sang read whatever he could get his hands on—novels, philosophy, science, history, even the speeches of Kim Il-sung. The bookstore in town sold novellas that told stories about brutal Americans, cringing and cowardly South Koreans, and heroic North Koreans. Occasionally there were Russian novels—works by Tolstoy or Maxim Gorky. His high school was supplied books by the Educational Instruments and Materials Provisions Office and his father had a respectable collection of Greek and Roman history. Jun-sang enjoyed reading about ancient warriors—he loved the story of how Hannibal fought to topple the Roman empire and then poisoned himself rather than accept defeat.

By the time he got to Pyongyang, he was ready for more modern fare. At the university, behind the librarian's desk, was a small selection of Western books that had been translated into Korean. They were forbidden to the general public; only top students could have access to them. At some high level of the government, somebody had decided that the nation needed an intellectual elite with some knowledge of Western literature. The books had no publisher identified on the title pages, but the rumor Jun-sang heard was that they were published by the Inmin Daehakseup Dang, the Grand People's Study House, a showcase national library at Kim Il-sung Square. The collection even included American books.

Jun-sang's favorite was *Gone with the Wind*. The melodramatic style of the book was not unlike the tone of Korean fiction. He was struck by the parallels between the American Civil War and the Korean War. It was amazing to him how vicious the fighting could be between one people—clearly the Americans were as impassioned as the Koreans. He thought the Americans better off for the fact that they ended up one country, not divided like the Koreans. He admired the heroine, Scarlett O'Hara, for her pluckiness. She reminded him a little of North Korea's own cinematic heroines who were always in the dirt, fighting for their land, but Scarlett was much more of an individualist—not a quality celebrated in North Korean literature. And North Korean heroines most certainly didn't have love affairs.

This was risqué stuff by North Korean standards. Jun-sang wanted to read more. He checked out everything he could find, from Sidney Sheldon's *Rage of Angels* to Gabriel García Márquez's *One Hundred Years of Solitude*. He even read *How to Win Friends and Influence People*, the 1930s self-help classic by Dale Carnegie. It was his first exposure to Western ideas about business, and it shocked him. He couldn't believe the advice that Carnegie was giving readers.

Learn to love, respect, and enjoy other people.

How could a product of the American capitalist system write something like this? Jun-sang asked himself. Weren't all capitalists enemies who lived by the law of the jungle—kill or be killed?

Jun-sang also borrowed books from his classmates. At a top university, many of the students had relatives in power who traveled abroad on business and picked up books and magazines. Korean-language material was available in China's Yanbian prefecture, which has a large ethnic Korean population. Through one of his classmates, Jun-sang got a sex-education booklet that had been published by the Chinese school system. Yet another eye-opener! Jun-sang realized that he and his other unmarried friends in their

twenties knew less about sex than the average Chinese schoolboy.
How was he to have known that women menstruated? It explained a
lot.

He was just as surprised to read a speech that had been delivered
at a Communist Party congress that criticized Mao for the Cultural
Revolution. That will be the day, he thought, when the Workers'
Party criticizes Kim Il-sung.

One day Jun-sang was approached by a classmate with whom he
occasionally had traded books. The student looked around ner-
vously before slipping a book to Jun-sang.

"It's a good one," he whispered. "Maybe you want to read it?"

The book was a slim volume about economic reform that had
been published by the Russian government. The boy's father had
gotten it at a book exhibition at the Russian embassy in Pyongyang.
It seemed to have been written in the early 1990s as Russia was trying to build a new free-market economy. Jun-sang realized immediately that he had something dangerous in his hands—North Koreans
were required to submit any foreign literature they found to the police. He, the boy, and the boy's father would be in serious trouble for
having a book of this sort in their possession. Jun-sang quickly put it
under the clothes in his locker. His dorm room had two bunk
beds—four students to a room—so he had little privacy. He made
sure to read the book under the covers with a flashlight.

He read:

> In the early stages, capitalism was an inhuman competition to
> produce wealth. There was no concept of dividing wealth
> fairly or welfare for the common worker. Economic develop-
> ment took place in a disorderly fashion. . . . But modern capi-
> talism has evolved considerably and corrected its previous
> faults. For example, antitrust laws ensure orderly production,
> but production that is not controlled by the state.

The book went on to describe pension systems and the concept
of insurance and welfare. It stated that socialist economic systems
throughout the world had failed because of their inefficiency. Jun-
sang found himself nodding as he read along.

—

IN 1996, JUN-SANG received his undergraduate degree. Rather than return to Chongjin, he decided to stay on at the university, taking a position at a research department. He was now officially an adult and had the right to leave campus. He moved out of his dormitory and took a private room. It was run-down, dirty, and poorly furnished, but he liked his landlords, an elderly couple who were hard of hearing and had poor vision. They suited Jun-sang's purposes perfectly.

Once he had a room of his own, Jun-sang took the last of his grandfather's money and bought a Sony television. He registered the television with the Electric Wave Inspection Bureau, as required by North Korean law. Since North Korea couldn't manufacture its own appliances anymore, imported sets had to be fixed to the government stations and then their tuners disabled—a North Korean version of crippleware that would prevent them from receiving any information from the outside world. North Koreans joked that they were like "frogs in the well." The world for them extended no further than the circle of light above their heads. Tech-savvy types had figured out how to get around the system. With radios it was easy—open up the set, cut the conveyor belt attached to the dial, and replace it with a rubber band that could turn the dial wherever you liked. Television required a little more expertise.

The bureau put a paper seal over the buttons of the television set that certified it had been preset on the approved station. To get around the seal without damaging it, Jun-sang used a long, thin sewing needle to push the buttons. There was a back door to his room leading out to the yard and there he constructed an antenna. He experimented with it at night after everyone was asleep, turning it this way and that until he had what he wanted: South Korean television.

Jun-sang listened to the television only late at night when the signal coming from some ninety miles away across the DMZ was clearest. He would wait until he was sure his landlords were asleep—the walls were so thin he could hear them snoring. The television wasn't equipped with an earphone jack so he turned the volume up only until it was just audible. He would crouch with his ear pressed to the speaker until his legs and neck were so cramped he couldn't hold the position any longer. He listened to television more than he watched it. He was always in a heightened state of alertness when his television was on. The Electric Wave Inspection Bureau was known to pay surprise visits at odd hours. A few doors down, a neighbor had dogs. If he heard them barking at night, Jun-sang would switch the television back to the central broadcasting channel and rush outside to take down the antenna.

The television inspectors did come. One of them was a sharp-eyed fellow who noticed that a piece of Scotch tape covered the paper seal. Jun-sang had put the tape on to cover a spot where the pin had left a mark.

"What's the tape for?" the inspector demanded.

Jun-sang's heart pounded. He'd heard of an entire family that was taken away to the gulag because one member watched South Korean television. A friend of his who was merely suspected of listening to South Korean radio was held for a full year of interrogation, during which time he never saw sunlight. When he was released, he was deathly pale, his nerves shattered.

"Oh, I put the tape on to keep the seal from coming off," he answered as nonchalantly as he could.

The inspector frowned and went on his way.

Jun-sang should have been more careful after his close call, but he could not contain his curiosity. He had an insatiable appetite for information, current information in real time. The television brought Jun-sang not only news of the outside world, but more information than he'd ever heard before about his own country.

Jun-sang learned astonishing things that he had suspected but never knew. He heard President Bill Clinton saying that the United States had offered fuel oil and energy assistance but that North Korea preferred to develop nuclear weapons and missiles. He found out that the United States was supplying the country with hundreds of thousands of tons of rice as humanitarian aid.

Members of a U.S. congressional delegation gave a news conference and said that two million people had died of starvation in North Korea. Human rights organizations estimated that 200,000 people were confined to a gulag of prison camps and that North Korea had the world's worst human rights record.

In 2000, South Korean television reported that the country's president, Kim Dae-jung, was going to Pyongyang for a historic summit with Kim Jong-il. During the summit, South Korean television broadcast Kim Jong-il's voice as he chatted with the South Korean president. Jun-sang had never heard the Dear Leader's voice before; on North Korean radio and television his words were voiced by professional announcers who read his words in the quivering, awestruck tone reserved for the leadership. It preserved the mystique. "What do you think of our historical sights?" Jun-sang heard the Dear Leader saying in a voice that sounded old, tinny, and distinctly human.

"He's a real person after all," Jun-sang said to himself.

Listening to South Korean television was like looking in the mirror for the first time in your life and realizing you were unattractive. North Koreans were always told theirs was the proudest country in the world, but the rest of the world considered it a pathetic, bankrupt regime. Jun-sang knew people were starving. He knew that people were dragged off to labor camps; but he had never before heard these figures. Surely South Korean news reports were exaggerated, just like North Korean propaganda?

JUN-SANG'S TRAIN rides home in particular reminded him of a description of living hell he had read in Buddhist scripture. The cars were so crowded that you couldn't get to the toilet. Men urinated out the windows or waited for stops to relieve themselves outside in the fields, but sometimes they couldn't make it and had to do it inside the car. Homeless children would run alongside the slow-moving trains begging, sometimes screaming for food. They would try to claw through the broken windows. There were long delays because the trains would break down trying to make the steep climb into the mountains north of Pyongyang. Jun-sang was once stuck for two days in a broken-down train in midwinter with an arctic wind gusting through the windowless car. He befriended other passengers—a woman with a twenty-day-old baby and a young man who was late for his own wedding. Together, they swiped a metal bucket and lit a fire inside, ignoring the conductor's commands to put it out. Had it not been for the fire, they all could have perished from hypothermia.

On one trip in 1998, when the North Korean economy was at its worst, Jun-sang was stuck at a small town in South Hamgyong province where he usually switched from the eastbound trains to the northbound line up the coast. The tracks were flooded and a cold, driving rain drenched the waiting passengers. Jun-sang took what shelter he could find on the platform. As he waited, his attention was drawn to a group of homeless children, the *kochebi*, who were performing to get money for food. Some of them did magic tricks, some danced. One boy, about seven or eight years old, sang. His tiny body was lost in the folds of an adult-sized factory uniform, but his voice had the resonance of a much older person. He squeezed his eyes shut, mustering all his emotion, and belted out the song, filling the platform with its power.

> *Uri Abogi, our father, we have nothing to envy in the world.*
> *Our house is within the embrace of the Workers' Party.*
> *We are all brothers and sisters.*
> *Even if a sea of fire comes toward us, sweet children do not*
>   *need to be afraid.*
> *Our father is here.*
> *We have nothing to envy.*

Jun-sang knew the song by heart from his childhood, except the lyrics had been updated. In the verse "Our father, Kim Il-sung," the child substituted the name of Kim Jong-il. It was beyond reason that this small child should be singing a paean to the father who protected him when his circumstances so clearly belied the song. There he was on the platform, soaking wet, filthy, no doubt hungry.

Jun-sang reached into his pocket and gave the boy 10 won, a generous tip for a street performer. It was less an act of charity than gratitude for the education the boy had given him.

He would later credit the boy with pushing him over the edge. He now knew for sure that he didn't believe. It was an enormous moment of self-revelation, like deciding one was an atheist. It made him feel alone. He was different from everybody else. He was suddenly self-conscious, burdened by a secret he had discovered about himself.

At first he thought his life would be dramatically different with his newfound clarity. In fact, it was much the same as ever before. He went through the motions of being a loyal subject. On Saturday mornings he showed up punctually at the ideological lectures at the university. The Workers' Party secretary droning on about the legacy of Kim Il-sung sounded like he was on autopilot. In winter when the auditorium was unheated, the lecturer would wrap up as quickly as possible. Jun-sang often snuck a peek at the other members of the audience. There were usually about five hundred people, mostly graduate students and postdoctoral fellows. During the lecture, they jiggled their feet and sat on their hands to stay warm. But their faces were still and expressionless, as blank as mannequins in a department store window.

He realized suddenly he wore the same vacant expression on his face. In fact, they all probably felt exactly the same way he did about the contents of the lecture.

"They know! They all know!" he nearly screamed, he was so certain. These were supposedly the finest young minds in the nation. "Anybody with a functioning brain cannot *not* know that something is wrong."

Jun-sang realized he was not the only nonbeliever out there. He was even convinced that he could recognize a form of silent communication that was so subtle it didn't even rise to the level of a wink or a nod. One of the university students, a young woman, gained some acclaim when she wrote in her diary about her admiration for the Dear Leader. An article appeared about her in *Rodong Sinmun* and she won an award for her loyalty. The university students ribbed her mercilessly. They thought she was a freak, but because they couldn't say so, they just teased her instead.

"Who's the lucky guy who will get to marry *you*?" they asked her. But that was as far as they could go.

North Korean students and intellectuals didn't dare to stage protests as their counterparts in other Communist countries did.

There was no Prague Spring or Tiananmen Square. The level of repression in North Korea was so great that no organized resistance could take root. Any antiregime activity would have terrible consequences for the protester, his immediate family, and all other known relatives. Under a system that sought to stamp out tainted blood for three generations, the punishment would extend to parents, grandparents, brothers, sisters, nieces, nephews, cousins. "A lot of people felt if you had one life to give, you would give it to get rid of this terrible regime, but then you're not the only one getting punished. Your family would go through hell," one defector told me.

It was impossible to start a book club or conduct a political discussion. Any free exchange of ideas would invariably lead to forbidden territory. In any group of three or four people, there had to be at least one spy for the various intelligence agencies. Jun-sang suspected that his best friend from high school was a government informer. The boy had been the school's best student, even better than Jun-sang, but he couldn't attend university in Pyongyang because a childhood case of polio had left him with a limp. When Jun-sang came home from Pyongyang, the friend would complain loudly about the government, encouraging Jun-sang to respond. There was something bold and contrived in his tone that made Jun-sang worry about entrapment. He avoided the friend entirely.

He reminded himself: You don't talk politics as long as you live in North Korea. Not with your best friend, not with your teachers or your parents, and certainly not with your girlfriend. Jun-sang never discussed his feelings about the regime with Mi-ran. He didn't tell her he was watching South Korean television, and reading pamphlets about capitalism. He certainly did not tell her that he had begun to harbor fantasies of defecting.

CHAPTER 14

THE RIVER

The Tumen River as seen from China.

THE LESS THEY COULD CONFIDE IN EACH OTHER, THE MORE
strained their relationship was.

In the past, Jun-sang and Mi-ran gossiped for hours about their
classmates, their colleagues, their families. As they strolled in the
dark, he recounted entire plots of films he had seen and books he
had read. He recited poems. He loved her natural curiosity, the way
she was unembarrassed by what she didn't know, which was so different from his striving colleagues at the university. Much of the
pleasure he took from reading was in the anticipation of telling Mi-
ran about it later. During their long months apart, he would store
up his best material, rehearsing it in his mind, imagining the way

her eyes would flicker with delight, how she would laugh out loud without the coy gesture of covering her mouth. Now he held back even though his head was bursting with ideas he couldn't share.

Not that he didn't trust her—he felt closer to Mi-ran than anybody outside his immediate family. As other friends drifted away, she loomed larger at the center of his life. What good would it do to tell her anyway? If she knew what he knew, wouldn't it just make her as unhappy as it had made him? How could she continue teaching hungry children to sing songs that praised Kim Jong-il if she knew how rich the South Koreans were? Why did she need to know about capitalist reforms in China or Russia? He worried about Mi-ran. With her bad class background, she had to be more cautious about her conduct than others. A slip of the tongue would be all it took to get her sent away. When they spoke together about her starving pupils, they used euphemistic language about the "situation" and the "Arduous March." Anything more explicit could steer them into the treacherous territory of identifying who was responsible.

The other matter left unspoken was personal. Jun-sang suspected Mi-ran was hurt by his decision to stay on at the research institute after his graduation in 1997. It was harder than ever to continue a relationship with the miserable train rides home and the equally pathetic postal system. Once he got home, the logistics were also daunting. Neither had a telephone and neither wanted to leave notes at the other's house. In order to make plans Jun-sang would have to arrange to catch Mi-ran outside her house or at the school. During a blizzard, Jun-sang trudged for hours through blinding snow to the school, using railroad tracks as his guide. By the time he arrived, his fingers stinging from the cold, he found out she had left for the day.

They saw each other twice a year—during summer and winter vacations. After long periods apart, it took time to overcome the initial awkwardness. Mi-ran had changed. The daring cropped hair she had when they first met was long gone. She now looked more like other young Korean women, with her hair grown out to shoulder length and pinned back. He was surprised to see that she had begun wearing makeup.

The fact of the matter was that they were full-fledged adults now—he was twenty-seven years old and she was twenty-five. The obvious question of their future went unanswered.

The subject came up unexpectedly during one of his visits. Mi-ran had attended a wedding party for one of her classmates earlier in the day. After dinner, she and Jun-sang met up behind her house and hiked up to the hot springs resort. It was a clear evening and the place was deserted. They circled the path under the trees and strolled past the artificial waterfall and the reflecting pool. They settled on their favorite bench with a view of the moon over the mountains.

Mi-ran was entertaining Jun-sang with a description of the wedding and her friend's new husband.

"I don't see why people need to get married so young," Jun-sang interjected. He had been reading classical Korean poems lately and from the vast repertoire rumbling around his head, he retrieved one about the woes of a young bride.

> *If a tiger in the mountains came upon us could it be any more*
> *   frightening than a mother-in law?*
> *Could the coldest frost be chillier than your father-in-law?*
> *Bean pods, even if they burst when you step on them, would never*
> *   stare as rudely as your husband's younger brothers.*
> *No, not even the hottest pepper could be as bitter as the life of*
> *   a married woman.*

Jun-sang thought the poem was hilarious. Mi-ran laughed, but hesitantly; he wondered if she took it as a cautionary message.

In fact, Jun-sang hadn't thought much about marriage, or at least he was trying to push such thoughts away. On the one hand, he couldn't imagine himself married to anybody but Mi-ran, even though marrying her would dash his chances of getting into the Workers' Party. Without the party, he had little chance of getting a permanent position at a university in Pyongyang. But that was under the current regime. What if he left North Korea, perhaps with her? What if the North Korean regime collapsed? Jun-sang knew from his late-night television watching that North Korea was the last Communist country of its kind, save perhaps Cuba. Just like the Berlin Wall had come down in 1989 allowing the Germanys to reunite, the Koreas might one day be together. Every time he walked past another body on the street swarming with flies or spotted another filthy child on the verge of death, he felt the end was near. They were living as though in a state of war, tragedy bombarding them from all sides. Under such conditions, Jun-sang couldn't plan for the next week, let alone think about marriage.

He was suddenly overcome with sadness for himself and for Mi-ran and the unhappy life in which they found themselves. He hadn't wished to offend her with the poem. More as a gesture of consolation than anything else, he did something he'd never done before: he leaned over and kissed her.

At least it was sort of a kiss. It was little more than a brush of the lips on her cheek that trailed off before reaching the mouth, but it was far more physical intimacy than they'd shared before. They had known each other for thirteen years, dating for the past nine, and had done nothing more than hold hands.

Mi-ran looked startled. She didn't seem to be angry, just nervous. She stood up abruptly from the bench and gestured for him to do the same.

"Come on," she said. "Let's keep walking."

MI-RAN WAS taken aback by the kiss. Although she had only the dimmest idea of the mechanics of sex, she knew that a kiss could lead to a place she didn't want to go. She had heard tell of girls sleeping with men and the terrible trouble they got into. There was no birth control to be had. Instead there were expensive and dangerous abortions.

Unlike her dreamy boyfriend, Mi-ran had thought plenty about marriage. Two of her three sisters were married with children and her high school friends were getting engaged. She had to think seriously about her future. She didn't think Jun-sang would ever marry her.

To be sure, her situation had improved. By the 1990s, Kim Jong-il had bigger enemies to tackle than the families who had fought on the wrong side of the Korean War fifty years earlier. Like a childhood scar disappearing under the wrinkles of old age, the stigma was fading. Even under North Korea's law, once three generations passed, the tainted blood would be diluted. Mi-ran and her younger brother had been admitted to teachers' college. Her oldest sister's good looks had trumped her poor class background and she had married well; her husband was a civilian military employee and they lived on a closed military base in one of the few areas nearby where the forests hadn't been ravaged. She kept the family supplied with pine mushrooms, a precious commodity that they could trade for other food.

Still, Mi-ran had to accept certain limitations. She doubted, for example, that she or anybody else in her family could ever get a residency permit for Pyongyang. If she and Jun-sang married they would at best live in Chongjin. She would feel responsible for his sacrifice. When she looked at him, so pale and serious behind the eyeglasses he had gotten at school, she worried how he would fare back in Chongjin. He might end up like his mentors, those starving intellectuals who could quote Tolstoy by heart but were utterly clueless about how to feed themselves.

Then there were his parents. She'd never met them, but she'd heard about them. They would surely throw a fit if Jun-sang tried to marry her. His father might threaten suicide; his mother would feign illness. Jun-sang was a dutiful son, if nothing else. He would never disobey his parents.

People who came from Japan usually married their own kind, anyway. They would fix him up with a girl who had Japanese money or he'd meet a smart, sophisticated girl at university. Mi-ran's romantic, poetry-quoting boyfriend was simply out of her league. Face the facts, she told herself.

She tried to imagine what her life would be like without him. Ordinary. Without poetry. Marriage to a factory worker or miner like her father. Children. Life forever in the mining village or at best in Chongjin. She could feel the walls closing in.

Her teaching job had turned to misery. There were only fifteen students left in her class, down from fifty when she'd started. She dreaded entering the decrepit building every morning, as the departed classmates cast a deep sadness over the school. The children didn't laugh the way they used to. Nobody could concentrate on their studies—not the students, not the teachers, who hadn't been paid since the year after Kim Il-sung's death. When Mi-ran asked the principal when salaries might resume, the woman chuckled.

"Maybe when we're reunited with South Korea," she quipped.

Mi-ran thought about pursuing another career. Maybe she could work at the market or find a job at one of the sewing factories. She had worked so hard to get into college, to become a teacher and slip into mainstream society. Now it seemed it had all been for nothing.

MI-RAN'S OTHER BIG worry was her father. Now in his mid-sixties, he seemed to be shrinking before her eyes. Tae-woo's sinewy body curved with age and he had grown gaunt. It embarrassed her mother, who prided herself on her ability to provide for the family. Tae-woo spent his days puttering around the house, sometimes starting a project, fixing a table or a cabinet, and then forgetting what he was doing midway. Once so quiet, he now talked constantly to whoever was in the house or to himself. He spoke of things that had gone unmentioned for nearly half a century. He reminisced about his childhood in South Chungchong province and about his beautiful sisters. He boasted about his father and an ancestor somewhere along the line who was a *yangban*, a nobleman. His rheumy eyes watered during these ramblings. During the wedding of Mi-ran's third sister, he did something that the family had never seen before: he got drunk.

Mi-ran's father had always distinguished himself from other North Korean men of his generation by his refusal to drink. It was in fact something of a defense mechanism. In the 1960s he had seen several friends—like himself, former South Korean POWs—get in trouble for talking too much while drunk. But now, Tae-woo felt he could be a little less careful. The wedding party was held at their home. They served Mi-ran's mother's home-brewed corn liquor. Tae-woo downed three cups of the potent brew. By the time the guests were leaving, he started singing a sentimental South Korean song from his childhood, oblivious to who might hear.

I used to hold my mother's hand.

Then I let go to reach for the fruit and cake.
Oh, how I miss holding my mother's hand.

MI-RAN'S FATHER DIED in 1997 at the age of sixty-eight. Mi-ran wasn't at home, but her brother was with him. He reported to the sisters that their father's last word was *mother.*

In the months before his death, Tae-woo had spoken more lucidly than before about his family. He insisted that his only son memorize the names of their ancestors on the family register, a ledger in which Korean families record their heritage. He had been the only boy himself in the family and so his own son would carry on the family line.

There was yet another last wish that would be harder to fulfill. Tae-woo wanted his family in South Korea to be notified of his death. The request sounded like the hallucinations of a dying man.

Notwithstanding the nearly half century that had passed since the Korean War, there was no postal service between North and South Korea and no telephone service. The Red Cross was not permitted to carry messages. (It was not until 2000 that some highly choreographed family reunions were held, but only for a fraction of those people separated by the Korean War.) Mi-ran and her siblings assumed their South Korean grandparents were long dead, but had not a clue about their father's sisters. To contact relatives in South Korea seemed utterly impossible.

THE YEAR AFTER Mi-ran's father died, her sister So-hee came rushing into the house. She was out of breath, her face flushed with excitement. She'd just spoken with a friend who had admitted to traveling back and forth to China. He knew people there who could help them get in touch with their father's family. Once you were inside China, he assured Mi-ran's sister, you merely had to pick up a telephone to dial South Korea.

Maybe they wanted to try?

Mi-ran and So-hee were suspicious at first. You could never trust anybody who wasn't family. This was exactly the way that the secret police entrapped people.

After a few days of deliberation, they decided the friend was sincere. He had relatives in China, as well as a whole network who could help. He knew somebody with a truck who would drive them to the border; a border policeman who knew exactly where to cross the river and who could bribe the appropriate people to look the other way; a cousin with a house just across the border where they would be safe. The plan was for Mi-ran and So-hee to go together for a few days. They confided in only one person, their newly married sister, who was sworn to secrecy. However, she couldn't keep such a big secret. She blabbed to their mother, who put her foot down.

"Unmarried girls can't go alone to China," she decreed. Already rumors had circulated that North Korean women were raped or kidnapped to work in the sex industry or killed and had their organs stolen. Mi-ran's mother wasn't to be crossed.

They huddled in a family conference, arguing about what to do. Mi-ran's brother insisted that, as the man of the family, he should go alone. Their mother wasn't okay with this option either. He was only twenty-two years old, the baby of the family, her only son.

Finally it was decided. Mi-ran, So-hee, and their brother would go, along with their mother. It would be a family trip. Her recently married sister didn't want to go, and they didn't dare tell the oldest sister, who was living with her husband and children in a military compound and would have never approved.

MI-RAN'S FAMILY HAD never been among the most faithful—her mother scoffed at the women who dusted the leaders' portraits every day—but they weren't actively opposed to the regime. The most daring among them, as it turned out, was Mi-ran's brother, Sok-ju, who unbeknownst to the others had been listening to South Korean radio with earphones at night. The others didn't care much about current events; they were all too busy working to think about the outside world.

Relative to other North Koreans, Mi-ran's family was thriving in the new economy. Her mother was still operating the corn mill.

They weren't hungry; they weren't in trouble with the law. They didn't have a pressing reason to leave North Korea. But opportunity presented itself and once they pursued it, one thing followed another, the plan gained momentum, and it was too late to turn back. The ramblings of a dying man had become an imperative that was propelling them toward the border.

They would go to China to contact her father's relatives in South Korea. They had no idea whether they could locate them or if their relatives would be glad to hear from them. They didn't dare think about actually *going* to South Korea.

All the elements of the plan fell into place within just a few weeks. In their harmonica house, with its paper-thin walls and nosy neighbors, they couldn't do anything that would betray the agitation within. They had to maintain an outward appearance of calm. Nothing could look like it was out of the ordinary. They couldn't sell off possessions to raise money for the trip. They couldn't nail boards over the windows to secure their house.

Mi-ran had one urgent task in preparation for leaving. The night before their departure she took out a carefully wrapped bundle from her clothing cupboard. It contained every letter she had ever received from Jun-sang. She had kept them with all the gifts he had given her over the years. Her most prized possession, the butterfly-shaped barrette decorated with rhinestones, she would leave behind. The letters had to be destroyed. She ripped each one into tiny pieces before throwing them out. She didn't want anybody to learn of the decade she and Jun-sang had spent obsessed with each other. Nobody knew except his brother and two of her sisters. Now more than ever it was important to keep the romance a secret.

Mi-ran told herself they were going just for a short trip to make the telephone call, but in her heart, she knew she might never come back—whether or not their South Korean relatives would accept them. After they were gone, they would be denounced as traitors. "She received an education through the benevolence of the party and she betrayed the fatherland," she could almost hear the party secretary saying. She didn't want her guilt to rub off on Jun-sang. After she was gone, his life could go on as it had before. He could find himself a suitable wife, join the Workers' Party, and spend the rest of his life in Pyongyang as a scientist.

He'll forgive me, he'll understand, she told herself. It's in his best interest.

MI-RAN LEFT THE next morning, a small backpack slung over her shoulder. She mounted her bicycle and casually waved good-bye to her mother and brother. The plan was for everyone to leave the house separately to avoid attracting attention. Later in the day, her mother would pop her head into a neighbor's front door to mention she was off to help one of her married daughters with a baby for a week or two. That would buy them a little time before the police were notified that they were missing.

They met up in Chongjin, where Mi-ran's sister had an apartment. Mi-ran and her sister went off together on foot to find the man with the truck who would drive them to the Chinese border. Mi-ran felt unnaturally calm, as if each motion were purely mechanical. She was doing what she had to do, detached from the consequences of her actions. But as she was walking with So-hee, she happened to glance across the street and her heart stopped.

She saw Jun-sang walking in the opposite direction, or at least it appeared to be him. Mi-ran had excellent eyesight, so even across six lanes of traffic she could swear it was him, even though it was October, when he would be ensconced in his research at the university. Her first instinct was to cross the wide street and hug him, which of course she couldn't do in public, but there was so much she needed to tell him. She wanted him to know that she cared for him, that she wished him only the best, and that she had him to thank for encouraging her to go to teachers' college. She would tell him that his enthusiasm for life had given her the courage to do as much as she had with her life, including what she was about to do. She was sorry if her actions might hurt him in the short term, but . . . She stopped herself. Just as soon as the words formed in her head, she realized it would all come gushing out and she wouldn't be able to keep the secret. It would compromise her family and his as well, if he were to know.

She kept walking on her side of the street, glancing over her shoulder every few seconds until the man who may or may not have been Jun-sang was out of sight.

THEY RODE IN SILENCE in the back of the truck, to Musan, the mining town where Mi-ran's father had been sent as a prison laborer after the Korean War. It was a ghost town now, its mines and factories closed. But beneath the lifeless exterior, the place was teeming with smugglers. The town is situated near one of the narrower stretches of the Tumen River and, along with Hoeryong and Onsong, was developing into one of the hubs for illegal border crossings into China. It was a growth industry, perhaps the only one in North Korea. The truck driver specialized in bringing people without passports or travel permits to the border. It was out of the question to take a train, since document checks were strict.

If anybody spotted the family, they wouldn't have suspected that they were fleeing their home. They wore their best clothing underneath their everyday clothes, hoping not to look like pathetic North Koreans once they got to China. Their attire also supported their cover story—they were attending a family wedding in Musan. They carried only enough luggage for a weekend excursion. Stuffed inside were a few family photographs and dried seafood, fish, squid, and crab, Chongjin's gastronomic specialties. The food was intended not for their own consumption, but for bribes. There were two checkpoints along the fifty-mile route to Musan. A few years earlier, they wouldn't have dared drive to Musan without permits; but this was 1998 and you could buy almost anything with food.

THE CROSSING HAD BEEN carefully scheduled for a moonless night, at the exact time that the border guards were most likely to be asleep. The location was on the outskirts of Musan, where the guardposts were spaced two hundred meters apart. The time and place of their crossing had also been coordinated with a guide on the Chinese side of the river who was expecting a "parcel" to arrive after midnight.

Mi-ran was traveling alone. Her mother, brother, and sister had gone earlier, per the arrangement. It was better if family members crossed separately. If caught alone, you could plausibly claim you had wandered over because you were hungry. With a little luck, you would get a light sentence, maybe a year in a labor camp. If an entire family was caught, it would be judged a premeditated defection and the punishment would be much, much worse. Exactly what, Mi-ran didn't know, since she'd never met anyone who'd run away. She tried hard to dispel such thoughts from her mind.

A guide escorted her out of Musan, down a dirt road that ran parallel to the river. When the road ended at a cornfield, he left her. He gestured to her to cross the field and keep walking in the direction of the river.

"Just go straight. Keep walking straight," the guide told her.

By now Mi-ran's unnatural calm had evaporated. Her body was trembling from fear and cold. The October day had been Indian-summer warm, but the temperature dropped to an autumnal chill by nightfall. Only a few stubborn leaves were still clinging to branches. The bareness of the trees left Mi-ran exposed. It was well past the harvest by now, and as hard as she tried to walk quietly, the dried corn stems crunched under her feet. She was sure somebody was watching, about to grab her by the scruff of the neck.

Without light to guide her, it was difficult to follow her orders to just go straight. Which way exactly was straight? Where was the river anyway? Shouldn't she have reached it by now? She wondered if she'd gotten turned around in the cornfield.

Then she almost collided with a wall. It stood directly in her path, looming high above her head and stretching as far in either direction as she could see. It was white concrete, like the wall around a jail or a military compound. Had she walked into a trap? She was certain now she'd walked the wrong way. She had to get out of here. Fast.

She edged her way along the white wall. As she followed it with her hands, the wall got lower and lower until it was easy enough to climb over. She understood now. It was a retaining wall for the river embankment. She scrambled down to the water.

Autumn is the dry season in Korea so the river was especially low, only reaching her knees, but it was so cold that her legs turned numb. They felt like they were made of lead as her sneakers filled with water. She had forgotten the instructions to roll up her pants. She was sinking into the silt. She lifted one leg, then the other. Step by step she inched forward, trying hard not to slip and topple into the water. *Keep walking straight,* she told herself, echoing the words of her guide.

Suddenly Mi-ran felt the water receding to her ankles. She pulled herself up to the riverbank and, sopping wet, looked around. She was in China, but she couldn't see anything. There was nobody there. She was completely alone in the dark. Her throat was clenched and dry, but even if she'd had the wherewithal to call out, she dared not.

Now she was truly panicked. She looked back behind her at North Korea. She saw from the other side the white wall that had so confused her. Beyond that the cornfield adjacent to the road where the guide had left her. If she could find that road, she could walk back to Musan. From there she could catch a train to Chongjin and the next day she would be home. She would go back to her teaching job. Jun-sang would never know she'd nearly run away. It would be as though none of this had ever happened.

As she contemplated her options, she heard a rustling in the trees. Then a man's voice.

"Nuna, nuna."

Her brother was calling her, using the Korean word for "older sister."

She reached out for his hand and was gone from North Korea forever.

CHAPTER 15

EPIPHANY

Apartment blocks in Chongjin.

AT UNIVERSITY IN PYONGYANG, JUN-SANG WAS UTTERLY DEPEN-
dent on the vagaries of the postal system to stay in touch with
friends and family back home. He had several regular correspon-
dents besides Mi-ran. His mother used to write him with tidbits of
information about her dogs. His father would prod him to study
harder: "For the sake of Kim Il-sung and the Workers' Party who
have given you so much," he would sign off his letters to please the
censors he assumed were reading them. During the bitter winter
months, when the railroad employees were suspected of burning
the mail to keep warm, Jun-sang would sometimes go for months
without a letter. So he didn't worry when several of his letters to Mi-
ran went unanswered. When October, then November, passed, and
December came without a word from her, he became concerned.

When he arrived in Chongjin for his winter vacation he was preparing to ask his brother in his most nonchalant voice if he'd seen Mi-ran around. But his brother preempted his question, blurting out, "She's gone!"

"Gone? Gone where?" Jun-sang couldn't accept what he was hearing. He hadn't had a hint that Mi-ran was planning a trip. She always told him everything she was doing, didn't she? Though he'd thought that her letters were perhaps a little chilly over the summer, that maybe she was brooding over his reluctance to commit to marriage, he couldn't believe she'd leave without a word. He squeezed his brother for information.

"They're all gone. There's a rumor they've gone to South Korea." It was as much as his brother knew.

He went to her neighborhood to investigate. First he circled around as though he were conducting surveillance; he couldn't bring himself to get any closer. His stomach was clenched; he could feel his pulse racing in his neck. A few days later he returned. He planted himself behind the wall where he used to wait for her to come out all those years they were dating secretly. He saw for himself: another family was living in her house.

Over the course of the vacation and in subsequent visits home, he kept returning to the house. It was not so much to gather information—nobody knew much beyond the rumors—but to do penance. What an idiot he had been. He hated himself; he had been every inch the indecisive intellectual, weighing every move until it was too late. It had taken him so long to ask her to marry him that she was gone. In truth, he had wanted to ask her to run away with him to South Korea, but didn't have the courage. Throughout their relationship, he imagined himself as the one in charge. He was the man, he was three years older, he had a university degree. He brought her poems from Pyongyang and told her about books and movies she'd never heard of. But in the end she was the brave one and he was a coward. Nobody knew for sure, but he could feel it in his heart—she was in South Korea.

Shit, she did it before me, he said to himself.

IN FACT, SHE DID it before almost anybody.

In the nearly half a century that elapsed between the end of the Korean War and Mi-ran's defection in October 1998, only 923 North Koreans had fled to South Korea. It was a minuscule number if you consider that while the Berlin Wall stood an average of 21,000 East Germans fled west every year.

Most of the North Koreans who defected were diplomats or officials traveling abroad. Hwang Jang-yop, a leading academic and official who had been one of Kim Jong-il's professors, walked into the South Korean embassy in Beijing on his way home from a business trip. Occasionally a North Korean soldier would defy all odds and wriggle through the DMZ to defect. A handful of fishermen sailed to South Korea.

The North Korean regime took extraordinary measures to keep its population locked up. Fences were erected along the beaches in Chongjin and other coastal cities in the early 1990s to prevent people from sailing off to Japan. When North Koreans left the country on official business, they had to leave behind spouses and children who were effectively held hostage to assure their return. Defectors had to be able to live with the knowledge that their freedom came at the expense of loved ones who would likely spend the rest of their lives in a labor camp.

That changed in the late 1990s. The famine and the economic changes in China gave North Koreans new motivation to escape. From the border, they could see shiny new cars scooting along the wharf by the Tumen River. They could see with their own eyes that life in China looked good.

The same networks that had helped Mi-ran cross the river quickly expanded their operations. They charted new routes across the Tumen, locating the narrowest crossing points and bribing the border guards. If you couldn't swim, you could pay somebody to carry you across. The numbers of defectors grew exponentially. By 2001, it was estimated that 100,000 North Koreans had sneaked into China, a small percentage of whom eventually defected to South Korea.

Traffic flowed both ways. North Koreans poured into China; Chinese goods poured into North Korea—not just food and clothing, but books, radios, magazines, even Bibles, which were illegal. DVDs stamped out by Chinese pirating factories were small and cheap. A smuggler could cram as many as a thousand DVDs into a single chest, with a layer of cigarettes on top as a bribe for the border guards. DVD players, too, were made in China and cost as little as twenty dollars, which was within the means of North Koreans earning money privately in the new economy. Big sellers were *Titanic, Con Air,* and *Witness.* Even more popular were South Korean movies and melodramatic and syrupy soap operas. South Korean situation comedies supposedly depicted the lives of working-class people, and North Korean viewers paid special attention to the kitchen appliances and the quality of the clothing of the characters. For the first time, ordinary North Koreans could watch, in their own language, dramas free of messages about Kim Il-sung or Kim Jong-il. They were offered a glimpse (albeit an idealized, commercial glimpse) of another way of life.

The North Korean government accused the United States and South Korea of sending in books and DVDs as part of a covert action to topple the regime. DVD salesmen were arrested and sometimes executed for treason. Members of the Workers' Party delivered lectures warning people against the dangers of foreign culture:

> Our enemies are using these specially made materials to beautify the world of imperialism and to spread their utterly rotten, bourgeois lifestyles. If we allow ourselves to be affected by these unusual materials, our revolutionary mind-set and class awareness will be paralyzed and our absolute idolization for the Marshal [Kim Il-sung] will disappear.

Information in North Korea, however, wasn't spread by books or newspapers or movies as much as it traveled by word of mouth. People who didn't have the means to watch foreign DVDs would hear about them from others. Unbelievable tales spread about the wealth and technological development of neighboring countries. It was said that the South Koreans had developed a car so sophisticated that it would start only if the driver blew into a breathalyzer to prove he was sober (untrue), and that ordinary Chinese peasants living across the border were so rich that they ate white rice three times a day (true).

A North Korean soldier would later recall a buddy who had been given an American-made nail clipper and was showing it off to his friends. The soldier clipped a few nails, admired the sharp, clean edges, and marveled at the mechanics of this simple item. Then he realized with a sinking heart: If North Korea couldn't make such a fine nail clipper, how could it compete with American weapons?

For one North Korean student it was a photograph in the official media showing a South Korean on a picket line. The photograph was meant to illustrate the exploitation of the worker in capitalist society; instead the student noticed that the "oppressed" worker wore a jacket with a zipper and had a ballpoint pen in his pocket, both of which were luxuries at the time.

A North Korean maritime official was on a boat on the Yellow Sea in the mid-1990s when the radio accidentally picked up a South Korean broadcast. The program was a situation comedy that featured two young women fighting over a parking space at an apartment complex. He couldn't grasp the concept of a place with so many cars that there was no room to park them. Although he was in his late thirties and fairly high-ranking, he had never known anyone who owned a private car—and certainly not young women. He assumed the radio program was a parody, but after a few days of mulling it over, it struck him that yes, there must be that many cars in South Korea.

He defected a few years later, as did the soldier who saw the nail clipper and the student who saw the photograph of the striker.

IN HER WILDEST DREAMS Dr. Kim never imagined leaving North Korea. It was not that she was ignorant or lacking in curiosity about the world—she was an avid reader and loved tales of exotic faraway lands—but as far as she was concerned, North Korea was the very best country of all. Why go anywhere else?

Throughout her childhood, Dr. Kim had heard from her father about his miserable life in China before he fled to North Korea in the early 1960s. Dr. Kim felt fortunate to have been born in North Korea and was especially grateful that the government had allowed her, the daughter of a humble construction worker, to go to medical school for free. She felt that she owed her education and her life to her country. It was her greatest ambition to join the Workers' Party and repay the debt she owed her nation.

"I would have donated my heart if the party told me. I was that patriotic," she would later say.

Dr. Kim was working extra hours in her volunteer job—as an assistant in the party secretariat—when she learned that the party did not feel the same way about her.

The winter after Kim Il-sung's death, Dr. Kim's volunteer work required her to arrive at the hospital by 7:30 A.M., before any of the hospital's other senior staff, so that she could tidy up the messy office of the party secretary, a female doctor in her fifties, a specialist in hepatitis, who was addressed as Comrade-Secretary Chung. The director's office was a small room with the requisite portraits of Kim Il-sung and Kim Jong-il and walls lined with filing cabinets. The old wooden desk had drawers that didn't quite close, so papers spilled out and were strewn across the floor. Newspapers, however, were meticulously arranged on the desk. They couldn't be thrown on the floor lest somebody step on a photograph of Kim Jong-il or Kim Il-sung. Comrade-Secretary Chung wasn't much of a reader or a writer; she was completely dependent on Dr. Kim to read the editorials in *Rodong Sinmun* and the local *Hambuk Sinmun* and prepare lectures for her. In return, Dr. Kim was confident the comrade-secretary would recommend her for party membership. She even dared to imagine that one day she might follow in the footsteps of her mentor and become the party secretary herself.

As she sorted through the mess, Dr. Kim noticed a wooden filing cabinet had been left open. Her curiosity got the better of her. A large envelope poked out of the files. She opened it and saw that it contained a list of names that she recognized as hospital employees, all of whom were to be placed under extra surveillance. Comments next to each name indicated what it was that made them suspect.

Mostly it had to do with class background—parents or grandparents who had been active churchgoers, children of former landowners, people whose families had emigrated from Japan, people with relatives in China.

Her own name was on the list.

Dr. Kim was incredulous. Her entire life, her behavior had been impeccable. She was a perfectionist by nature and held herself to an exacting standard. As a student, her grades were perfect. She was always the first to volunteer for extra work and to attend extra ideological sessions. Her father had come from China and still had relatives there, but Dr. Kim had never met or corresponded with them.

It had to be a mistake, she told herself.

Eventually the truth sank in. Comrade-Secretary Chung was stringing her along, exploiting her hard work and talent with absolutely no intention of letting her join the party. Even worse, Dr. Kim began to suspect that she was indeed under surveillance. She felt that the party officials at the hospital looked at her with interest.

Her suspicions were confirmed about two years later when she received a surprise visit at the hospital from a national security agent. The man worked for the Bowibu, the police unit that investigated political crimes. At first Dr. Kim thought he had come to inquire about a patient or co-workers, but he was asking questions only about her, her family, and her job, until finally he came to the point. His purpose in visiting was to find out if she was planning to defect.

"Leave North Korea?" Dr. Kim was indignant. She'd never considered such a thing. Of course, she had heard rumors of people who'd left, but she looked down on anyone who didn't have the stamina to endure the Arduous March and would betray their country.

"Why would I want to leave?" she protested.

The agent enumerated the reasons. She had relatives in China. Her marriage had broken up. The hospital wasn't paying salaries.

"You! We're watching you. Don't run!" he told her gruffly before he left.

Later, she replayed the conversation in her mind. The more she thought about it, the more that the Bowibu man's reasoning made sense. He had planted the idea and she found she couldn't shake it.

Her life in North Korea was miserable. Her ex-husband had remarried soon after their divorce. Her six-year-old son lived with her former in-laws, as was typical in Korean divorces; by law and tradition, children belong to the father's family and are listed only on the father's family register. Dr. Kim could visit her son only on the occasional weekend, when she would fret about how small and skinny he was. Her ex-husband and in-laws didn't have much food at home.

She wasn't faring much better. Other doctors supplemented their earnings by selling medicine or performing operations, particularly abortions. Dr. Kim didn't have the training or the stomach for such things. Instead she cobbled together meals from her patients' gifts of food, but after a while they didn't have much to give.

Dr. Kim had quit pediatrics in 1997. She couldn't bear looking into the eyes of starving children any longer. She switched to research, hoping that it would keep her from having to deal with dying people, but there were no conditions in which to do research. After breakfast, the doctors were preoccupied with finding food for dinner, and after dinner, they worried about the next breakfast. She began leaving work early to scavenge in the mountains for edible weeds. Sometimes she'd chop wood to sell. Her weight had fallen below 80 pounds. Her breasts shriveled and she stopped menstruating. From afar, she looked more like a twelve-year-old child than a woman in her early thirties. The first few days she'd gone without eating she'd felt so hungry she would have stolen food from a baby. But after four days or so, she felt nothing but a strange sensation that her body was not her own, that she was being lifted into the air and dropped down again. She was profoundly exhausted. She had no strength to get up in the morning. She quit her volunteer position at the party secretariat and by early 1998 had stopped going to work entirely. She tried various ways to make money—she sold alcohol or coal at the market. She didn't lament the waste of her medical school training. At the height of the famine, it was enough just to stay alive.

On one of her excursions to the market, she ran into an old

friend. They had been classmates in high school, both of them the kind of popular, smart girls who might have been voted "most likely to succeed." Her friend had been a class officer. They made polite small talk, telling each other that they looked well even though they were both sallow and emaciated. Then Dr. Kim inquired about her classmate's family. Her husband and her two-year-old son had died, just three days apart, she said matter-of-factly.

Dr. Kim tried to offer her condolences.

"Oh, I'm better off. Fewer mouths to feed," she told Dr. Kim.

Dr. Kim couldn't decide whether her friend was callous or insane, but she knew that if she stayed in North Korea any longer, she would either be the same, or she'd be dead.

Before he died, Dr. Kim's father had given her a list of his relatives' names and last known addresses in China. It was a suicide note of sorts—her father had scribbled it in a shaking hand during the delirium of his self-imposed starvation. At the time, Dr. Kim was offended by the list, but she hadn't thrown it away. She dug out the little box in which she had stored it, carefully unfolded the paper, and looked at the names.

"They will help you," her father had said.

DR. KIM LEFT FOR China alone. She couldn't afford to hire a guide or bribe the border guards, so she had to rely solely on her own wits and instinct. By March 1999 enough people were making the trip that you could pick up tips in border towns about the best spots to cross. The early-spring landscape was just beginning to thaw out from an exceptionally bitter winter, and the Tumen was still frozen in spots. Dr. Kim went to a spot that she'd heard you could walk across. Every few feet she would throw a heavy stone to test the thickness of the ice. At least on the Korean side, it was solid. She slid one foot forward, then the next, delicate as a ballerina. She made it about halfway before her stone disappeared into a patch of slush. She followed anyway and the freezing water came up to her waist. She cleared a path with her hands as if breaking through icebergs.

Dr. Kim staggered up the riverbank. Her legs were numb, encased in frozen trousers. She made her way through the woods until the first light of dawn illuminated the outskirts of a small village. She didn't want to sit down and rest—she feared succumbing to hypothermia—but she knew she didn't have the strength to go much farther. She would have to take a chance on the kindness of the local residents.

Dr. Kim looked down a dirt road that led to farmhouses. Most of them had walls around them with metal gates. She tried one; it turned out to be unlocked. She pushed it open and peered inside. On the ground she saw a small metal bowl with food. She looked closer—it was rice, white rice, mixed with scraps of meat. Dr. Kim couldn't remember the last time she'd seen a bowl of pure white rice. What was a bowl of rice doing there, just sitting out on the ground? She figured it out just before she heard the dog's bark.

Up until that moment, a part of her had hoped that China would be just as poor as North Korea. She still wanted to believe that her country was the best place in the world. The beliefs she had cherished for a lifetime would be vindicated. But now she couldn't deny what was staring her plainly in the face: dogs in China ate better than doctors in North Korea.

CHAPTER 16

THE BARTERED BRIDE

North Korean wives of Chinese men, Tumen, 2003.

I T SURPRISED NO ONE THAT OAK-HEE WOULD LEAVE NORTH KOREA
at the first opportunity. From the time she was a schoolgirl, Mrs.
Song's oldest daughter stood apart from the Kim Il-sung idolatry
that consumed her nation. As soon as she came home from school,
Oak-hee would yank off the red scarf of the Young Pioneers. She
didn't bother to fake tears at Kim Il-sung's death in 1994.

Over the years, as her family got hungrier, she grew angrier. She
blamed the government for mismanaging the economy and for the
deaths of her brother and father. North Korean television incessantly played a song called "The Comrades' March" ("We live in a
socialist country with no worries about food or clothing. / Let's
straighten our chests and look at the world with pride") and ran patriotic footage of waving flags, which Oak-hee found ridiculous.

222 I NOTHING TO ENVY

"No worries?" she would snort as she switched off the television.

But the truth was that Oak-hee's initial decision to defect from North Korea had as much to do with escaping her marriage as it had to do with escaping the system.

The marriage had been tumultuous from the beginning. Oak-hee and Yong-su fought like other couples about sex and money, and when times got tough they fought about food and politics. Yong-su always won. If the argument wasn't going his way, he would deliver a hard slap that would send her reeling across the room as the last word.

Despite his drinking, Yong-su managed to keep his job as a conductor and apartment thanks to his family's clout. The conductor's job was among the most desirable within the railroad. When he was working the routes to the border, Yong-su could supplement his income by carrying goods to sell to Chinese traders. He'd pay 5 won for copper wire and scrap metal to workers who stripped it from their idled factories and resell it for 25 won. At first Oak-hee was surprised because her husband had, in the past, fancied himself something of a party official, even though he'd been rejected for party membership, and liked to deliver impromptu lectures on the evils of egoism and capitalism to his wife and anyone else who'd listen. He would chastise her for flippant remarks about Kim Jong-il. Now he waved away his earlier compunctions.

"Anyone who does what the party says is stupid. Only money matters now," he told her.

Yong-su's scrap-metal scam made him a relatively wealthy man in bad times. From his trips to the border he would bring home big bags of rice and bottles of soy sauce; for a time, they had stockpiles of corn in their apartment. Whenever Oak-hee would suggest that they take some food to her starving parents and brother, however, he flew into a rage.

"How can you think about giving away our food at a time like this?" he yelled.

Yong-su didn't trust Oak-hee not to help her family, so he would leave only a bare minimum of food and money in the apartment even though his work took him away for days at a stretch and the railroad schedules were unpredictable. In 1998, he left Oak-hee and their son and daughter, then eight and six years old, for a week with nothing to eat. On June 5, a holiday called Children's Day, their son was supposed to participate in a sports fair at his school. The children were told to bring a box lunch, but the house was completely empty. Oak-hee rushed around the city trying to beg food from her relatives, but nobody had much to give. She finally found her sister selling biscuits at the market and took a handful. She ran to the school at lunchtime to find her son standing in the playground waiting, his eyes filled with tears.

"I'm so sorry, sweetheart," she told him, handing him a small bag of biscuits.

Yong-su, a former musician, had a nice singing voice and a charming manner around women. Now, with some money in his pockets, he and his friends would pick up women and stay up late drinking. One night, when Oak-hee and the children had been asleep for hours, she heard Yong-su drunkenly stumble into the apartment and then a woman's peals of laughter. Oak-hee didn't know if it was a girlfriend or a prostitute, but she wasn't about to get out of bed to find out.

After that, Oak-hee began plotting her escape in earnest. It was possible for her to file for divorce, but it would mean losing everything. Although the Workers' Party gave lip service to freeing women from their lowly place in traditional feudal society, the North Korean system was still stacked against them. In a divorce, the man kept the home and the children—no matter if he had been abusive or unfaithful. Oak-hee would be especially disadvantaged because of her family's class status and without a father to negotiate on her behalf. Oak-hee figured her best hope would be if she was able to go to China to earn some money of her own. If she had enough for her own apartment, she might gain some leverage to force Yong-su to give her custody of the children.

One night Yong-su came home drunk and in a particularly ugly mood. He hit Oak-hee, knocking her down, and then delivered a kick so hard she thought she heard her rib crack. Suddenly there was a knock on the door—it was a traveler asking for directions, which happened frequently given their proximity to the station. While her husband was answering, Oak-hee got up off the floor and retreated into the kitchen. She slipped out the back door and down the steps wearing only her nightgown.

The clock on the train station showed the time as 10:00 P.M. It was the end of August, the night warm and pleasant. When she was far enough away that she was sure her husband hadn't followed, she stood outside contemplating her next move. Usually after fights, she would run off to her mother, who would put warm compresses on the split lips and the black eyes. The next morning, when Yong-su sobered up, he would cry and apologize and beg her to come home, which she always did. For ten years, they had been living that way. If she was ever going to change, now was the time to do it.

Oak-hee didn't dare enter Chongjin Station, where her husband's co-workers might recognize her. Instead she walked along the train tracks north through the warm night out of the center of the city until she reached the first station on the outskirts, Suseong. So many people were homeless by now that nobody paid attention to a woman wearing only a nightgown.

She remained at the station for two days. Her ribs throbbed from the beating. Hunger and dehydration gave her a blinding headache. She felt too dizzy to stand up. She saw a crowd forming around the station, people getting excited. A train was departing for the border town of Musan. She summoned up the energy to claw her way into the throng surging toward the doors and windows of the train. People grabbed the seats, then filled the aisles, stood in the toilet and on the gangways between the cars. They hung out the windows and clung to the undercarriage. The train was so crowded that the conductor couldn't pass through to collect tickets or check travel permits. Oak-hee reached Musan after a day's journey. She had no documents, no money, no food, no clothing.

What she did have was the body of a relatively healthy thirty-two-year-old woman. Oak-hee had never been a great beauty. Her mother had always pegged her as the smart daughter—her middle sister was the one everyone said looked like a movie star—but Oak-hee had weathered the famine better than many. Short and buxom like her mother, she had the type of physique that gave the illusion of plumpness. Her tiny nose made her look young, and her teeth were white and straight. Even if she had been so inclined, Oak-hee was too old to be a prostitute, but that was never something she'd consider. There was, however, another way for North Korean women to sell themselves that was somewhat more palatable.

Just across the Tumen River, walls of corn stretched for miles. The villages had plenty of food, but what ran in short supply were women. The traditional preference for sons and the restriction on family size had resulted in a lopsided birthrate of about thirteen males for every ten females. In their late teens, many young women migrated to the cities to fill the jobs at China's booming factories, which paid better than farmwork. Bachelors in the countryside, particularly those over thirty-five and without money or great personal charm, had difficulty finding wives. They turned to marriage brokers who charged roughly three hundred dollars for their services, more if they delivered women who were good-looking and young. But looks and youth weren't a prerequisite; healthy women into their sixties were also in demand to cook and keep house for older widowers.

North Korean women had a certain mystique to the Chinese. Despite the toll taken by the famine on their bodies and complexions, North Korean women were thought to be among the most beautiful in Asia. South Korean men talked about *buk nyeo, nam nam*—northern women, southern men—which allegedly was the most desirable genetic combination. Chinese men found North Korean women more modest and obedient than their Chinese counterparts.

Oak-hee knew all about the Chinese marriage market. When a woman in Chongjin mysteriously disappeared, people would whisper, "That whore probably sold herself to the Chinese."

The Musan train station was where the sales were initially brokered. A woman alone merely had to linger there before she was approached with an offer. The man who solicited Oak-hee turned out to be an old friend of her husband's. The deal he offered Oak-hee was this: A guide would escort her safely across the river into China. She would be given clothing, underwear, food, and a place to stay until she was matched up. The broker would find her a respectable man with whom she would live as wife, even though all parties were aware that the marriage wouldn't be recognized by Chinese law. In return, she would agree to stay with the man chosen for her. She would get no cut of the money.

Oak-hee accepted with one condition. She insisted that the man not speak Korean. Most North Korean women preferred men from the ethnic Korean population so they could communicate, but not Oak-hee.

"No Koreans," she told the broker. "I want to live in a new world where nobody knows me."

The man selected for Oak-hee was a farmer in his mid-thirties. He was very short—about five foot one, same as she. He had a dull look that made Oak-hee suspect that he was mildly retarded and he was so shy he couldn't look her in the eyes. No wonder he wasn't married, she thought. They were introduced at a small restaurant on the Chinese side of the border. Another North Korean woman who was traveling with her had been sold to a man who was taller and more animated; he smiled and laughed with the other men being set up. Oak-hee felt a pang of envy, but she reminded herself that this was her choice—she wanted a man she could never love.

Tens of thousands of North Korean women have been sold to Chinese men. By some estimates, three quarters of the roughly 100,000 North Korean refugees living in China are women and more than half of them live in arranged unions with Chinese men. Stories abound of those who were beaten, raped, held in chains, or worked like slaves. Oak-hee was far more fortunate. Oak-hee's man, whose name was Minyuan, had none of the charm of her husband, but he had a sweetness that made him seem almost too innocent for this world. The first time he took her to bed, he carried her and washed her feet in a basin of warm water. He cooked her special meals and wouldn't permit her to do the dishes. His parents similarly doted on her.

Oak-hee lived with the man for more than two years. She learned enough Chinese so they were able to communicate. She pored over a children's geography book so she could orient herself. She had been sent more than six hundred miles southwest of where she'd crossed the border, to Shandong, a fertile cotton-and-wheat-farming province west of Qingdao. She memorized the bus routes into the city. The entire time she was plotting her escape.

She got pregnant twice, but had abortions. Although Minyuen badly wanted a child, she convinced him it would be ill-fated. The Chinese government didn't recognize marriages to North Korean women, so the couple's child would not be registered as a citizen and would not be able to go to school.

"I already have two children in North Korea. I have to go back to them one day," she told him. Minyuen nodded sadly.

When it was time for her to go, Minyuen took Oak-hee to the bus station and gave her a hundred dollars. He cried. She expected him to beg her to stay, but he didn't. He wasn't as dull as she'd first thought. He told her only, "Please be careful."

IN FACT, OAK-HEE'S journey would be dangerous. By 2000, the Chinese were fed up with North Korean defectors. Too many, they feared, would take away jobs from Chinese citizens and upset the ethnic balance of northeastern China. Human rights advocates argued that China had a moral and legal responsibility to the people who had come in search of food and safety, but the Chinese insisted that those who'd crossed the river were illegal "economic migrants" and not entitled to protection under the U.N. Convention on the Status of Refugees, to which China was a signatory. The Chinese pointed to a previously secret agreement signed in 1986 with the North Korean Ministry of State Security requiring that both countries cooperate against illegal border crossers.

The Chinese launched periodic campaigns to catch North Korean defectors. They set up roadblocks near the border and did random checks of identity cards. After a few months in China, North Koreans typically fattened up and bought new clothes; they weren't so easily distinguished from the Chinese. So the Chinese allowed North Korean police into the country to sniff out their countrymen. Defectors themselves were recruited as spies to infiltrate places where other defectors were hiding. The Chinese offered rewards of forty dollars to those who would denounce North Korean women living with Chinese men. The women would be taken from their homes, their de facto husbands, and children. The men would pay a fine, but get to keep the children. At least eight thousand women were arrested in one such roundup in March 2000. (As of 2009, the crackdown on North Korean defectors continued.)

Oak-hee had been safe in her Chinese husband's village because it was far enough from the North Korean border to be outside the dragnet. But in order to make money she would have to go back to the border area, where there were Korean speakers and greater opportunities. She was desperate to make money—it was her only chance to buy her independence and get custody of her children. Well fed and well rested, she figured she could get a job in a restaurant or factory, and then maybe start her own business. She took a bus north, not to where she had crossed the river, but to Dandong, the largest city on the Sino-Korean border.

Dandong was a boom town. Its Yalu riverfront sparkled with the glass facades of new office and apartment buildings amid the tangle of cranes. Its prosperity was all the more striking in contrast to the desolation of North Korea directly across the river. Dandong, however, quickly proved an unwise choice for Oak-hee. The main rail link from Beijing to Pyongyang ran through the city, and much of the official trade was carried over the river by the China-Korea Friendship Bridge. North Korea's state-owned trading companies had offices in Dandong. The city was crawling with undercover security agents.

Oak-hee was arrested in January 2001 and transferred across the river to a police station in the city of Sinuiju. After two years in China, Oak-hee was shocked at the state of her country. The police station had no heat in the dead of winter. Police and prisoners shivered together in solidarity. A police officer wrote out the charges against her on a piece of wood because he had no paper. Her timing was lucky, though. An amnesty was approaching for Kim Jong-il's birthday; thousands of low-level prisoners were to be released. Oak-hee was let go after only two weeks.

As soon as she got out, she crossed the river again into China.

Before her arrest, Oak-hee had worked at a brick factory, then at a restaurant. The dollar or two she earned a day seemed like a fortune—it was equivalent to one month's wages in Chongjin—but it didn't go very far in China. This time, Oak-hee needed work that would pay more, even if it was riskier. She decided to work for a broker like the one who had fixed her up with the farmer. Her first assignment required her to sneak back into North Korea and search for a child that had been left behind and bring him across the Tumen to be reunited with his family. Oak-hee took the job.

The child was believed to be living in Musan, from where she had defected originally. She knew the city well and could speak the local dialect, so she thought she could wander around for a few days without attracting much attention, but she was mistaken. On her first day in Musan, a policeman picked her out of the crowd.

"Hey, you," he yelled at her. After more than two years of living in China, Oak-hee was pale and plump. She used scented shampoo and soap. She looked and smelled different from everyone else. Furthermore, she was also carrying a transistor radio she had purchased in China that picked up South Korean programs. The police officer confiscated the radio and (after asking her to show him the frequencies for South Korean radio and demanding her earphones) turned her over to the Bowibu.

OAK-HEE WAS PUT in a holding room with more than one hundred other people who had been rounded up. They were told to kneel and remain motionless. Guards passed between the rows, hitting anybody who adjusted themselves to relieve pressure on their knees. After being hit once herself, Oak-hee allowed only her eyes to dart about. She studied her fellow prisoners. She could tell immediately who had already been in China. They were fairer-skinned, better-dressed, and healthier-looking, like herself. The others were gaunt, sallow, often shoeless; they were probably caught before they'd managed to make it across the river.

Oak-hee took it as a good sign that both groups were mixed together. Her best chance of survival was if the authorities didn't know she had been working for a broker. She hoped, too, that the policeman who confiscated her radio had kept it for himself and didn't report it. The penalty for defection varied, depending on class background and what the defector had been doing in China. A defector who'd crossed the river in search of food got a lighter sentence than one who'd been living and working there. People accused of brokering women, of trading DVDs, of meeting with South Koreans, or of going to church in China could be charged with "betrayal of the fatherland," which warranted execution or the gulag.

Eventually, the guards sorted the people in the holding room by their hometowns. As it happened, many came from Chongjin. The guards didn't have handcuffs, so they tied the prisoners in groups of three, binding their thumbs with plastic shoelaces. The lacing was wrapped so tightly it cut off circulation, turning the thumbs blue. The prisoners were escorted onto a special train where they squeezed three into a seat meant for two. Oak-hee saw a man across the aisle laboring to dig something out of his pocket. He had managed to keep his cigarette lighter. He used it to melt the laces and all three men scrambled out of a window faster than the guards could react. The women didn't dare to move except when one had to go to the toilet; in that case all three went together, joined at their thumbs.

As the train screeched to a halt, Oak-hee realized she was at Chongjin station. It was September 2001, nearly three years from the day she had run away in her nightgown. Now she had returned in shame, bound by throbbing thumbs like a prisoner in a chain gang.

"*Baka, baka*"—Bow, bow, screamed the guards as the prisoners climbed down from the train.

Oak-hee was all too willing to keep her head down. What if

her husband or one of his co-workers saw her? They were marched through the waiting room of the station, across the plaza where her mother sold cookies, and then practically under the window of her apartment. In the past, she herself had stared at this spectacle through her window, scanning the crowd of prisoners to see if she recognized anyone.

They were led down Chongjin's main road, through a crowd of curious onlookers, and then over two bridges, past the industrial district and the swampy lowlands, the only place in the city with rice paddies. Turning toward the ocean, they came to a compound surrounded by concrete walls and barbed wire. The place was known as the Nongpo Detention Center, built during the Japanese occupation to imprison Korean resistance fighters. The very name Nongpo inspired dread. It had been used during the 1970s and 1980s to incarcerate malingerers who shirked work. Now it was filled to capacity with people caught trying to defect.

Female prisoners filled three large rooms, so crowded that the women had to sleep in rows on the floor on their sides. Those who couldn't fit had to sleep out by the toilets. Every few days more prisoners arrived, usually about a hundred at a time. The guards strip-searched the new arrivals, separating those obviously pregnant and sending them off for abortions, no matter how advanced the pregnancy. The assumption was that the babies' fathers were Chinese.

At Nongpo, women outnumbered men two to one, which reflected the gender split in the defector population. As Oak-hee got to know the other women, she was struck by how similar their stories were to her own. Many had run away from husbands and children, rationalizing their actions by the thought that they could bring money and food back for their families. Oak-hee was disgusted by these women, as she was with herself. She had never forgiven herself for leaving her children.

What bitches we've become. The hunger has turned us so wicked, she thought.

She had plenty of time for reflection in the camp. Long hours of slave labor were followed by long nights of self-criticism sessions and lectures. Prisoners were fed meagerly and dealt the occasional brutality. In the scheme of things, Nongpo was probably better than other prison camps. On Saturday afternoons, women were allowed to draw water from a well in the courtyard to bathe. They would pick lice from each other's hair. For all her time there, Oak-hee saw only one woman who was badly beaten. In a fury, she tried to climb one of the camp walls. It was more of a tantrum than a bona fide escape attempt, as she had no chance of succeeding, but the guards pulled her down, and kicked and punched her into semi-consciousness as the other prisoners watched.

In all, the women at Nongpo appeared to Oak-hee to be less terrified than angry. As they performed their forced labor—making bricks, weeding the fields—their faces were fixed in a grimace of resentment. *Our whole lives we have been told lies. Our lives are lies. The whole system is a lie,* Oak-hee thought, and she was sure the other women thought as she did.

Even the prison camp officials had given up on reeducation. They merely went through the motions, reading the lectures handed out by the Workers' Party without enthusiasm. Everybody seemed to be in on the lie.

One day as the women were picking corn, the camp director came to deliver an impromptu lecture in the cornfield. It was the usual fodder. He urged them to arm themselves with the ideology of Kim Il-sung against the temptations of capitalism and to commit themselves to their nation.

Then he asked for a show of hands: Who would promise not to run away again to China? The women squatted in sullen silence. Oak-hee looked around. Not a single woman raised a hand.

After an uncomfortable silence, the prison director spoke up. "Well, if you go to China again, next time don't get caught."

In fact, Oak-hee was already plotting her next move. One day she was assigned to weed the vegetable fields outside the concrete walls of the compound but within the barbed-wire perimeter fence. Oak-hee spotted an elderly woman tending goats on the other side of the fence. Glancing around her to check that there was no guard near her, Oak-hee spoke to the woman through the fence. She offered her a deal: Oak-hee would give the woman her underwear if she would tell Oak-hee's mother where she was. Underwear is scarce in North Korea and Oak-hee's was new, having been purchased recently in China. The old woman agreed.

Oak-hee squatted down and removed her underpants. She rolled them up into a ball, inserted a small note with her mother's address, and handed them over the fence.

CHAPTER 17

OPEN YOUR EYES,
SHUT YOUR MOUTH

World Cup celebration, Seoul, 2002.

MRS. SONG WAS NOT SURPRISED TO LEARN THAT OAK-HEE WAS at Nongpo. She'd thought it was only a matter of time before her daughter landed in prison. She hadn't heard anything from Oak-hee since she'd run away from her husband three years earlier, but Mrs. Song had assumed she was in China with the rest of those whores and traitors. If she'd betrayed the fatherland, she deserved to be in prison. But a daughter is a daughter. Mrs. Song couldn't let her first-born languish in Chongjin's most notorious detention center.

After so many years spent surviving on the edge, Mrs. Song had swallowed many of her scruples. She'd also developed street smarts. She learned long ago that you could bribe your way out of almost any predicament. As long as you weren't caught cursing Kim Jong-il, you could get out of a death sentence with enough money. So she went to the black market and bought ten cartons of cigarettes at 50 won each. Then she asked around until she found the national security office in charge of Nongpo, all the while muttering under her breath that her wayward daughter had cost her a week's income.

A few days later, Oak-hee appeared at her front door and collapsed into her mother's arms.

Mrs. Song shrieked when she saw her. It was October, already cold, and Oak-hee was nearly naked and barefoot. Her shoes had been cut apart by the security guards at Nongpo, who thought she might be concealing money in the soles. She'd torn off her shirt sleeves to use as menstrual rags. She'd given away her underwear. What remained of her clothing was in shreds. Her hair crawled with lice. But when Mrs. Song gave her a bath, she could see that Oak-hee was healthier than she'd been before she left the country. Even after weeks of eating only gruel and the kernels of raw corn she picked in the fields, Oak-hee had good muscle tone. Her complexion was pink, glowing.

Oak-hee talked incessantly. In a torrent of manic energy, she spoke about everything in China—the white rice they ate for breakfast, lunch, and dinner, the markets, the fashions. Her discourse was part travelogue and part political screed. Mrs. Song and her two younger daughters gathered around to listen.

"What's life like in South Korea?" they asked.

Oak-hee didn't know firsthand, but she'd watched plenty of South Korean television while in China.

"South Korea's a rich country. Even the Chinese can't dream of the riches in South Korea," Oak-hee told them. "I swear I'll go to South Korea before I die."

The sisters sat crossed-legged on the floor as Oak-hee held forth. At times they were fascinated, at other times horrified. The middle sister, who was married to a railroad security guard, was the most straitlaced of the three. Her big eyes opened wider and wider as Oak-hee went on. Hesitantly, because she'd always been intimidated by Oak-hee, she interrupted.

"But our general has worked so hard for us . . ." She pointed to the father-and-son portraits her mother had dusted just that morning.

"Can't you see? Your general has turned you all into idiots," Oak-hee snapped.

The youngest sister, Yong-hee, divorced and living with their mother, was more sympathetic to Oak-hee's opinion, but she worried about her sister's outspokenness. The family had gone through enough heartbreak; they didn't need more trouble. Although Mrs. Song's house was freestanding, someone might be lingering outside.

"Just be careful. Let's all be careful what we say, okay?" she warned Oak-hee.

After her mother and sisters had heard their fill of her stories, Oak-hee started talking to other people. The *ajummas* who lived in the neighborhood clucked their tongues, but were curious just the same. They dropped by in the afternoon to welcome Oak-hee back and gathered around to listen.

"Open your eyes. You'll see our whole country is a prison. We're pitiful. You don't know the reality of the rest of the world."

Whenever an image of Kim Jong-il came on the television, Oak-hee flew into a rage. "Liar! Cheat! Thief!" she would scream at the television.

Mrs. Song finally lost her temper. Oak-hee's loose talk put the family at risk—it was treacherous. If it wasn't her own daughter speaking like that, Mrs. Song would have felt compelled to report her under her obligations to the *inminban*. Despite all that had happened, Mrs. Song remained a believer.

"Shut up. You're a traitor to the country," Mrs. Song screamed at Oak-hee.

Oak-hee was startled—her mother rarely raised her voice—but she was not about to shut up. She taunted her mother in return.

"Why did you give birth to me in this horrible country?" Oak-hee shouted. "Who do you love more? Kim Jong-il or me?"

Mother and daughter fought incessantly. After forty days at her mother's house, Oak-hee was sufficiently recovered from her ordeal in the prison camp to move on. She told her mother and sisters that she had learned from her earlier mistakes and would try again to make money in China. Only this time she wouldn't get caught. Mrs.

Song grudgingly loaned Oak-hee more money. She was sick with worry, but at the same time relieved to see her daughter go.

EIGHT MONTHS PASSED without word from Oak-hee. Then, in June, a woman came to Mrs. Song's door claiming to have news of her daughter. Mrs. Song braced herself. Oak-hee must be back in prison, she thought. She would have to bail her out again. But no, the woman said Oak-hee was working near the Chinese border and was doing very well indeed. She wanted to repay her mother and had some clothing and gifts for the family, but she feared she might get arrested if she came back to Chongjin. Wouldn't Mrs. Song please come to visit her instead?

Mrs. Song hesitated. She didn't know this woman. She hadn't traveled since the accident in 1995 that had unleashed so much grief on her family. She didn't really need money; her cookie business was doing well. The Songpyeon market now had stalls for the vendors and a roof. She paid rent and had a license. She felt like a proper businesswoman. She had remarried, too—sort of. It was more of an arrangement with an elderly widower who needed somebody to help keep house, but the man was kind and relatively well-to-do. Mrs. Song was living more comfortably than ever before. She had no reason to make a risky trip to the Chinese border, but she was still smarting over the 500 won she'd spent bailing Oak-hee out of prison. The strange woman promised Mrs. Song she wouldn't have to take the train—Oak-hee had arranged for a private car. Mrs. Song was impressed. She accepted.

On a hot, rainy day in June 2002, Mrs. Song left for Musan. She packed just an overnight bag. She would spend the night and ride back in the morning. But when they arrived there was no sign of Oak-hee. Mrs. Song had been told only that Oak-hee was working at the border. The woman hadn't specified which side of the border, but now she made it clear: Oak-hee was in China.

"You'll have to go to China to get the money and clothing. Your daughter is waiting for you," the woman told her. She introduced Mrs. Song to a man she said was her husband. "Don't worry. He'll take you over."

Mrs. Song had come so far. Could she turn back? They took another car up a road toward Hoeryong, another border town. Then they waited for dark.

By the time they arrived at the river, it was ten o'clock and still raining. The river was swollen, sloshing over its banks and turning them into slippery mud. Mrs. Song could barely tell where land ended and the river began. Two men in the uniforms of North Korean border guards had joined them. One lifted her like a child onto his back and the other took the arm of the first to balance them as they teetered across the river. They stumbled a few times and nearly lost their footing. Mrs. Song was sure she would be dropped and swept away by the currents. Like most North Koreans of her generation, Mrs. Song couldn't swim. But before the scream building within her could surface and give voice to her wishes—*take me back, take me home*—they were climbing out of the river. One guide gave the border guards some money and then disappeared into the water to cross back to North Korea. Mrs. Song and the other guide made their way through the darkness into China. They climbed a hill through the night and by daybreak were walking into a small village.

Then they got into a taxi, something Mrs. Song had never done before. Cars, trucks, scooters, and carts converged down narrow streets heading toward the market. Horns blared. It was 8:00 A.M. and the shops were opening. The security gates over the display windows rolled up with the screech of metal against metal. The shopkeepers switched on music that rang out from big speakers over the doorways. Loud, horrible music, Mrs. Song thought. She wanted to put her fingers in her ears. If this was capitalism, she didn't like it. Too noisy. How could Oak-hee live in such a terrible place?

Mrs. Song's guide stopped to buy eggs, sausage, and pigs' feet for their breakfast. They headed out of town and drove down a dirt road to a cluster of houses that made up a village. They went inside one of the houses. The guide introduced Mrs. Song to the owner of the house and his teenage daughter. They were ethnic Koreans of Chinese citizenship and spoke in virtually the same dialect as Mrs. Song. They showed her around. The house wasn't anything remarkable—redbrick walls, a tile roof, a homemade wooden fence that formed a courtyard out front—but it was crammed with all sorts of appliances: a stereo, a water purifier, a color television, a refrigerator. The man kept opening the refrigerator door, pulling out different things to eat and drink. Beer, fruit, kimchi. When they laid out the food the guide had brought, there was more to eat on that table than Mrs. Song had ever seen outside of a wedding feast. Everything she might possibly desire was here, everything but Oak-hee.

"Where's my daughter?" Mrs. Song asked.

The man looked at her and mumbled something unintelligible. Mrs. Song asked again, this time more sharply.

"She's gone to look for work," he answered. Mrs. Song wasn't sure that she believed him. Her hosts were nice, maybe too nice: Mrs. Song thought they were hiding something, but she was too exhausted to push further. She fell into a fitful sleep. When she woke up and there was still no sign of Oak-hee, she was gripped by a terrible suspicion: I've been kidnapped.

MRS. SONG DIDN'T KNOW if she should try to run away. Where would she go? She didn't know where she was. The original guide had left. Should she confront her hosts with her suspicions? And what had happened to her daughter? The couple kept reassuring her that Oak-hee had been delayed and would be back soon. The next day Oak-hee finally called. She spoke over a scratchy line and it sounded like she was far away. She tried to reassure her mother that everything was fine, that she would see her very soon, that she should rest.

"Where are you anyway?" Mrs. Song asked suspiciously.

"In Hanguk," Oak-hee answered.

Mrs. Song had never heard of the place.

"Where is that? Near Shenyang?" asked Mrs. Song, referring to one of the largest cities in China's northeast, about three hundred miles from where she was staying.

"Farther. I'll call you tomorrow to explain."

North Koreans call their country Chosun and their estranged neighbor Nam Chosun, literally South Korea. The South Koreans use an entirely different name for their country. They call it Hanguk.

In the next telephone call, Oak-hee clarified that she was actually in South Korea. Mrs. Song couldn't believe it. She was so angry she shook with rage. She worried she was having a heart attack. Of all the bad things that Oak-hee had done in her life, from her childhood pranks to her foul mouth to her stint in prison camp, this was over the top. She had crossed over to the side of the enemy. She had paid these people to trick her mother into defecting. Mrs. Song had never been so angry in her life.

"You traitor! You're no daughter of mine," she screamed into the phone before slamming down the receiver.

Over the next three days, Oak-hee called repeatedly. Mrs. Song refused to take the calls. Finally she relented.

Oak-hee sobbed into the telephone.

"Mother, I love you. I want you to come live with me here." Oak-hee told her a little bit about her life. She had a job. The South Korean government had given her money when she arrived to get settled.

"If it's so wonderful in Seoul why are you crying?" demanded Mrs. Song.

Mrs. Song figured that the South Koreans, puppets of the Yankee imperialist bastards, had corrupted her daughter with money. Once they'd extracted enough information from Oak-hee, they'd torture and kill her. That's what Mrs. Song had heard about South Korea's treatment of North Korean defectors. She had no reason not to believe it.

"It's not like that, Mom," Oak-hee protested. "I'm crying because I miss you. I want you here."

Mrs. Song didn't want to listen. She told Oak-hee she wanted to return to North Korea as soon as she recovered from the journey. She would rest up for a few more days and build her strength.

She lounged around the house, napping, eating, and watching television. The house had a huge white satellite dish that received South Korean television. South Korea's soap operas were very popular and Mrs. Song quickly got hooked on one called *Glass Slipper*, about two orphaned sisters separated as children. When that wasn't playing, she'd flip through the channels to look for the soccer tournament.

The 2002 World Cup was being co-hosted by South Korea and Japan. Not since 1988, when South Korea hosted the Olympics, was there so much footage from Seoul. Mrs. Song wasn't that interested in soccer, but she was intrigued by the glimpses of South Korea she saw in the background. She couldn't help but notice the cars, the high-rises, the shops. During the commercial breaks, there were advertisements for mobile telephones and other things that Mrs. Song had never heard of.

When the South Korean team beat Poland, tied the United States, and beat Portugal, Italy, and Spain to reach the semifinals—the first Asian team to do so—millions poured out into the streets to celebrate. They wore red T-shirts and horns with little red lights for the team's fan club, the Red Devils. There they were, Koreans just like her, speaking the same language, but looking so beautiful, so happy, and so free.

It was hard for Mrs. Song to trust anything she saw on television. She knew well enough from a lifetime in North Korea (not to mention twenty-five of those years married to a journalist) that images could be manipulated. The Workers' Party lectures had warned her that foreign television broadcasts were designed to undermine the teachings of Kim Il-sung and Kim Jong-il. ("The South Korean puppets under the control of the U.S. CIA wickedly connive to use these specially made materials to beautify the world of imperialism," read one such lecture.) She suspected (correctly) that her generous hosts were being paid by Oak-hee to brainwash her into going to South Korea.

But it couldn't all be made up. And she couldn't dispute what she saw for herself in China—the abundant foods, the cars, the appliances.

Her hosts had an automatic rice cooker with a sensor that turned it off when the rice was done. Most of their appliances confused her, but the rice cooker was an endless source of fascination. Long ago, she'd owned a crude rice cooker, nothing like this one. It had been confiscated by the police because you weren't supposed to use electricity for cooking.

Every morning when she heard the beeping of the rice cooker, signaling that breakfast was ready, Mrs. Song marveled at the technology. It was true, she thought, North Korea was years, maybe decades, behind China. And who knew how far behind South Korea? She wondered what her poor late husband would have thought of all she was seeing here in China. Although she hadn't left the house since she'd arrived, she felt like she was having a great adventure just exploring the kitchen and turning on the television. She would have liked to share it with her husband. She thought of Chang-bo especially when she was eating. How that man loved to eat! He would have so enjoyed the sausage. Her eyes watered at the thought. Then her thoughts drifted to her son. Her memories were so tinged with guilt and shame that she couldn't even speak about him. So strong, so handsome—such a tragedy to have lost him at twenty-five. How much life he had missed. How much they had all missed, herself too, her daughters, locked away in North Korea, working themselves to death. For what? We will do as the party tells us. We will die for the general. We have nothing to envy. We will go our own way. She had believed it all and wasted her life. Or maybe not. Was it really over? She was fifty-seven years old, still in good health.

These were the thoughts drifting through her head one morning as the thin light of dawn seeped into her room. As she stirred to consciousness, she heard the chirp of the rice cooker in the kitchen. She sat up with a start. This was her wake-up call. She was ready to go.

CHAPTER 18

THE PROMISED LAND

Mrs. Song at the market in Seoul, 2004.

ON A TUESDAY MORNING IN LATE AUGUST 2002, MRS. SONG WAS buckled into the seat of an Asiana Airlines flight from Dalian to Incheon, the international airport in South Korea. She was traveling under a false name and carrying a forged passport. She knew only one other person on the plane—a young man sitting a few rows away. He'd come to her hotel room at 6:00 A.M. to give her the passport, which had been stolen from a South Korean woman of about the same age, the original photos extracted with a razor blade and replaced by Mrs. Song's. If questioned, she was to say she was a South Korean tourist who had spent a long weekend in Dalian, a popular seacoast resort just across the Yellow Sea from Korea. To support her cover story, Mrs. Song was outfitted in new clothes that would have looked outlandish in North Korea—capri-style jeans and bright white sneakers. She carried a sporty backpack. Her handlers had pierced her ears—something women in North Korea didn't do—and her hair had been cut short and permed in a style favored by South Korean women of a certain age. Mrs. Song had spent two weeks in China being fattened up and groomed so that she wouldn't look like a refugee. The only thing that might give her away was her guttural North Korean accent. She was advised not to make small talk. To avoid striking up a conversation with a fellow passenger, she was told to remain in her seat for the duration of the eighty-minute flight.

She sat perfectly still, her hands folded on her lap. She wasn't nearly as nervous as one might expect under the circumstances. Her serenity came from the certainty that she was doing the right thing. She was at peace with her decision to defect. The morning at the farmhouse when she awoke to the sound of the rice cooker, her confusion had lifted. She had decided to accept Oak-hee's invitation to South Korea. She wanted to see with her own eyes the world she had glimpsed on television. Her daughters, her grandchildren would have their chance—the situation in North Korea couldn't last forever—but she had only so many years left. She would seize this opportunity, but first she wanted to go back to Chongjin to say a proper good-bye to her younger daughters. She wanted to explain her decision and give them the money that Oak-hee had left for her in China—almost a thousand dollars. "I can't let your sisters think I'm dead," she told Oak-hee. Oak-hee argued against it, worrying that her mother would lose her nerve or that her younger sisters would dissuade her, but Mrs. Song was insistent.

Her stay in Chongjin lasted one month because the Tumen River flooded during the rainy season; still Mrs. Song did not for a moment waver. She maintained a sense of purpose that carried her through the riskiest moments in her defection. The smugglers that Oak-hee had hired to bring her to South Korea were astounded that this sweet little grandmother carrying a doctored passport could board an international airliner without breaking into a sweat.

Getting out of China and onto the plane was the most dangerous part of the journey. Had the Chinese immigration authorities detected her forged passport, she would have been arrested and sent back to North Korea to face prison camp. Only one hurdle remained after the plane landed in South Korea. Her passport wouldn't be convincing enough to fool the South Koreans, who would quickly discover it had been reported stolen. In fact, the young man on her plane would reclaim it before they landed and disappear into the crowd.

"Pretend you don't know me," he told her. She would have to wait in the ladies' room until he was safely out of the airport. Then she would go to the immigration counter and tell them the truth.

She was Song Hee-suk, fifty-seven years old, from Chongjin. She had lost half her family during the famine and was now seeking a new life for herself with her daughter in South Korea. There was nothing more to hide.

IN ARTICLE III OF its constitution, South Korea holds itself out as the rightful government of the entire Korean peninsula, which means that all of its people—including North Koreans—are automatically citizens. The right of North Koreans to citizenship was upheld by the Supreme Court in 1996. The reality, however, is more complicated. In order to exercise the right of citizenship, North Koreans must get to South Korea by their own volition. A North Korean cannot demand the right at the South Korean embassy in Beijing or at one of the various consular offices. Out of residual loyalty to its Communist ally and also to prevent millions of North Koreans from streaming across the border, China will not permit asylum seekers to present themselves at these diplomatic offices. The Chinese are aware that an exodus of East German defectors through Hungary and Czechoslovakia in 1989 forced the opening of the Berlin Wall and the collapse of the East German government.

The South Korean government, too, is content to keep the number of refugees down to manageable levels. A flood of defectors coming south would be a great financial and social burden.

Those who make it into the country use various subterfuges. If they have money or connections, they can get fake passports and fly to South Korea. Alternatively, they can slip out of China into neighboring countries such as Mongolia or Vietnam, where the embassies are not as restrictive about accepting defectors. A small number have made it into European embassies or U.N. offices in China and requested asylum.

Only a small fraction of the 100,000 or more North Koreans in China are able to make it to South Korea. In 1998, there were just 71 North Koreans who requested South Korean citizenship; in 1999, the number rose to 148; in 2000, there were 312 defectors; and in 2001, there were 583. In 2002, 1,139 North Koreans were admitted. Since then, anywhere from 1,000 to 3,000 have been arriving steadily each year.

By the time Mrs. Song arrived, South Korean officials were accustomed to North Koreans showing up unannounced without documents at the airport. Her arrival at Incheon would set off a flurry of activity, but no panic.

MRS. SONG WAS disoriented the minute she stepped off the plane. She had been in an airport only once before—boarding the plane that morning in China—and it was nothing like this. The $5.5 billion Incheon airport had opened the year before, not far from the beach where General Douglas MacArthur's troops landed in 1950. It is one of the largest airports in the world, a colossus of glass and steel. Sunlight streamed through the glass panels of the long arrivals corridor. People glided effortlessly along a moving walkway from the gates. Mrs. Song didn't know where to go, so she fell in step with the other passengers while keeping a safe distance from the man who had been her escort. When the other passengers queued up at the immigration counter, she ducked into the ladies' room, which she found as confusing as the rest of the airport. She couldn't figure out how to flush the toilet. The faucets over the sinks turned on and off automatically, without a touch. She poked her head out of the ladies' room to see if the man had gone, but she spotted him from behind, waiting to go through immigration, so she stayed put. She arranged her newly permed hair and freshened her makeup, gazing into the mirror at the unfamiliar face staring back at her.

The next time she checked, he was gone. She ventured out in search of a security official to approach. She practically collided

with a very tall man whose badge and photo ID were at Mrs. Song's
eye level. She bowed low, as one does when beseeching an official,
and spoke her rehearsed line.

"I have come from North Korea. I am requesting asylum here,"
she said.

The man was a janitor. He looked startled, but he knew what to do.

"How many of you are there?" he asked, knowing that most defectors arrived in groups. She told him she was alone. He steered her
to an office next to the immigration counter. Telephone calls were
made and within minutes agents arrived from the National Intelligence Service (NIS), South Korea's equivalent of the CIA.

Mrs. Song's interrogation lasted for nearly a month. She was
transferred from the airport to a dormitory set up for newly arrived
defectors by the intelligence service. She wasn't allowed to leave the
premises, but Oak-hee was permitted to visit her. The NIS's first
task was to ascertain that Mrs. Song was neither a spy nor a fraud, as
undercover North Korean agents whose mission was to monitor the
population of defectors had been caught over the years. The NIS
was also screening for Korean-speaking Chinese posing as North
Koreans to obtain South Korean citizenship and resettlement benefits that were worth more than $20,000. Mrs. Song was debriefed for
two hours every morning, after which she had to write out notes of
what had been discussed. She was asked to detail the location of
major landmarks in Chongjin—the offices of the Workers' Party,
the security offices, the boundaries of the *gu* and *dong,* the districts
and neighborhoods into which all Korean cities are organized. She
found that she actually enjoyed the debriefing sessions: they gave
her a chance to reflect on her life. In the afternoon, she would nap
and watch television. The smallest creature comforts delighted
her—the refrigerator stocked with complimentary juice boxes, each
individually wrapped with its own straw.

She would later recall her stay with the NIS as the first real vacation of her life. After that, the hard work would begin.

IT IS NOT EASY for people earning less than a dollar per month to
be integrated into the world's thirteenth-largest economy. South

Korea's per capita income of roughly $20,000 per year is fourteen to fifty times greater than North Korea's.

A good deal of propaganda on both sides of the DMZ is devoted to how North and South Koreans are the same—*han nar*, one people, one nation—but after sixty years of separation the differences between the people are significant. South Korea is one of the world's most technologically advanced countries. While most North Koreans are unaware of the existence of the Internet, South Korea has a higher percentage of homes on broadband than do the United States, Japan, and most of Europe. North Korea has been frozen culturally and economically for the last half century. Their languages are no longer the same; the South Korean version is now peppered with words borrowed from English. Physically, too, the people have grown apart. The average South Korean seventeen-year-old male, fed on milk shakes and hamburgers, is five inches taller than a North Korean defector the same age. North Koreans talk and eat like South Koreans did in the 1960s.

As the number of defectors increased in the 1990s, the South Korean government grew increasingly concerned about successfully integrating them into society. The nation's think tanks assigned teams of psychologists and sociologists, historians and educators to come up with a plan. Although the number of defectors was small (as of late 2008, there were 15,057 in a country of 44 million), someday there might be millions if Korea were to be reunified. "If this relatively small group of North Korean defectors fails to adjust, our prospects for reunification are gloomy," said Yoon In-jin, a South Korean sociologist involved in the studies. "If they succeed in making a new life here, we have hope of integrating. For that reason, we have to make every effort to help them so we can learn from their trials and their errors."

The South Koreans studied various historical models. They looked at schools in Israel for newly arrived Jews from the former Soviet Union and North Africa, people who had exercised their right of return to the Jewish state but knew little of its language and culture. They also studied the problems of East Germans adjusting to life in the reunified Germany.

In 1999, they opened Hanawon on a secluded campus fifty miles south of Seoul. Something of a cross between a trade school and a halfway house, the center teaches North Koreans how to live on their own in South Korea. They are taught how to use an automatic teller machine and how to pay an electric bill. They are taught the Roman alphabet in order to read advertisements that use bits of English. North Koreans also must *unlearn* much of what they were taught before—about the Korean War and the role of the Americans in World War II. The defectors take classes on human rights and learn the mechanics of democracy.

In the classroom it all made sense, but once outside the confines of Hanawon, Mrs. Song would become terribly confused. Her class was taken on a field trip to buy clothes. They got haircuts. They went to a food court, where everybody was given money to buy their own lunch. They all got noodles; nobody could figure out what the other foods were.

Sometimes when Mrs. Song left the campus, she felt almost dizzy from the excitement. There was so much noise, so many lights that she couldn't focus. Her eyes flitted between the huge animated screens fixed to the buildings—some twenty feet high—and the billboards. She couldn't understand most of the billboards. HDTV, MTV, MP3, MP4, XP, TGIF, BBQ—it seemed like a code impossible to decipher. But the people themselves were what mystified her most. She knew they were fellow Koreans, but they looked like another race entirely. The girls wore such short skirts and tall boots made of real leather. So many had dyed hair—boys and girls with red and yellow hair, just like foreigners. They wore little plastic plugs in their ears, with wires draped into their pockets. Most shocking was seeing boys and girls walking arm in arm and even kissing each other on the street. Mrs. Song looked around, but nobody else seemed to notice. One day she went to a subway station in Seoul, where she watched crowds of people riding the escalators, marching down the corridors, switching between lines. She wondered how they knew which way to go.

Mrs. Song spent three months at Hanawon. At the end of her stay, there was a graduation ceremony. She was given a stipend of $20,000 to get started. And then she was on her own.

—

WHEN I MET MRS. SONG in 2004 she'd been out of North Korea for two years. I was interviewing people from Chongjin for the *Los Angeles Times*. We arranged to meet at the paper's office in Seoul. I opened the door to an immaculately dressed, tiny woman, who exuded confidence. She wore a large jade ring, and a pink polo shirt tucked into neatly pressed beige trousers. Everything from her cheery pastels to her perfectly coiffed hair suggested a woman in control of her life.

After she left Hanawon, Mrs. Song took a job as a housekeeper. She was used to working full-time in North Korea and felt she would be depressed if she stayed idle in her new life. She decided not to live with Oak-hee, but to get her own apartment, and rented a studio in a high-rise in Suwon, a city twenty miles to the south of Seoul where the rents were cheaper. By living frugally and continuing to work, she was soon able to afford to travel—something once beyond the reach of her dreams. She joined tour groups that catered to older women and explored every corner of South Korea. She even went back to China—this time as a tourist. She traveled to Poland with a group of fellow North Korean defectors who were speaking at a human rights conference. She made friends. She even dated a little. She loved going to the market to try new foods— mango, kiwi, papaya. She enjoyed eating out. She didn't develop a taste for pizza or hamburgers, but she came to love the South Korean style of cooking beef and pork and barbecuing it at the table.

Every six months or so Mrs. Song and I would get together for a meal. When I worked on articles about North Korea I found her to be a particularly reliable commentator. She was by no means an apologist for the North Korean regime—"That rotten bastard!" she once said of Kim Jong-il, the only time I ever heard her use profanity—but she was not as embittered as most defectors I'd met. There were things she missed about North Korea—the camaraderie among neighbors; the free health care before the system broke down. She was nostalgic for her life as a young married woman. Her eyes would mist and her round face would soften when she spoke of her late husband.

"When I see a good meal like this, it makes me cry," Mrs. Song apologized one night as we sat around a steaming pot of shabu-shabu, thinly sliced beef cooked in broth and dipped in a sesame sauce. "I can't helping thinking of his last words, 'Let's go to a good restaurant and order a nice bottle of wine.' "

When it came to her son, she was entirely unable to speak. If I broached the subject, she would avert her eyes. Oak-hee told me later that her mother had never forgiven herself for rejecting him when he fell in love with the older woman and for being unable to provide for him.

But that was the past, a place where Mrs. Song mostly chose not to dwell. She relished her freedom and was determined to get the most out of her remaining years. She was bursting with curiosity. "I feel much younger now and much bolder," she told me. As many questions as I asked about North Korea, she asked about the United States and other places I'd traveled. She would show up for our appointments full of energy and enthusiasm, always wearing a new, crisp, and cheerful outfit. After so many years sacrificing for others, she now took care of herself. When she developed a paunch—much to her astonishment after so many years of deprivation—she went on a diet. She always wore makeup. One day when I'd taken the train to Suwon to meet her, we spotted each other from across the crowded waiting room. As soon as we pushed in close enough to be within earshot, she called out, unable to restrain her excitement a moment longer, "Look at me. I did my eyes!"

She'd had plastic surgery to add the extra little crease in her eyelids to make herself look more Caucasian. It was the ultimate South Korean experience. Mrs. Song had arrived.

FOR ALL HER eagerness to defect, Oak-hee wasn't as happy in South Korea as her mother. Oak-hee was a more troubled person, quick to find fault with herself and others. It was always startling to see mother and daughter together: their heart-shaped faces and compact bodies so alike, their personalities so fundamentally different. Oak-hee dressed in black—black jeans, shiny black blouses, high-heeled black boots. With her angular wire-rimmed glasses and plucked eyebrows, the effect was severe. Mrs. Song and her daughter were affectionate, stroking each other's hair and hugging as though they'd only just been reunited, but they still fought about politics. Over lunch, a friend of mine who worked for an aid agency asked if they thought humanitarian aid was reaching the intended recipients in North Korea. Oak-hee thought that aid was being siphoned off by the military and party cadres and served only to strengthen Kim Jong-il's hold over North Korea.

"But if it saves even a few lives—" Mrs. Song said.

Oak-hee cut her off. "You're propping up an evil regime."

Mrs. Song pressed her lips together into a straight line and didn't speak much for the rest of the meal.

Oak-hee often seemed wrapped in a cloak of bitterness. She'd had money problems from the time she'd come to South Korea, in fact even before she left China. She had fallen in with a low-life crowd of Chinese and Koreans who made their living in the shadowy world of forgery, smuggling, and loan sharking. Mostly, though, they trafficked in people. They smuggled women across the river into China and they supplied stolen passports to get others into South Korea. When Oak-hee left North Korea the last time, she had no money to get herself from China to South Korea. One of the smugglers agreed to provide a passport and a plane ticket, in return for a fee of $14,000 to be paid from the defector's stipend she would receive from the South Korean government. They signed the deal with thumbprints since neither knew the other's real name.

The week after she was released from Hanawon, the smuggler called Oak-hee on her mobile phone. She'd just bought it—mobile telephones were invariably a defector's first purchase—and couldn't figure how he'd found her or gotten the number. He was insistent that she pay up immediately.

"I'm in Seoul. I'll meet you in front of your apartment," he told her.

Oak-hee panicked. The resettlement money was less than she had expected. Defectors in their twenties and thirties got smaller packages than older people because they were presumed to be able to work. She'd already paid $3,000 for the deposit on an apartment.

She agreed to meet the smuggler in front of a police station. After considerable negotiation, she convinced him to accept a lower fee, $8,000, just about all the money she had left.

After that, Oak-hee took a job in a funeral home, hoping to get her finances in order. She just might have, if she hadn't been struck by a terrible longing.

She missed her mother. All along Oak-hee had been mulling the idea of bringing over her mother, and after she arrived in South Korea it became a fixation. She'd been surprised to see how well older people were treated.

"In North Korea, they don't want you when you're too old to work," she said. "They'd just as soon get rid of you. In South Korea, I saw old people singing and dancing. I thought of my mother and how hard she had worked her whole life. I thought she deserved to live a little."

Knowing that Mrs. Song would not be easily convinced to leave North Korea, Oak-hee turned to the same gang. Together, they came up with the plan to lure Mrs. Song into crossing the border to China. Oak-hee was worried that her mother could end up in a prison camp if something went wrong, and wanted her mother to be taken along the safest and least-frightening route. Defections were arranged like package tours and Mrs. Song went first class. Her package included the private car that drove her from Chongjin to the border, the bribes to the North Korean border guards who carried her on their backs across the river, and the stolen South Korean passport. "I could have done it cheaper," Oak-hee explained, "but I wanted her to travel like a VIP."

Oak-hee plunged deeper into debt. She signed up for extra shifts at the funeral home, but the overtime wasn't enough to cover her payments. She tried to think of other ways of making money. She was a thirty-eight-year-old woman whose only professional experience had been exhorting people to work harder for Kim Il-sung— hardly a marketable skill in South Korea.

She turned to the karaoke business. *Noraebang,* as they are called, literally song rooms, are designed for guests, usually male, to relax by singing. The clubs provide private rooms with sound systems, microphones, video monitors, soft drinks, and snacks. The real attraction, however, are the hostesses who sing along, dance, pour drinks, and engage in a little flirtation—or more. Oak-hee's role in this enterprise was to recruit young women, drive them to and from the clubs, and make sure they didn't get into trouble with customers. Her territory was the vicinity around Suwon. Most of the karaoke bars' clients were construction workers living in temporary housing who had nothing else to do at night. Oak-hee had some twenty girls under her wing, all of them North Korean. They were mostly in their early twenties and had been recruited straight out of Hanawon.

"They come to South Korea and they have no skills," Oak-hee explained. "They learn quickly that they work in an office or a factory and make nine hunded dollars for a month's work. Here they can make a hundred dollars in one night," Oak-hee explained one evening when I accompanied her on her rounds. She was driving a Hyundai van, the floor strewn with crumpled cigarette packs and cassette tapes of psalms. It was 5:00 P.M. and Oak-hee was just starting work. She followed the rush-hour traffic out of Suwon, then exited the highway onto a two-lane road lined with fields and greenhouses. At little towns along the way, she stopped to pick up women, some of whom looked like schoolgirls playing dress-up in their spiky-heeled sandals. Although her business is considered illegal by the police, Oak-hee insisted her girls were not prostitutes. "I don't force them to do anything. I tell them, 'All you have to do is sing and dance and snatch money from the customers.'" The business was easier here than in the big city. "They have to do more in Seoul than they do out here. In Seoul, the men in business suits pay for drinks and then they expect something from the girls. These construction workers are rough, but naïve."

The job paid Oak-hee well enough to have allowed her to bring out both of her sisters, at a cost of tens of thousands of dollars. Her youngest sister came with her five-year-old daughter. Her middle sister brought her husband and two young sons. The sisters now both work in the karaoke business, too.

The only family members Oak-hee had not been able to get out were those she loved the most—her own children. She was racked with guilt over this. "I sacrificed my babies to save myself," she berated herself. The last time I saw her was in the summer of 2007; her son was eighteen years old, and her daughter sixteen. She hadn't seen them since the night in 1998 when she fled Chongjin in her nightgown. However, she regularly sent them money through brokers in China who would take a commission and then get a smuggler to carry it across the border. Shortly after she left North Korea, an illegal phone service started up in towns close enough to the border to pick up Chinese mobile telephone signals. As a result, Oak-hee was able to speak with her estranged husband every few months. He would travel to Musan to use a smuggled Chinese phone, but he would not let her speak to the children. He also refused her offer to bring them to South Korea because he suspected, correctly, that she would no longer send money if she had the children.

"I had a dream the other night about my children," she told me the night she was driving between the clubs. "I'm holding my son's hand. I'm carrying my daughter on my back. We are all running, trying to escape from North Korea. There is a tall man wearing a railroad conductor's uniform, walking toward us. I'm not sure, but I think it is my husband and he's trying to stop us." She woke up to the fact that she was a world away without them.

CHAPTER 19

STRANGERS IN THE HOMELAND

Kim Hyuck, 2004.

THE QUALITIES MOST PRIZED IN SOUTH KOREA—HEIGHT, FAIR
skin, affluence, prestigious degrees, designer clothes, English-language
fluency—are precisely those that the newly arrived defector lacks,
which accounts for the low self-esteem typically found among North
Koreans in the South, such as Oak-hee. South Koreans weren't much
better off fifty years ago, but North Koreans remind them of a past
they would rather forget. The defectors also augur a frightening
future, with good reason—South Koreans fear that the collapse of
Kim Jong-il's regime will see their country overrun by 23 million
people in need of food and shelter. Although political correctness

dictates that all Koreans yearn for their missing kin ("reunification is our desire, even in our dreams," South Korean schoolchildren dutifully sing), some view the prospect with dread. Think tanks in Seoul regularly churn out reports estimating how much it would cost to reunify, with figures ranging from $300 billion to $1.8 trillion. Young people, born long after the end of the Korean War, have less sentimentality about the missing other half of Korea. They would rather ignore the impoverished, nuclear-armed dictatorship looming above them. In the blur of their busy lives, working the longest hours of any developed nation, playing hard, driving their Hyundais fast, and listening to their iPods loud, it is easy to forget.

For all the support provided by the government, defectors can sense the pity and fear and guilt and embarrassment with which the South Koreans view them. The mixed welcome is part of what makes them feel like strangers in their homeland.

DR. KIM HAD no intention of defecting to South Korea. When she crossed the Tumen River in 1999, her sole destination was China. Her plan was to find the relatives whose names and last-known addresses her father had scribbled down before his death. She figured they would help her to find some kind of work. She could eat enough to recover her strength, then save up money to bring over her son. Eventually, she wanted to return to Chongjin and her job at the hospital. Despite the gnawing hunger and her quarrels with the Workers' Party, she still felt she owed a debt to the country that had provided her schooling.

As it happened, Dr. Kim's resolve weakened during her first hours in China when she saw the big bowl of white rice and meat set out for the dog. With each passing day, there was a fresh observation that would heighten her outrage over the lies she'd been fed. Everything that transpired propelled her further and further away from the fatherland and from the beliefs she once held dear, until it became impossible for her to return.

As she nudged open the gate to the farmhouse, the dog started barking furiously, waking its owners. They were ethnic Koreans, an older woman and her adult son. They knew from Dr. Kim's frozen clothing and emaciated features that she was a newly arrived refugee. They invited her inside, gave her dry clothes and a hot meal. These strangers could have received several hundred dollars had they sold her as a bride—she was thirty-four years old and reasonably attractive—but instead they put her up for two weeks and helped her find her father's relatives. There, too, she was met with astonishing generosity. The relatives she'd never met accepted her immediately as their kin.

At first, Dr. Kim had no trouble blending in with the other ethnic Koreans. She learned a little Chinese. She got a job in a restaurant making packaged lunches for workers. But by 2000, the Chinese police had redoubled their efforts to arrest North Korean defectors. Dr. Kim was caught three times. Each time her relatives bribed officials to gain her release. After the last arrest, Dr. Kim decided it was too dangerous to remain in northeastern China. She took a train to Beijing to look for a job. Passing herself off as an ethnic Korean from Yanbian, she answered an advertisement for a Korean-speaking nanny.

Dr. Kim's employer was a working mother, a South Korean professor who had come to China with her five-year-old for a one-year sabbatical. Dr. Kim liked the professor and embraced the opportunity to live in a comfortable apartment and help raise a child. She proved to be an extremely competent nanny and housekeeper. As the end of the academic year approached, the professor proposed that she stay on with the family when they returned to South Korea. Many affluent South Korean families employed ethnic Koreans from China as their nannies.

Dr. Kim felt she had no choice but to confess. She blurted out her life story—the divorce and the loss of custody of her son, her father's suicide after Kim Il-sung's death, the years of semistarvation, the dying children at the hospital.

"Oh my God. You're a doctor!" the professor said. The women hugged and cried together. "If I had known, I would have treated you differently."

"If you'd known, it would have been impossible for me to work for you. And I needed the job."

The confession brought a rapid end to Dr. Kim's career as a

nanny, but the professor proved true to her word. She promised to bring Dr. Kim to South Korea anyway. A few months after her departure, she put Dr. Kim in touch with a broker.

In March 2002, Dr. Kim arrived at Incheon Airport, euphoric at the prospect of starting a new life. But these feelings did not last long. Dr. Kim was convinced by a man she met at church to invest most of the $20,000 resettlement money in a direct sales operation in which she was supposed to peddle soap and cosmetics to acquaintances. Dr. Kim hadn't learned enough in her month of orientation to recognize a scam; the sales proposition turned out to be a pyramid scheme, and she lost nearly all of the government stipend. Then she experienced another setback: she learned that South Korea wouldn't recognize her medical training. If she wanted to practice medicine, she would have to start all over again, applying to medical school and paying for it herself because she was too old to qualify for a government scholarship. Dr. Kim grew bitter. Seven years of medical school and eight years of practicing medicine were all for nothing. She veered between self-pity and self-hatred. She felt residual guilt over deserting North Korea. She fantasized about suicide.

When I met Dr. Kim in 2004, I asked her if she regretted coming to South Korea.

"I wouldn't have come here if I knew what I know now," she answered, the only defector I'd ever met who would admit as much, although I suspect others felt similarly. I couldn't help noticing that Dr. Kim still looked like a North Korean. She wore her hair pulled back and tied with a black velvet ribbon and painted her bow lips a shade of red that was straight out of a 1960s Technicolor movie. She reminded me of the Workers' Party members I would see in downtown Pyongyang.

When I met up with her a few years later, she had thoroughly reinvented herself. I scarcely recognized the woman who walked into the chic new Japanese restaurant in Seoul in the summer of 2007. She wore her hair in a shoulder-length shag, she wore blue jeans, and from her ears dangled long beaded earrings.

"I got tired of that tacky North Korean look," she told me.

She looked much younger, like a student, and in fact, she was. After years of fighting the South Korean medical board, she bit the bullet and at age forty began a four-year medical program. She was living in a dormitory with classmates nearly two decades younger. Her studies, she told me, were difficult, not because her training in North Korea had left her ill-prepared but because the South Korean medical school used English terminology that was completely unfamiliar to her. The only foreign language she had studied was Russian. She looked rejuvenated by the experience, though. After graduation, she planned to resume her medical career, this time specializing in geriatrics. Her mother had died a miserable death from Alzheimer's. Dr. Kim dreamed of opening a nursing home, perhaps even a chain of nursing homes. She hoped that one day, when the North Korean regime had fallen, she might be able to take South Korean ideas of elder care back to Chongjin. Perhaps it was a pipe dream, but it helped her bridge the divide between her past and present selves and ease the guilt about what she'd left behind.

THE SAD TRUTH is that North Korean defectors are often difficult people. Many were pushed into leaving not only because they were starving, but because they couldn't fit in at home. And often their problems trailed after them, even after they crossed the border.

This was especially true of Kim Hyuck. When he arrived in South Korea at the age of nineteen, he was the same as he had always been—poor, short, homeless, and without family or connections to help him make his way.

Hyuck was released from the labor camp Kyohwaso No. 12 on July 6, 2000. He was so weak from malnutrition that he could barely walk a hundred meters before needing to rest. He stayed at a friend's home while contemplating his next move. Initially, Hyuck had planned to resume working as a smuggler, though taking better care not to get caught, but the labor camp had shattered his confidence. At eighteen, Hyuck had already lost the illusion of invulnerability that allows teenage boys to be so fearless in the face of danger. He didn't want to be caught again; he didn't want to get beaten. He was tired of running. There was nothing for him in North Korea; and if he escaped to China he would be hunted down. He decided his only chance was to make a break for South Korea. He had no idea how he would get there, but he had heard rumors about South Korean missionaries who helped homeless youth like himself. So when he crossed the Tumen for the last time, on Christmas Eve, 2000, he set out to find a church.

The most Christian country in Asia after the Philippines, South Korea sends missionaries spreading the gospel and dispensing humanitarian aid throughout Asia, Africa, and the Middle East. In contrast to the general ambivalence most South Koreans show defectors, the missionaries are passionate about the plight of North Koreans. Thousands of South Korean missionaries—sometimes joined by their Korean-American counterparts—have flocked to northeastern China, where they work quietly so as not to provoke the Chinese authorities, operating small, unregistered churches out of private homes.

At night, their red neon crosses glow eerily in otherwise dark patches of countryside. Other safe houses for North Koreans are known only by word of mouth. Since the U.N. High Commissioner for Refugees and the mainstream nongovernmental organizations cannot overtly violate Chinese laws against sheltering North Koreans, the missionaries fill an important void by providing food and shelter to refugees.

Hyuck found his way to a church in Shenyang, the largest city in northeastern China. The church was run by a South Korean businessman who owned a furniture factory and was rumored to have the connections and money to arrange safe passage to South Korea.

"I want to learn about Christianity," Hyuck lied.

Hyuck submitted himself to the routine. He and a handful of other defectors rose at 5:00 A.M. and prayed. Then there was breakfast, exercise, Bible study, dinner, and then more prayer before they went to sleep at 9:00 P.M. It went on like that every day, except on weekends, when they would occasionally play soccer. Like other North Koreans his age, Hyuck had never heard of Jesus Christ. The churches in Chongjin had been closed down decades before he was born; older people who still practiced did so in private. What little he'd been told about Christianity came from his elementary school's reading primers in which missionaries appeared as stock villains, duplicitous and cruel. Hyuck was still cynical about Christianity. He felt that the South Korean church was forcing him to swallow its propaganda in return for food and shelter. Then again, he felt somewhat guilty about deceiving them by pretending to be a believer. Gradually, his attitude softened. After a while, as he murmured the words of the prayers, he felt the comfort he had not enjoyed since his early childhood when he recited a poem about Kim Il-sung and had something greater than himself to believe in.

Only this time when he said "Uri Abogi," our father, he meant God, not Kim Il-sung, and when he spoke of the son, he meant Jesus, not Kim Jong-il.

After five months at the church, the leader suggested to Hyuck that it was time for him to move on. The church was under constant surveillance by Chinese police and feared for the safety of the refugees. The man gave Hyuck 1,000 yuan (about $125) and asked him to lead a group of refugees to the Mongolian border. From there, they could try to reach South Korea.

If Mrs. Song's passage by airplane with doctored South Korean passports was a first-class defection, the Mongolian route was akin to going steerage class. But for someone without money, it was the best way to go. Unlike the Chinese, the Mongolians allowed the South Korean embassy in Ulaanbaatar, the Mongolian capital, to accept North Korean defectors. In fact, if North Koreans managed to sneak across the Chinese border into Mongolia, they would be arrested by Mongolian border police and turned over to be deported—to South Korea. Getting arrested in Mongolia was in essence a free plane ticket to Seoul. As a result, Mongolia had become a major depot on what had become a veritable underground railroad ushering North Koreans into South Korea.

Hyuck and the other refugees took a train to Erenhot, the last town in China before the Mongolian border, a desert outpost with more camels and sheep than people. There were six North Koreans in all, including a three-year-old and a ten-year-old boy whose father was already in South Korea. Their plan was to hook up at a safe house with another group of North Koreans who were coming up from Dalian on a separate train. One of the people in the other group knew the terrain and would lead them across the border.

But everything went wrong. While still on the train, Hyuck got a panicked phone call informing him that the other group had been arrested. His group had no choice—it was too late to turn back. They couldn't go to the safe house because it was probably under surveillance. They had to throw away their mobile phones because they could give away their location to police. Hyuck and the other adults conferred. They had been briefed on the route and had a hand-drawn map. They decided they would head for the Mongolian border anyway.

The refugees hid out near the train station in Erenhot until 9:00 P.M., waiting for the light to seep out of a long summer day so they could make their way in the dark. Their instructions were to follow the main railroad line that headed north to Ulaanbaatar, using the tracks as their guide, but keeping their distance so as not to be seen. Once they reached a deserted stretch of border, they were to slip under the seven-foot-high wire fence into the no-man's-land that separated the countries.

It was only five miles from the Erenhot train station to the first border fence and from there just a mile to the first Mongolian watchtower, where they were to surrender themselves to the authorities. They should have been able to make it on foot before daybreak, but the desert was disorienting by night—with only stars to guide them and an endlessly repeating pattern of thistle, rock, and sand the color of muddy coffee. The adults quarreled about which way to go.

Were they supposed to be walking east or west of the railroad tracks? They chose east, which turned out to be a critical mistake. The border ran in a northeasterly direction then curved sharply to the north; they were walking parallel to the border without getting closer to a place to cross. Only at daybreak did they realize their mistake. The Gobi Desert temperatures were soaring into the 90s. By the time they changed direction, found the wire fences delineating the border, and slipped through, it was late afternoon. Their shoes were in tatters from the rough terrain and their feet were bleeding. They were sunburned. The six liters of water they'd brought were finished. Hyuck and the others took turns carrying the three-year-old, but when the ten-year-old started flagging, they couldn't do anything but drag him along. They finally found an abandoned hut near a small pond. One of the women stayed with the boy while

Hyuck ran off to get water. As he approached, he heard the woman screaming. The boy was dead.

The Mongolian border police found the North Koreans in the evening. The presence of the dead boy badly complicated the handling of their case. The coroner needed to confirm that he had indeed died of dehydration and that there had been no foul play. For the ten weeks that the investigation dragged on, Hyuck and the other adults were held in a Mongolian prison. It was an inauspicious beginning to Hyuck's life in the free world.

Hyuck arrived in South Korea on September 14, 2001, on a flight from Ulaanbaatar with a dozen other defectors. He almost broke down when an immigration official at Incheon Airport stamped the temporary passport he'd been given in Mongolia and told Hyuck, "Welcome to the Republic of Korea."

As with many defectors, though, Hyuck's elation quickly vanished. His interrogation was especially grueling because of the time he spent in prison camp. The South Korean government was increasingly wary of criminals in the defector population. Then, just as he thought he would be freed, he was sent to the Hanawon camp for a month. He couldn't tolerate being held in confinement.

Hyuck's personality was as much of an impediment in South Korea as it was in North Korea. He was quick to anger. He bristled at authority. He couldn't sit still. His stature, too, put him at a disadvantage in a height-obsessed society. His legs were underdeveloped and his head too large for his body—a physique typical of people who have been deprived of food during their formative years. When denied nutrition, the body directs its resources toward the head and torso at the expense of the limbs. In famine literature, the syndrome is called "stunting." A 2003 study by the World Food Programme and UNICEF found that 42 percent of North Korean children were permanently damaged in this way.

At the time of our first meeting in 2004, Hyuck was living in Buyeo, a provincial town about two hours south of Seoul. There were no other defectors around, no one to help him settle in. He said his nerves couldn't cope with the noise and congestion of a big city. He was broke, having lost the $20,000 in resettlement money almost immediately. He'd given the money to a broker who claimed he could find Hyuck's older brother. After more than a year of being strung along, Hyuck concluded that his brother was probably dead. "My brother was nearly six feet tall. There's no way he could have survived," he told me. One advantage of being short was that you needed less food.

Hyuck flitted between jobs. He delivered ice cream for a while before he discovered that a South Korean employee of the same company was being paid more, and he quit in a huff. He took a course to be an auto mechanic and worked as a trainee for a few months, but that didn't stick either. He then decided that his true destiny in life was to be a professional boxer, but when he went to a boxing gym in Seoul, he was rejected for being too short. That damaged his ego and made him worry he'd never be able to find a girlfriend.

He was desperately lonely. He had a hard time connecting with new people. If South Koreans were sympathetic toward him, he found them condescending. Even though he hated the North Korean regime, he found he'd get defensive when South Koreans criticized it. This was a common predicament for defectors.

The basics of etiquette in South Korea eluded him. North Koreans don't have the custom of making small talk with strangers and are taken aback by those who do. Whenever Hyuck left the safety of his own apartment, he was startled by neighbors who would greet him casually. He would avert his eyes or scowl in return.

"I didn't know that when somebody exchanges a few words with you, you're supposed to respond. I didn't understand that that's how you eventually build a friendship with your neighbors or that maybe those people could help me." Hyuck would later laugh as he recalled his social blunders during those first years in South Korea.

When I saw him again in 2008, he had moved to Seoul and enrolled in college, hoping to get a degree in history and business. He was twenty-six years old. Although he lamented not having a girlfriend, he had many friends, including a cousin from Musan who'd recently defected. The process of showing the ropes to somebody greener than himself boosted Hyuck's confidence. He told me that he'd recently met a man who owned a private school near the university that taught English. They'd just struck up a conversation on the street. Instead of running away, Hyuck told the man he was a North Korean defector, and the man invited Hyuck to study at the school for free.

He had arrived.

CHAPTER 20

REUNIONS

Jun-sang in Myongdong pedestrian market,
carrying a copy of *1984,* Seoul, 2007.

THE TAINTED BLOOD THAT HAD DOOMED MI-RAN TO A MARGINAL life in North Korea proved her greatest asset once she crossed the border. The family ties to South Korea would prove invaluable. Unlike other defectors, reborn alone in a strange new world, Mi-ran had kin waiting to receive her.

Beneath the crisp efficiency of modern life in South Korea, Confucian traditions still hold sway. Mi-ran's father, as an only son, was the custodian of the family line, and after his passing, his offspring assumed that role.

When Mi-ran's family crossed the Tumen River into China in 1998, the first thing they did was telephone the municipal office in Seosan, South Chungchong province, where her father was born. Everybody had moved out of the village decades before as part of the mass migration to the cities. The village itself had mostly disappeared when the land was flooded to build a reservoir. But in Korea, home is the place where your father was born, regardless of whether or not anybody still lives there. The municipal office had the addresses of Tae-woo's two younger sisters, still both alive and living near Seoul, and offered to forward a letter to them. Mi-ran's twenty-three-year-old brother, although the youngest in the family, as the only male was designated to compose the letter. He wrote in formal language: *I am writing as the only son of your brother. I wish to inform you that he passed from this world last year in Kyongsong county, North Hamgyong province.* He included the address and phone number of a house in Yanji, a small city near the border, where they were staying.

Within a few weeks, they got a telephone call from one of the sisters. She was skeptical. Nearly half a century had elapsed without so much as a telephone call, a letter, even a rumor that their brother had survived the Korean War. In 1961, eight years after the end of the war, the South Korean Ministry of Defense recorded him as having been killed in action in 1953. As far as the family was concerned, he had died childless at the age of twenty-one. His name was on the tablet for the war dead at the National Cemetery. How were the sisters to know that this wasn't a hoax, a crude attempt to extort money from them? Mi-ran's sister, who had picked up the telephone, told the aunt some of what she knew. Little tidbits of family lore, birthdays and nicknames. The South Korean relatives suggested a DNA test. Mi-ran and her siblings agreed.

The family reunion lasted two weeks. Both aunts came to China along with assorted relatives, ten people in all. As soon as they all laid eyes on one another, they realized that the DNA testing had been superfluous.

"We just kept on staring. We marveled at the backs of our heads, the shape of our hands, the way we talked and walked," said Mi-ran.

"My father's sisters thought they'd lost their entire lineage because my father was an only son," Mi-ran's brother recalled. "When Father's sisters came to China and I saw them, my body was shaking. They were women, but they looked exactly like him."

There was no turning back. Mi-ran's mother had wanted to return to Chongjin to be with the two daughters who'd stayed behind and her grandchildren, but they feared that the North Korean government would discover they had met with their relatives from an enemy state while in China—a capital offense in itself. They had no place to go but South Korea.

Their aunts went to the South Korean consulate in Shenyang, asking to have the North Korean relatives flown to Seoul—the least they could do for the widow and children of a South Korean veteran held prisoner of war for so long—but the consulate balked at the request. Kim Dae-jung, who would later win the Nobel peace prize, had taken office as South Korea's president in February 1998 and had launched the "sunshine policy" to ease tensions with North Korea. Relations between South Korea and China, too, were sensitive. The officials feared that bringing in Mi-ran's family could have adverse diplomatic consequences.

The relatives fortunately had the means to take matters into their own hands. The sisters ran a small hotel, and one of their sons owned a bathhouse on the outskirts of Seoul. He flew back and forth between China and South Korea, rustling up plausible forgeries for the North Korean relatives. He got one for Mi-ran from a cousin of about the same age. Her photograph had been stripped out and replaced with Mi-ran's. An aunt "lost" her passport so that it could be used for Mi-ran's mother. These were illegal acts and, in fact, one of the cousins would later serve a month in jail for passport fraud, but they worked. Mi-ran, her sister, her brother, and her mother arrived safely in South Korea in January 1999.

With family to receive her, Mi-ran wasn't perceived as an outsider so much as a South Korean who had spent her first twenty-five years somewhere else. She was North Korean enough to be a novelty, but not enough to scare South Koreans. At five foot three she was positively statuesque for a North Korean woman and a respectable height for a South Korean. She still had those high cheekbones and the striking Romanesque nose that had stopped Jun-sang when he spotted her at the movie theater. She possessed that certain mystique North Korean women hold for South Korean men. Good looks, family connections, poise, and her natural intelligence made all the difference. She was quickly accepted into a graduate program in education. She was articulate, able to tell a story in a clear narrative style, and she was frequently asked to give talks and interviews about the North Korean school system

Just before she turned thirty, she was introduced to a strapping young man whose broad-cheeked smile and round glasses conveyed warmth. He had a good job as a civilian military employee. With the encouragement of both families, they married. In late 2004, she gave birth to her son. They celebrated his first birthday in traditional Korean style, with a lunch for nearly a hundred friends and relatives. The upper floor of a catering hall in eastern Seoul was festooned with blue and white balloons. Mi-ran, her husband, and the baby were dressed in colorful *hanbok,* the costume worn for ceremonial occasions. Mi-ran's outfit was made of a shimmering ivory silk with embroidered bands of red and black around the neckline. She was radiant and poised, a gracious hostess. She had achieved the Korean dream, actually the dream of many women I knew—the handsome husband, the baby boy, the graduate degree practically in the bag.

In her dress and manner of speaking, she was indistinguishable from a South Korean. She had lost the guttural accent that is a telltale trait of a North Korean. She and her husband bought an apartment in Suwon, the satellite city for upwardly mobile families who can't afford the $1 million home prices in Seoul. She lived in a housing complex that was a forest of identical concrete slabs, each high-rise distinguished only by the numbers stamped on the sides. As these compounds went, it wasn't a bad place. The buildings were new and clean, the facades a pleasant cream color. Sunlight streamed through a picture window into the living room of Mi-ran's second-floor apartment. It was bright and spacious inside, with a separate bedroom for the baby, a home office with a Samsung computer on the desk, and an open-plan kitchen with modern appliances.

When I came to visit, she cooked lunch as her son, by now a chubby toddler, watched cartoons in the living room.

"If I had him in North Korea, I'd have had to feed him rice milk with a little sugar if I could afford it," she said.

We chatted about the turns her life had taken. She was juggling the competing demands of her graduate studies and her family. Her in-laws expected her to be a traditional Korean wife. Child care was expensive; she found it hard to finish her work. She was taking an aerobics class in an effort to shed her pregnancy weight. Her skin often broke out from the stress. Her problems appeared to be not so different from those of all the other working mothers I knew.

Deep down, however, Mi-ran was the same person who had occupied the lowest rung of North Korean society, the poor, female progeny of tainted blood. She had been shaped by a thorough indoctrination and then suffered the pain of betrayal; she'd spent years in fear of speaking her mind, of harboring illicit thoughts. She had steeled herself to walk by the bodies of the dead without breaking stride. She had learned to eat her lunch, down to the last kernel of corn or grain of rice, without pausing to grieve for the children she taught who would soon die of starvation. She was racked with guilt. Guilt and shame are the common denominators among North Korean defectors; many hate themselves for what they had to do in order to survive.

In Mi-ran's case, the guilt was not merely an abstraction. It wasn't until I'd known her for more than two years that she told me what had happened to the sisters left behind. During the summer of 1999, about six months after the defecting family members arrived in South Korea, national security police had arrested both sisters almost simultaneously at home. Mi-ran's oldest sister, Mi-hee, the family beauty who'd married a military official and who had been so generous about providing food during the famine, and her sister Mi-sook had led blameless lives; they were loyal to their parents, their husbands, and their children, and loyal to Kim Jong-il. They were taken away in the middle of the night—the very same scenario of Mi-ran's recurring nightmare, except that the children were left behind with the husbands, who were instructed to file for divorce. The sisters were presumably taken to one of the labor camps for long-term prisoners. Given the severity of the food shortage in 1999, it was likely they were dead.

The fate of the sisters weighed heavily on the family, darkening every happy moment. Even as Mi-ran gave birth to a healthy baby boy and her brother, Sok-ju, was accepted at a university in Australia, the family couldn't rejoice. It seemed especially unfair. Defectors who came a few years later were able to send money in, and their relatives back home lived free from retaliation and better than the average North Korean. Perhaps the sisters received especially harsh treatment because Mi-ran's family had been among the first to leave and because of their poor class background. Mi-ran's mother, the iron-willed woman who held everything together through the famine, fell apart after she reached South Korea. Although only sixty-two years old when she arrived, her health and nerves failed her. She hired a shaman, a traditional fortune-teller, who informed her that her daughters were still alive, but it only increased her agitation.

Mi-ran's mother turned to religion. As a girl in Chongjin in pre-Communist times, she had attended a church, and now she rediscovered the faith of her childhood. She prayed constantly, begging forgiveness for betraying her girls.

Not being a believer herself, Mi-ran had no such solace. Her guilt troubled her sleep and intruded on a schedule that was so busy she wasn't supposed to have time to think. Her sisters had paid the ultimate price so she could drive a Hyundai.

She also thought about the boyfriend she had left behind. She credited him for pushing her to resist the destiny of her low birth, of giving her confidence as a woman and as a teacher. He'd never once spoken a word to her against the North Korean regime, but he had taught her to think for herself, which in the end kept her mind open and clear.

Mi-ran spoke frequently about Jun-sang when we met. I suspected she enjoyed reminiscing about her first love—something she couldn't talk about with her mother and certainly not with her husband. When she recalled how Jun-sang first spotted her at the movie theater, or how they walked all night in the darkness, the words tumbled out like those of an excited schoolgirl gossiping with a friend.

"Can you imagine? Three years to hold hands, six years to kiss? Not even a kiss, really, just a peck on the cheek."

We joked that unrequited, or in this case unconsummated, love affairs are the only ones that last forever. It seemed as though her longing was not so much for her ex-boyfriend as for the innocence of her earlier self.

I asked her if she knew what had happened to Jun-sang.

"I guess he's married by now." Her voice trailed off and she shrugged with affected disinterest. She didn't regret that they weren't still together, she told me—she loved her husband—but she was sorry she had left North Korea without an opportunity to say good-bye. She remembered that last day in Chongjin, when she thought she spotted him across the street but dared not approach for fear of blurting out her plans to leave.

"You know, he and I, we have a special bond. I think someday we will meet again."

We had that conversation in mid-October 2005, shortly after her son's first birthday party. Three weeks later, Mi-Ran called, her excitement palpable through the receiver. She announced the news:

"He's here!"

WE MET UP FOR coffee a week later at a Starbucks in Seoul, a few blocks from my office.

The way Mi-ran had described him, I had imagined a big, handsome man, larger than life. Here instead was a skinny fellow in jeans and glasses. And yet there was something extraordinary about him. His teeth gleamed white like a movie star's. His flat cheeks and flaring nostrils gave him an exotic Tatar look that reminded me of Rudolf Nureyev. When our cappuccinos were ready, he jumped up to retrieve them from the counter. He moved lithely; he was comfortable in his body. Mi-ran, on the other hand, was visibly nervous. She wore a short denim skirt and more makeup than usual.

I was about to remark that he seemed oddly at ease for some-

274 | NOTHING TO ENVY
body who'd just arrived from a country without coffee shops, but it
turned out that Jun-sang had been in South Korea for almost a year.
When he learned that Mi-ran was married—from a National Intelligence Service agent he met during his debriefing—he decided it
would be best for both of them if he didn't reach out to her. It was
not for lack of interest. In fact, he had been devastated by her departure, far more than she had imagined. Her defection triggered a
major crisis of confidence for him. He was tormented by the ab-
surdity of their situation. Why had they been so secretive with each
other? How was it that they had both nurtured a desire to defect but
didn't tell each other? On top of that, he felt cowardly for not defecting earlier. His pride was injured not because she'd left him, but because she had proved herself the braver one.

"I'd always thought I was ahead of her in my thinking, but I was
wrong," he admitted. Mi-ran interrupted, for a moment, to soothe
his ego. "I had doubts and mistrust of the government back then too,
but he had more information than me about the outside world." She
smiled at him, then allowed him to continue his story.

After Mi-ran left, he buried himself in his work at the research institute and was offered a permanent job and a chance to join the
Workers' Party. His parents and siblings encouraged it. This was
about as good as it could get in North Korea. His life in Pyongyang
was comfortable. His rented room was warm and he had enough to
eat. But he resisted settling down. He didn't date the university girls
who would have made suitable matches. He didn't attend the extra
lectures that would have boosted his chances of party membership.
Every night after work, he came home and drew the curtains tight
so he could watch South Korean television.

In 2001, Jun-sang asked permission to quit his job at the institute.
He told his boss and his colleagues that his parents were in poor
health and that as the oldest son he needed to care for them, a plausible explanation. The truth was that he wanted to be back in
Chongjin, where his activities would be less monitored and where
he'd be that much closer to the Chinese border. He did odd jobs and
worked briefly at the nursing home near where he and Mi-ran used
to walk at night. Rather than squander his money, he spent most
evenings at home with his parents, even though it meant he had to

endure the reproachful silence of his father, resigned now to disappointment in his once-promising son.

Despite all the deliberating and planning, however, things did not go as smoothly for Jun-sang as they had for Mi-ran.

Jun-sang spent three years saving money for his escape. He was a methodical person who weighed the consequences of his every word and action. He meticulously planned every detail, right down to what he would wear for the occasion—an expensive shirt with a pattern of bubbles that his uncle had sent from Japan. It was too loud to wear in Chongjin, and he figured that if he wore it in China nobody would think he was a beggar from North Korea. He put his best Japanese trousers and a backpack in a plastic bag. The crossing was set for June, when the river ran high. He had picked one of the deeper stretches, since it was less guarded. The broker who was escorting him across brought along empty plastic bottles to use as floats. Jun-sang and another defector, a forty-year-old woman, stripped down to their underwear, modestly turning away from each other even though it was pitch-dark. Jun-sang wrapped his clothing in plastic bags to keep it dry.

The water came up to his chin and the current was stronger than he'd expected. The water came up over the other defector's head; she didn't know how to swim. Jun-sang gripped her hand tightly and fought the current. Suddenly his bare feet touched sand and he climbed out in his sopping underwear. The woman followed. He was in China. He looked back across the river at the jagged silhouette of the North Korean mountains emerging from the sky, touched with the first light of the morning. He felt a brief stab of grief, but couldn't stop to dwell on it. He put on his clothing, which had gotten wet despite the plastic, and followed the broker into the mountains away from the river until they lost sight of North Korea.

He'd never realized it could be so cold in June. His feet chafed inside his wet shoes and swelled up with blisters. When they finally reached the village where they hoped to rest and eat, it turned out that a North Korean had been caught stealing a few days before and the locals were hostile toward defectors. They hustled out of there quickly, fearing they would be reported to the police. The woman who was traveling with Jun-sang suggested that they push on to her final destination, a village where she had been living with a Chinese farmer. During the walk, she told Jun-sang her story. She had been with the man for several years and they had a year-old baby. She'd been arrested seven months earlier and sent to a labor camp in North Korea. Now she was eager to get back to her husband and son. She assured Jun-sang that her husband would put him up until he was ready to move on.

The farmhouse proved to be no refuge. When they arrived, the Chinese farmer kicked and slapped the woman and attacked Jun-sang with a hoe, screaming furiously. He apparently thought that Jun-sang was her lover.

Alone and lost, Jun-sang wandered through the countryside. He finally spotted a bicycle rickshaw and hopped in, repeating the one word of Chinese the broker had taught him—*shichang*, market. He got out at a small outdoor market and found a woman selling kimchi. She had to be Korean, he figured, and he asked her if she knew anybody who would hire him. Her eyes flitted between his eyeglasses and his gaudy Japanese shirt.

"You look like a young man who's never done any hard work," she told him dismissively. Nevertheless, after some reassurance, she introduced him to an ethnic Korean businessman who owned a brick factory and offered Jun-sang work.

Jun-sang spent his days carrying heavy trays of bricks that were so hot they would singe his eyebrows if he stood too close. At night in the workers' dormitory, he wrote in a notebook he'd bought. It was the first time he kept a journal—in North Korea, it had been too dangerous to confide honest thoughts to paper. He wrote about his time at the university. He wrote poems. After the mind-numbing work at the factory, the journal reminded him of the reasons he had left home.

He spent two months at the brick factory, saving money to pursue his goal of reaching South Korea. He took a bus down to Qingdao, which had a large South Korean business community and a consular office.

South Korean consulates in China were well guarded precisely in order to keep out people like Jun-sang, but he thought he could talk his way in if he dressed properly. He used his remaining money to buy a suit and new eyeglasses. Full of self-confidence, he showed up at the building, marched right past the security guard downstairs, got into the elevator, and pressed the button for the seventh floor, where the consulate was located. But the elevator buttons for the seventh and eighth floors didn't work without a key. Stepping out at the sixth floor, he spotted another security guard so he ducked back into the elevator. Finally, he got off at the ninth floor and raced down the stairs. As he ran out of the building he could hear the guards talking in urgent tones into their walkie-talkies.

He was lucky to get out of there without being arrested.

Jun-sang had no more money and no more ideas. He thought about returning to North Korea—and just might have had he not discovered the Internet.

Though Jun-sang had been an elite student at one of North Korea's best universities, he had never used the Internet. His university had decent computers, IBM compatibles running Pentium 4 processors, and he'd been on the North Korean "intranet," a closed system available only to academics to browse various academic papers and a censored encyclopedia the country had purchased, but the country remained an Internet black hole, one of the few in the world that had chosen to stay offline. At a computer club in Chongjin kids could play games, nothing more.

Jun-sang had heard of the Internet, and once in China his curiosity about it intensified. He even had a vague idea that it could solve his problems. But how to get on? At the Qingdao bus station, he loitered, listening for a Korean speaker, and then approached a young man. The guy turned out to be a South Korean exchange student. "No problem. I'll teach you how to use it. It's very easy," he told Jun-sang, leading him to an Internet café.

The Web was a revelation to Jun-sang. With every click, the world was opening up to him. He felt certain for the first time that he had been right after all to escape to China. Here he was, a graduate of one of the best universities in the country, indeed one of the most computer-literate North Koreans, yet he was like a child in his knowledge. He typed into a South Korean search engine the words *North Korean human rights* and *North Korean defectors*.

Over the next several weeks, Jun-sang stayed late at night at the café, eating instant noodles and reading. He learned that other

North Korean defectors had similar problems getting to South Korea and studied the strategies they'd used, what worked and what failed. He educated himself about the South Korean laws governing North Koreans and about the diplomatic complications that prevented South Korea from accepting defectors at its embassy and consulates inside China. He studied maps of China, plane and train schedules, and wondered how he would get out.

Then one day he read about a pastor in Incheon who'd written with much compassion about the underground railroad that brought defectors out through Mongolia. Jun-sang, who had set up an e-mail address with the help of the student, excitedly dashed off a message: *I am in Qingdao. Can you help me get to South Korea?*

JUN-SANG'S ROUTE was the same as Kim Hyuck's. Hundreds of others had by this time defected along these lines and the border crossings and safe houses were well mapped out. Jun-sang would need $2,500 for the journey, which his uncle in Japan wired him. He took the train to Erenhot, then crossed the desert terrain of the border into Mongolia, where the border police turned him over to the South Korean embassy. He arrived in South Korea in October 2004, whereupon he was turned over to the National Intelligence Service for debriefing.

Then it was Jun-sang's turn to ask questions. It was not his first question, but one of the first: Can you tell me how to get in touch with Mi-ran? He knew for sure she was in South Korea because he'd searched for her name in the Internet café in Qingdao and had read an interview she'd given. The NIS kept close tabs on North Korean defectors and would surely have information about her.

The NIS agent hesitated. Under the rules, defectors are not supposed to be given information about other defectors for fear one might be a North Korean spy.

"We can't release that unless you're immediate family. Sorry."

"She was my fiancée, my first love," Jun-sang pleaded.

The agent was sentimental, and offered to make inquiries. The next day he came in and told Jun-sang he would give him her phone number, but he felt Jun-sang ought to know that she was married.

He was astounded. In retrospect, Jun-sang conceded that it was ridiculous for him to assume she was single and the height of arrogance to think she might be waiting for him. Mi-ran was by this time thirty-one years old. They'd had no contact for more than six years.

"At the time, honestly, it hadn't crossed my mind that she might be married," Jun-sang recalled.

He tried to comfort himself. He remembered a poem by the nineteenth-century Hungarian poet Sandor Petofi that he'd recited as he crossed the Tumen River:

Liberty and love
These two I must have.
For my love I'll sacrifice
My life.
For liberty I'll sacrifice
My love.

The poem had moved him long ago when he'd read it in Pyongyang, and he'd memorized the words. He had sacrificed his love for Mi-ran to remain in Pyongyang. He'd never put her first in his life. He'd come to South Korea for freedom and that alone.

OVER THE FOLLOWING MONTHS, Jun-sang went through the same rites of passage as the other defectors. He left the orientation program, got an apartment and a mobile telephone, and wandered the streets and markets in bewilderment trying not to be overwhelmed. He had only a few friends and sometimes regretted not knowing how to find Mi-ran. After he'd learned she was married, he told the national security agent that he didn't want her phone number.

"It's better to leave her alone. She's married," he told himself.

One evening he went to the apartment of someone he'd met at Hanawon. It was an informal gathering of defectors who'd occasionally get together to drink beer. Among them was a brooding young man he recognized immediately as Mi-ran's kid brother. Jun-sang used to slip him candies in an effort to ingratiate himself. Sok-ju was just a child at the time and now didn't recognize Jun-sang.

They struck up a conversation that evening and spoke again in subsequent gatherings. After a while, Sok-ju grew suspicious.

"How do you know so much about me and my family?" he asked. Then, before Jun-sang could respond, he slapped his knee and answered his own question. "Yeah, you're that guy who used to hang around my sister . . ."

A WEEK LATER, Jun-sang was pacing the sidewalk in front of identical high-rise apartments. He and Mi-ran had agreed to meet at a subway station in eastern Seoul. When Sok-ju had figured out who he was, Jun-sang had little choice but to call her. As soon as she realized it was Jun-sang on the phone, he could hear the indignation in her voice. "How come you didn't call me sooner?" Mi-ran said. "We could have helped you."

He felt foolish. He'd been in South Korea for nearly a year, a period when he was flailing about, desperately lost and lonely. He could have used a friend, particularly an old friend who knew him and understood where he came from. Though he felt himself aggrieved, a man who'd been jilted without notice, he ended up apologizing.

Now he checked the time again and again on his mobile telephone—nobody he knew wore a watch. He wondered if he had taken the wrong subway line or was waiting at the wrong exit. He was still confused by all the subway lines that shot out from the ever-expanding nexus of downtown Seoul, each station bigger than the last, with endless tile-lined corridors and multiple exits that were indistinguishable from one another. This one was in a newly built apartment district where Mi-ran said her mother lived. Jun-sang scanned the sidewalk to see if he recognized anybody in the crowd streaming toward him. It was a clear day in that brief, perfect interlude between the soggy summer and winter. The sidewalks were crowded, mostly with women, since it was a weekday and most South Korean women don't work after they have children. Jun-sang watched the women in their tight jeans, yakking on their mobile telephones with fuzzy toys dangling off the ends. Some pushed elaborate strollers that must have cost as much as bicycles. Strollers were almost unknown in North Korea—kids who couldn't walk were strapped on the back with long cloths. Jun-sang wondered if Mi-ran was like these pampered young mothers. In a fleeting moment of panic, he wondered if she could have walked right by without his recognizing her. Then he heard his name called and he spun around, startled.

"Have you been waiting long?" Mi-ran said, rolling down the window of her car.

Jun-sang was still susceptible to Hollywood imagery. For years he had anticipated their reunion and hadn't quite let go of the scene of the couple running toward each other on a foggy train platform. He'd imagined all kinds of scenarios but they never involved a car—certainly not a car with Mi-ran behind the steering wheel.

She was stopped in the bus lane and leaned over to push open the passenger-side door, beckoning for him to climb in. She spoke rapidly, apologizing for her lateness, the traffic, how she couldn't find a parking space. She kept her eyes on the road, while his darted over her. Her features were the same—he couldn't believe he ever thought he might not recognize her. Maybe, though, she wasn't as radiant as he remembered, or maybe her beauty had been magnified by the years of longing. Her complexion betrayed the strain of mothering a one-year-old; a sprinkling of acne around her chin was barely concealed by makeup. He could see the touch of the *ajumma* about her. She wore a flouncy apricot-colored skirt and a baggy short-sleeved blouse. The clothing was complicated, like her life; the simplicity of girlhood had vanished long ago.

"You're so calm," he broke the silence.

"No, no, I'm nervous inside," she responded.

They drove to a quiet restaurant on the outskirts of the city. They began with polite inquiries about family, but there was no subject that didn't lead to tragedy. Jun-sang didn't dare ask about her sisters. He'd heard that they'd been taken away. And she couldn't ask him about his parents, whom he might never see again. They quickly wound their way to the subject of Mi-ran's abrupt departure. As they spoke, he felt the anger swelling up.

"You might have tried to send me a clue," he told her.

She protested that she wasn't sure at the time she was defecting—

that it could have just been an excursion to China to see relatives—
and even though he didn't quite believe her, he felt better hearing
her say it.

She learned that he had not been in Chongjin in October 1998
when she'd left—the glimpse she thought she had of him from
across the street was just a product of her imagination.

"If you were going to come to South Korea, why didn't you
come sooner?" she asked.

Jun-sang was at a loss to answer. At this point in the conversation,
Mi-ran was crying and the implications of her words were clear. She
was married and had a baby. It was too late.

AS THE MONTHS dragged on, the novelty of having rediscovered
each other wore off. When we spoke, one often sounded exasper-
ated with the other. Jun-sang complained rather peevishly that Mi-
ran wasn't as beautiful as she used to be. Mi-ran had promised to
introduce him to some women but never did. When they communi-
cated, it was by e-mail or text message. The instant gratification of
modern communication killed some of the magic between them.
Their relationship was one that thrived in the adverse conditions of
North Korea. Emotions somehow meant more when they were hand-
written on precious scraps of paper and conveyed on slow trains running out of fuel.

"Now that I can call him on the phone whenever I want or send
him a text, I'm not so interested," Mi-ran admitted. "It's hard for me
to understand now why I spent so many years obsessing about this
guy."

The reversal in their social status didn't help. In North Korea,
Jun-sang had the better class background, the money, the fancy
Japanese sweaters, and the Pyongyang education. Now he was fresh
off the boat with no money and no connections. His North Korean
education was useless in South Korea. Everything he'd learned
about science and technology was obsolete. He had no immediate
prospects of a good career and was stuck doing odd jobs such as
delivering food on a motorbike. On his rounds one day, he was
knocked over by a taxicab. He picked himself up off the pavement

and, finding no damage to himself or the bike, rode off. When he got back to the restaurant and recounted what had happened, his boss roared with laughter. If Jun-sang hadn't been such a clueless greenhorn, he would have collected some settlement money from the driver.

Jun-sang shrugged it off. He didn't let little jabs from South Koreans bug him. His confidence ran deep, to the core. He was never self-pitying and never expressed regrets about defecting, although he worried about not seeing his parents again. He took enormous satisfaction in the tiniest freedoms in his new life. He dressed in denim precisely because he'd been unable to in North Korea. He grew his hair down to his shoulders. ("It was always my dream to grow my hair long. I figured I'd have to do it before I turn forty so I don't look like a loser," he told me.) He read voraciously. In North Korea, he'd managed to get something of a liberal arts education, but there were gaps. I often gave him books to read. His favorite was a translation of *1984*. He marveled that George Orwell could have so understood the North Korean brand of totalitarianism.

The last time I saw him, we met at Lotte World, a huge shopping and entertainment complex in the southern part of Seoul. It was a Sunday afternoon just before the lunar New Year and the place was jammed. We pushed our way through the crowds, looking for a place to talk, until we found seats at a revolving sushi bar, the latest rage in South Korea. Plucking our sushi from the conveyor belt, Jun-sang told me he had gone back to school to get a pharmacist's license. During school vacations, he installed ventilation systems on a construction site in the suburbs. These seemed like odd choices for somebody of his background. I suspected he would be doing something different by the next time we met.

North Korean defectors often find it hard to settle down. It is not easy for somebody who's escaped a totalitarian country to live in the free world. Defectors have to rediscover who they are in a world that offers endless possibilities. Choosing where to live, what to do, even which clothes to put on in the morning is tough enough for those of us accustomed to making choices; it can be utterly paralyzing for people who've had decisions made for them by the state their entire lives.

Defectors are also nagged by the impermanence of their situation. Many, if not most, wish to return to North Korea. Most of them fled with the conviction that Kim Jong-il's regime was on the verge of collapse and that they would return within a few years to a free North Korea. It was a reasonable assumption. In the mid-1990s, in the aftermath of Kim Il-sung's death and the dissolution of the Soviet Union, it was a matter of virtual consensus in the foreign-policy establishment that the end was imminent. Those who visit Pyongyang and snap photos of the towering monuments, the goose-stepping soldiers, and the kitschy socialist billboards are invariably astounded that the place has survived into the twenty-first century. "See it while it lasts" is how one travel agency advertises its tours to North Korea.

While the persistence of North Korea is a curiosity for the rest of the world, it is a tragedy for North Koreans, even those who have managed to escape. Jun-sang has little chance of seeing his parents again unless the regime collapses in their lifetime. Mi-ran's best hope for her sisters is that they can survive until the day the gates to the labor camps are opened and the long-term political prisoners are set free.

This is where I leave the story. North Korea remains the last bastion of undiluted communism in the world. Mrs. Song has just retired. Oak-hee runs her karaoke business in Suwon. Dr. Kim is in her last year of medical school and Jun-sang in his first year of pharmacy school. Mi-ran gave birth to her second child, a daughter, in December 2007. I can only excuse myself for leaving the story incomplete because the people in it, like Korea itself, remain works in progress.

EPILOGUE

WAITING

A bus stop on Chongjin's main street, 2008.

DURING THE FIVE YEARS THAT I SPENT IN SEOUL REPORTING
for the *Los Angeles Times,* I attended numerous dinners with fellow
journalists, diplomats, and academics. Invariably the conversation
would turn to North Korea, with the participants speculating about
when Kim Jong-il's regime might collapse.

In fact, the longevity of the North Korean regime is something
of a mystery to many professional North Korea watchers. During
the 1990s, imminent collapse was the virtually unchallenged consensus. ("The Coming Collapse of North Korea" was the title of an op-
ed essay by the noted North Korea scholar Nicholas Eberstadt,
published in June 1990.) Against all odds, North Korea survived the

breaching of the Berlin Wall, the breakup of the Soviet Union, the market reforms in China, the death of Kim Il-sung, the famine of the 1990s, and two terms of George W. Bush's presidency. Bush famously lumped North Korea into the "axis of evil" along with Iran and Iraq, and insinuated that he would send Kim Jong-il packing as he did Saddam Hussein.

Yet in 2009, Bush is gone and Kim Jong-il is still in power, albeit in poor health. He is the last of the twentieth-century dictators, a living anachronism. Kim runs his country as though it were the thick of the Cold War, churning out bombastic propaganda, banning most foreigners from visiting, threatening real and imagined enemies with nuclear weapons and missiles. On May 25, North Korea conducted its second nuclear test, detonating a bomb assessed by U.S. intelligence to be several kilotons at an underground site in North Hamgyong Province, fifty miles southwest of Chongjin. As of this writing, sixteen years' worth of diplomacy on the part of successive U.S. administrations has failed to produce an agreement under which North Korea would give up its weapons programs in return for diplomatic recognition by the United States and a permanent settlement to the Korean War. The regime's defiant stance was displayed just weeks later in the harsh sentencing, to twelve years' hard labor, of two U.S. journalists captured while reporting too close to the Tumen River border. They were pardoned only after the personal intervention of former president Bill Clinton, who visited Pyongyang in August to secure their release.

At sixty-seven, Kim Jong-il is graying and gaunt. Over the summer of 2008 he was reported to have suffered a stroke, and recent photographs show him with one arm hanging limp, as though partially paralyzed.

Despite his infirmities, it is by no means a foregone conclusion that the end is near or even that Kim's death would bring about the demise of the regime. At the meeting of the People's Assembly, Kim's brother-in-law, Jang Song-taek, was named to the National Defense Commission. The move was widely read as a signal that Jang could serve as North Korea's nominal leader in the event of Kim's passing, perhaps merely as a caretaker until Kim's favored youngest son, Kim Jong-un, now twenty-six, is old enough to take charge.

North Korea watchers spend a lot of time debating whether conditions inside the country are getting better or worse or changing at all. Like other occasional visitors to Pyongyang, I am reluctant to make pronouncements about the state of the nation based on my observations because the government goes to such extraordinary lengths to choreograph what foreigners see of their country. I made two trips to North Korea in 2008, as well as two trips to the border in early 2009, and came away with mixed impressions. In Pyongyang I was surprised to see half a dozen new buildings under construction in the capital and others covered with scaffolding in the middle of renovations. The sounds of chain saws and jackhammers filled the air. It was nothing compared with other Asian capitals, where the cityscapes are in a perpetual state of reinvention, but nonetheless remarkable for Pyongyang, a city so stagnant that it seems stuck in a time capsule of the 1960s. Other than a few more monuments to the leadership, virtually nothing new had been built in Pyongyang in decades. Now 100,000 new units of housing are under construction, with the goal of completion in time for the 2012 festivities marking the centennial of Kim Il-sung's birth, my North Korean guides told me. North Korea watchers believe some of the funding is coming from the Middle East. Pyongyang's most notorious clunker, the 105-story pyramid-shaped Ryugyong Hotel, is getting a facelift, too, as part of a $400 million deal with Orascom. The Egyptian conglomerate also introduced a mobile telephone network in late 2008, which gives the city at least the appearance of modernity.

Other glimpses of progress? The Rakwon Department Store, which is largely reserved for foreign diplomats and the elite, had a nicely stocked basement supermarket with frozen Australian beef and American breakfast cereal. People on the streets of Pyongyang looked to be better and more colorfully dressed than I'd seen on previous visits. My most recent trip was during a warm week in September, and several women were wearing slinky high-heeled sandals. I also saw for the first time a middle-aged woman who was slightly overweight—not close to achieving an American standard of obesity, but odd enough in Pyongyang that I pulled out my camera and tried to catch a shot before she turned a corner.

Pyongyang is often said to be a Potemkin village, an elaborate artifice for the benefit of foreigners. Wherever we go, we stumble over suspiciously well-dressed people posing in various improbable situations—for example, young women with brightly rouged cheeks in traditional dresses sitting on concrete benches under the main statue of Kim Il-sung, pretending to read books. It takes a while before you notice what's wrong with the picture. During my last visit, I watched a delegation of soldiers in their crisp uniforms approach the statue with a bouquet of flowers. When they bowed down low to show their respect, their pants hitched up just enough to reveal that they didn't have socks. Socks for the military have been in chronically short supply.

When the New York Philharmonic went to Pyongyang last year, the city was lit up as if it were Christmas—floodlights bathed Kim Il-sung Square and garlands of tiny white lights were draped over the main streets. The delegation of more than three hundred people, including musicians and journalists, stayed in the Yanggakdo Hotel (often nicknamed "Alcatraz" for its location on an island in the river that prevents tourists from wandering off). It had been outfitted for the occasion with broadband Internet access for journalists filing reports on the concert. When we checked in, the rooms were so overheated that many of us stripped down to T-shirts. At each meal, we were feted to excess. Dinner was a multicourse banquet of salmon, crab gratin, lamb, sliced pheasant, and Viennese-style chocolate cakes. Our breakfast buffet table was decorated with ice sculptures and carved melons and filled with a generous array of foods. Still, it was a great show. Even the most cynical journalists among us got the impression that North Korea was on its way up, steadily recovering from the Arduous March of the 1990s.

Of course, we'd been had. It was a blip, a brief interlude of light in the grim, dysfunctional country that North Korea really is. The Internet access disappeared. The lights went out. The week after the concert, I spoke by telephone to the U.N. World Food Programme's representative in Pyongyang at the time, Jean-Pierre de Margerie, who told me, "As soon as you guys left, it was pitch-dark again."

The World Food Programme, which has the largest presence in North Korea of the various aid agencies, has a grim assessment of the economic situation. A survey of 250 North Korean households conducted in the summer of 2008 found that two thirds were still supplementing their diets by picking grass and weeds in the countryside. Most adults didn't eat lunch for lack of food. When questioned about where they would get their next meal, those surveyed replied that they didn't know or offered vague answers such as "I'm hoping my relatives who live on a cooperative farm will deliver some potatoes tonight," according to de Margerie. Some of the interviewees cried as they were being questioned.

The U.N. agencies don't envision another famine like the one in the 1990s; instead they describe a population that has been chronically undernourished for years. "Teachers report that children lack energy and are lagging in social and cognitive development. Workers are unable to put in full days and take longer to complete tasks," a group of U.S. aid agencies wrote in another report last summer. Hospital staff told the agencies they were seeing 20 to 40 percent increases in digestive disorders caused by poor nutrition.

As soon as you leave Pyongyang, the real North Korea comes into view, albeit through the windows of buses or fast-moving cars. Even aid officials stationed in Pyongyang are not allowed into the countryside without an escort. On an excursion through Nampo (the west-coast city where Mi-ran saw her first dead body) in September 2008, I saw people who appeared to be homeless sleeping on the grass along the main street. Others squatted on their haunches, heads down, apparently having nothing better to do at ten o'clock on a weekday morning. Walking barefoot along the sidewalk was a boy about nine years old wearing a mud-stained uniform that hung below his knees. That was the first time I'd seen one of the notorious wandering swallows, the *kochebi*.

There was evidence all along the twenty-five-mile drive between Pyongyang and Nampo of the extent to which North Korea's able-bodied population was enlisted in the production of food. Middle-aged office ladies were marched out to the countryside, carrying pocketbooks and shovels slung over their shoulders. On the side of the road, older people sifted through the grass on their hands and knees in search of edible weeds. The countryside reeked of the night soil that is still used instead of chemical fertilizer. Donations of fertilizer from South Korea dropped precipitously last year due to political tensions. There were few motorized vehicles in the fields. Trucks belching smoke looked as if they had been retrofitted to burn wood and corncobs instead of gasoline. People carried huge sacks on their backs, hunched over as they walked along rusted railroad tracks that clearly hadn't been used in years.

Even in the best of times North Korea can produce only about 60 percent of the food needed for its population, and it currently cannot afford to import the rest. The food shortage worsens the farther away from Pyongyang you get. The assessment prepared jointly last year by the U.N. World Food Programme and the Food and Agriculture Organization named North Hamgyong once again as the province most vulnerable to shortages.

THE NORTH KOREAN ECONOMY continues to stagnate. South Korean investment in North Korea has shrunk since the conservative Lee Myung-bak was elected president in December 2007. South Korean tours to the scenic Mount Kumgang area just north of the DMZ—one of North Korea's largest sources of hard currency— were suspended for more than a year after the accidental shooting of a South Korean tourist in the summer of 2008. Strained relations between the Koreas have threatened another promising project north of the border, the Kaesong industrial park where South Korean factories employ more than 38,000 North Korean workers.

The belligerent mood in Pyongyang goes hand in hand with the economic hard line. Decades after the rest of the Communist world capitulated to capitalism, Kim Jong-il is trying to run the economy the same way his father did in the 1950s. If anything, he's been taking the country on a great leap backward, rolling back the market reforms of the past decade. The markets that had brought North Koreans imported fruits and bright T-shirts are under constant pressure from the Workers' Party, and some fear they might soon be closed down entirely. Market hours in much of the country have been restricted to 2:00 P.M. to 6:00 P.M. The government has banned all vendors except for women aged fifty and over; all the men and younger women must report to their official jobs at state-owned enterprises. There are increasing restrictions on what can be sold, too. Along with rice and corn, soybeans have been banned from the markets lest they be taken into China and resold to the enemy in South Korea. Special police roam the markets confiscating banned goods.

"Our General wants to bring back socialism the way it used to be," a trader who gave his name as Kim Young-chul told me. He was one of several people from North Hamgyong province I interviewed in June 2009 near the border. The North Korean government, he said, had launched a new campaign against all products "made in China" that has practically emptied the markets of cosmetics, candies, cookies, and medicines.

"We're supposed to buy North Korean products instead of Chinese, but North Korea doesn't make anything—it all comes from China—so there is nothing to buy," he said.

Lee Myong-hee, a woman in her fifties, complained that the restrictions were squeezing the life out of the economy.

"If they don't give us food and clothing and we're not allowed to buy things, how are we supposed to survive?" she demanded. She was from Kilju, the city closest to the nuclear test site, and had come out of North Korea five days before the test. She was frantic with worry—about radiation leakages, about impending U.N. sanctions, about the economy. As fat tears rolled down the hollows of her cheekbones, she asked, "Isn't it a waste to be spending money on nuclear weapons when people are starving?"

Although China remains North Korea's largest trading partner, the back-and-forth across the Tumen River has slowed. In the run-up to the 2008 Summer Olympics in Beijing, China installed barbed-wire fences and security cameras along the river. The pillboxes for North Korea's border guards have been moved closer together to prevent defections and illegal trade. A Chinese businessman who owns a factory in Chongjin told me that the North Korean government had recently banned the export of steel plates to China, decreeing that vital resources should not be taken out of the country.

Chongjin might be the most entrepreneurial city in North Korea, but it is under constant pressure from the central authorities, who have anxiously watched it drifting away from their control. As the city's fortunes over the past decade have become more entwined with the border trade and less with the dictates of Pyongyang, its residents and even its provincial officials have become less pliable. In March 2008, when the edict barring women under age fifty from the market was first imposed, people simply refused. Female vendors held a rare public protest at the management offices of Chongjin's big Sunam market, chanting, "Give us food or let us trade."

Market authorities were forced to back down, although this year they are again trying to enforce the restrictions. Many people I've met from Chongjin describe the prevailing sentiment: why can't the government just go away and let us run our lives? It's not something that's said so much as intuitively understood. A coal miner from Chongjin whom I met in 2004 in China told me, "People are not stupid. Everybody thinks our own government is to blame for our terrible situation. We all know we think that and we all know that everybody else thinks that. We don't need to talk about it."

SEVERAL OF THE PEOPLE whose lives I've followed in this book are able to contact their families in Chongjin occasionally through the illegal telephones in Musan, Hoeryong, and other border towns that pick up Chinese signals. "Things are so, so hard for people," Mrs. Song told me after speaking to one of her brothers on the phone in March 2009. "There is not much food on the market and the inflation is terrible. They are barely making ends meet." She says her siblings live better than most because of money she sends through China, but much of it is confiscated by officials.

"The families of defectors are some of the richest people in the neighborhood," Oak-hee told me. "My husband says security agents always come by looking for something. They even come by to shave because they know he's the only one who has razors."

The widening gap between rich and poor has led to a rise in crime. The husband of Mrs. Song's second daughter worked as a security guard for the railway until 2006, when he and his wife came to South Korea at Oak-hee's invitation. At the time of his defection there were so many thieves stealing food from the cargo warehouses that guards were issued guns with real bullets and shoot-to-kill orders. Similar rules apply to the narrow plots planted alongside the tracks to grow corn for the families of railroad workers. Chongjin also has a surprisingly large drug problem because of the widespread availability of "ice," or crystal methamphetamine, which is produced in small factories and sold inside the city and at the Chinese border. It's cheap and it cuts the appetite, making it a drug well suited for the North Korean lifestyle.

Chongjin is not experiencing the little boomlet of new construction that I observed in Pyongyang. Except for a couple of gas stations along the main road, nothing of significance has been built downtown in years. The newest building is a garish pink structure put up in the late 1990s to house a permanent exhibit of Kimjongilia, a flower named for the Dear Leader. Facades along the main Road No. 1 have been repainted in pastel shades of wintergreen and peach, but the cornices are crumbling—a constant danger to pedestrians below. New posters spaced at regular intervals along the roadside tout the government's latest slogan about rebuilding the economy: *kyungjae jeonsun*, the economic front line.

In the last few years, a number of private restaurants have started up inside empty buildings that once housed state-owned restaurants or companies, as have *noraebang*, karaoke bars. Most of these kinds of businesses, however, don't last long before they are shut down.

"I didn't see any signs of progress. In fact, Chongjin looks like a city moving backward in time. Everything is in a state of disrepair and it appears to be getting worse," said Anthony Banbury, Asia regional director for the World Food Programme, who visited in August 2008. "At most of the factories, there is no sign of activity. At best one smokestack out of eight is puffing smoke."

Eckart Dege, a German geographer who generously contributed photographs to this book, in September 2008 was permitted to visit both Chongjin and Kyongsong county, where Mi-ran grew up. He also detected little economic activity except for a large group of civilians on the road to Kyongsong who were rebuilding a road entirely through manual labor. "There were thousands and thousands of people carrying dirt from the hills in shovels and laying it down in little heaps, as though they were building the pyramids," Dege said.

Inside the city, he noted the unusually large number of people squatting in a position that is almost emblematic of North Korea, knees bent up to the chest, balancing on the balls of the feet. "In other places in the world people are always doing something, but here they were just sitting."

It is a North Korean phenomenon that many have observed. For lack of chairs or benches, the people sit for hours on their haunches, along the sides of roads, in parks, in the market. They stare straight ahead as though they are waiting—for a tram, maybe, or a passing car? A friend or relative? Maybe they are waiting for nothing in particular, just waiting for something to change.

—*Barbara Demick*
September 2009

ACKNOWLEDGMENTS

My deepest gratitude goes to the six North Koreans profiled in this book. They gave generously of their time, endured prying questions, and relived painful memories for no motivation other than to help me and my readers understand their world. I am grateful to the members of their families as well for their help. Jinna Park deserves special thanks for her love of language and patience in interpreting most of the interviews that went into this book. The late Dr. Jae Nam introduced me to the first people I met from Chongjin. I could not have learned as much about North Korea as I did without the help of a very courageous woman I will call K, who gave up a comfortable retirement in the United States and who, despite her advanced age, worked tirelessly with her husband on behalf of North Korean refugees. She is one of many people whose names should be mentioned here.

Besides the people featured in this book, there were many other North Korean exiles who helped fill in the blanks about their country: Joo Sung-ha of Dong-a Ilbo, who will someday write his own book; Kim Do-seon; Kim Yong-il; Cho Myong-chol; Kim Hye-young; and Kim Tae-jin.

I also relied on the work of many nongovernmental organizations devoted to North Korean issues. The Seoul-based Good Friends publishes an excellent newsletter on North Korea. Lee Young-hwa of Rescue the North Korean People provided guidance and steered me to photographs and videos that enriched the descriptions of Chongjin. Other excellent sources included Tim Peters, Michael Horowitz, Suzanne Scholte, Han Ki-hong of *Daily NK*, Sunny Han, Reverend Kim Young-shik, Chun Ki-won, Human Rights Watch, and the Citizens' Alliance for North Korean Human Rights. Do Hee-yun's research into POWs and abductees helped me to capture the story of Mi-ran's father.

Among the people in the humanitarian aid community, I wish to thank Katharina Zellweger of the Swiss Agency for Development and Cooperation; the American agronomist Pil-ju Kim Joo; and from the

United Nations' World Food Programme, Jean-Pierre de Margerie, Gerald Bourke, and Tony Banbury.

Korea experts who were unusually generous with their time were Michael Breen and Scott Snyder, as well as Stephan Haggard, Marcus Noland, Nicholas Eberstadt, Bob Carlin and Leonid Petrov, Brian Myers, Daniel Pinkston, Donald Gregg, David Hawk, and Brent Choi. I was helped enormously by the scholar Andrei Lankov, whose writings are quoted frequently in this book. Fellow journalists Donald Macintyre and Anna Fifield were as obsessed with North Korea as I was and shared with me their ideas and inspiration. Charles Sherman offered constant encouragement for this project, as did other friends and colleagues in Seoul, including Jennifer Nicholson, Jennifer Veale, Scott Diaz, Sue-Lynn Koo, Patricio Gonzalez, Pascal Biannac-Leger, Lachlan Strahan, and Lily Petkovska. Others whose work in Korea helped to shape this book were Moon Il-hwan, Tim Savage, Paul Eckert, Jasper Becker, Choe Sang-hun, Kim Jung-eun, Donald Kirk, and Bradley Martin, whose own book, *Under the Loving Care of the Fatherly Leader,* is cited frequently here. Chi Jung-nam and Lim Bo-yeon accompanied me on many interviews with North Koreans.

I'd like to thank the people who provided photographs for this book: Eckart Dege, a geographer who traveled to Chongjin and Kyongsong county in autumn of 2008; photographers Jean Chung and Eric Lafforgue; and journalists Anna Fifield and Jonathan Watts. Jiro Ishimaru of AsiaPress helped me track down photographs of Chongjin that were taken by North Koreans at great risk.

Among those whose research went into this book were Lina Park Yoon, Park Ju-min, Hisako Ueno, and Rie Sasaki. Howard Yoon was a great help in shaping the book proposal.

My friends Julie Talen and Tirza Biron served as writing coaches, helping me transform a style learned at daily newspapers into one suitable for a book. Without Jim Dwyer, I don't know that I could have gotten this book published. Margaret Scott and Terri Jentz talked me through the book proposal and writing processes. Others who contributed valuably to this book were Gady Epstein, Molly Fowler, Ed Gargan, Eden Soriano Gonzaga, Lee Hockstader, Aliza Marcus, Ruth Marcus, Nomi Morris, Evan Osnos, Catherine Peterson, Flore de Preneuf, David Schmerler and Isabel Schmerler, Lena Sun, Jane Von Bergen, Nicholas Von Hoffman, Eric Weiner, Laura Wides-Munoz, and Tracy Wilkinson. Many years later, I am still thankful to my college writing teacher, the late John Hersey, who taught his nonfiction writing students to seek structures and models in the work of other writers. His own book *Hiroshima* was an inspiration to me as I wove together the stories of the six people in this book.

I was extremely lucky to find as my agent Flip Brophy, who rose from a bad bout of the flu over Christmas 2006 to take on this project and whose support has gone beyond the call of duty. My publishers, Julie Grau and Celina Spiegel, understood the concept of the book completely from day one. And Laura Van der Veer helped put the pieces into place.

At the *Los Angeles Times*, I wish to thank Simon Li, who first hired me to cover Korea, and editors Dean Baquet, John Carroll, Marc Duvoisin, Doug Frantz, Marjorie Miller, and Bruce Wallace, who encouraged the kind of investigative reporting that made me proud to work for the newspaper. Julie Makinen expertly edited a series of articles about Chongjin that were the germ of this book. Mark Magnier, John Glionna, Valerie Reitman, Ching-ching Ni, Don Lee, and David Pierson were among many colleagues at the *Los Angeles Times* who were particularly helpful.

At Princeton University, where I spent 2006–2007 as a Ferris fellow at the Council of the Humanities, Carol Rigolot gave me a place to write at Henry House. Among the other fellows, Lisa Cohen, Martha Mendoza, T. R. Reid, and Rose Tang gave valuable advice, along with my friends on the faculty, Gary Bass, Maryanne Case, Gabe Hudson, and Jeff Nunakawa.

Finally, special thanks to my mother, Gladys Demick, who, when I told her I was moving to Korea with her only grandchild, instead of complaining, replied, "What a great opportunity!" Her encouragement has been the foundation of my career. And to my son, Nicholas, who cannot remember any time in his young life when he was not competing with North Korea for my attention, and who must have asked me dozens of times, "Aren't you done with that book yet?," I can finally answer yes.

NOTES

THIS BOOK IS PRIMARILY AN ORAL HISTORY. I HAVE MADE BEST EFFORTS to confirm the accounts of my subjects through other sources and have added information obtained through my own reporting on North Korea.

I made nine trips to North Korea between 2001 and 2008, three of them to Pyongyang and nearby areas; the others were to areas just north of the demilitarized zone, such as Mount Kumgang, when it was open to tourists. In the course of my reporting for this book and for the *Los Angeles Times,* I interviewed approximately one hundred North Korean defectors, most of them now living in South Korea or in China; about half were originally from Chongjin. I also reviewed hours of video footage taken secretly in Chongjin, some of it shot by the courageous North Koreans Ahn Myong-chol and Lee Jun, who carried concealed cameras in their bags. I am indebted to the Osaka-based organization Rescue the North Korean People for allowing me to screen the footage and to AsiaPress for granting me rights to the still photography. In addition, an excellent series of photographs of both Chongjin and Kyongsong taken in 2008 by the German geographer Eckart Dege proved very helpful in corroborating the descriptions of my subjects and in bringing the landscape and vistas to life.

CHAPTER 1: HOLDING HANDS IN THE DARK

Credit for the term "Great Vituperator" belongs to the North Korea scholar Aidan Foster-Carter. "Great Vituperator: North Korea's Insult Lexicon," *Asia Times,* May 26, 2001.

Kim Jong-il's ideas about film are spelled out in his book *On the Art of Cinema* (Pyongyang: Foreign Languages Publishing House, 1973). His love of cinema was manifested in its most extreme form in 1978, when he arranged the kidnapping of his favorite South Korean actress, Choi Eun-hee, and her ex-husband, Shin Sang-ok. Choi and Shin had been recently divorced before their abduction—they remarried in

North Korea at Kim's "suggestion." They made films for North Korean studios until 1986, when they defected to Vienna. A memoir they wrote together in 1987 about their experiences is one of the few firsthand accounts of Kim Jong-il.

For more on cinema in North Korea, see Andrei Lankov, "The Reel Thing," in *North of the DMZ: Essays on Daily Life in North Korea* (Jefferson, N.C.: McFarland, 2007). Lankov quotes a 1987 report on Pyongyang radio stating that the average North Korean goes to the cinema 21 times per year. South Korean sociologists who surveyed defectors found they'd gone to the movies 15 to 18 times per year. The average South Korean visits the movie theater 2.3 times per year, according to Lankov.

I also wrote about North Korean cinema for the *Los Angeles Times* in 2008 when I attended the Pyongyang Film Festival. "No Stars, No Swag, but What a Crowd!" *Los Angeles Times*, October 11, 2008.

CHAPTER 2: TAINTED BLOOD

The accounts of Tae-woo's childhood came from interviews I conducted on February 28, 2008, with two of his childhood friends still living near Seosan, South Korea.

Background about rural life in South Korea before the war comes from Cornelius Osgood, *The Koreans and Their Culture* (New York: Ronald Press, 1951).

Dean Rusk wrote of the fateful division of Korea in his memoir *As I Saw It* (New York: W. W. Norton, 1990).

For a South Korean perspective on the war, a helpful source was Bong Lee, *The Unfinished War: Korea* (New York: Algora Publishing, 2003).

The place where Tae-woo was captured is alternately known as Kumhwa or Kimhwa. Descriptions of the terrain come from a memoir by a former commander of U.N. forces in Korea: Matthew B. Ridgway, *The Korean War* (New York: Doubleday, 1967).

The soldier was U.S. Army PFC. Gene Salay, who was interviewed by the *Morning Call* (Allentown, PA): "So this is what it feels like to die: An interview by David Venditta." July 27, 2003.

An invaluable source was a memoir by another POW, named Huh Jae-suk, who escaped North Korea in 2000. He was captured by Chinese troops in 1953, one week before Mi-ran's father, at the same place,

Kumhwa, and also worked in the mines: Huh Jae-suk, *Nae Ireumeun Ttonggannasaekki-yeotta* [My Name Was Dirt] (Seoul: Won Books, 2008).

Information and statistics about South Korean POWs come from the U.S. House of Representatives, Asia and Pacific Subcommittee of the House International Relations Committee, "Human Rights Update and International Abduction Issues," April 27, 2006. The subcommittee heard extensive testimony from South Koreans who had been held as prisoners of war in North Korea.

Among many news reports on this issue, particularly helpful was "Hardly Known, Not Yet Forgotten, South Korean POWs Tell Their Story," Radio Free Asia, January 25, 2007.

Among other books on the Korean War and on the division of the Koreas:

Blair, Clay, *The Forgotten War: America in Korea, 1950–1953* (Annapolis: Naval Institute Press, 1987).

Hastings, Max, *The Korean War* (New York: Simon & Schuster), 1987.

Oberdorfer, Donald, *The Two Koreas: A Contemporary History* (Basic Books, 1997).

Stueck, William, *The Korean War: An International History* (Princeton, N.J.: Princeton University Press, 1995).

The categories assigned to the "hostile class" in North Korea come from "White Paper on Human Rights in North Korea," pp. 103–12, published in 2005 by the Korea Institute for National Unification, a South Korean government-funded think tank. It was prepared by South Korean intelligence based on testimony by defectors. Kim Dok-hong, a party official who accompanied Hwang Jang-yop, the most prominent party official ever to have defected, told me in a 2006 interview that records were kept in a giant underground warehouse in Yanggang province.

Excellent accounts of the system are also found in the following:

Hunter, Helen-Louise, *Kim Il-song's North Korea* (Westport, Conn.: Praeger, 1999).

Oh, Kongdan, and Ralph C. Hassig, *North Korea Through the Looking Glass* (Washington, D.C.: Brookings Institution Press, 2000).

Scalapino, Robert A., and Chong-sik Lee, *Communism in Korea, Part II: The Society* (University of California Press, 1972).

The recruiting of young women to work at Kim Il-sung's and Kim Jong-il's mansions was done by the fifth division of the Central Workers' Party. The most credible account of the recruitment of young women by the *okwa* comes from this exhaustively reported modern history of North Korea: Bradley Martin, *Under the Loving Care of the Fatherly Leader: North Korea and the Kim Dynasty* (New York: Thomas Dunne Books, 2004), pp. 198–202.

About the migration from Japan to North Korea, statistics come from Yoshiko Nozaki, Hiromitsu Inokuchi, and Kim Tae-young, "Legal Categories, Demographic Change and Japan's Korean Residents in the Long Twentieth Century," *The Asia-Pacific Journal: Japan Focus,* September 10, 2006.

Jun-sang's family background is not unlike that of Kang Chol-hwan, a former prisoner of the North Korean gulag whose family came from Japan with similar dreams of building a new homeland. His memoir is one of the best-known recent books about North Korea: Kang Chol-hwan and Pierre Rigoulot. *The Aquariums of Pyongyang: Ten Years in the North Korean Gulag* (New York: Basic Books, 2002).

CHAPTER 3: THE TRUE BELIEVER

Chongjin is a city with a largely fictional official history, because of the government's desire to downplay the Japanese role in its development. I am grateful to Andrei Lankov for providing me with an unpublished essay, "The Colonial North," about this remote area. Kim Du-seon, a former trade official from Chongjin who defected in 1998, has become the informal repository in South Korea of information about the city. He filled in some details of its history and topography.

The best published source I have found on Chongjin's history is *Choson Hyangto Daebaekkwa* [Encyclopedia of North Korean Geography and Culture] (Seoul: Institute for Peace Affairs, 2003).

Accurate population figures are difficult to come by. The last North Korean census was conducted in 1993 and the population is believed to have declined since then because of deaths during the famine, defections, and a low birthrate. The U.N. Population Fund and the Central Bureau of Statistics are as of this writing conducting another census.

Information about the rise of Kim Il-sung comes from Dae-Sook Suh, *Kim Il-sung: The North Korean Leader* (New York: Columbia University Press, 1988).

The cult of personality that developed around Kim Il-sung is elo-
quently described by the historian Charles Armstrong. He writes: "The
Kim cult combined images of Confucian familism with Stalinism, elements of Japanese emperor worship, and overtones of Christianity.
Confucian familism, and particularly the virtue of filial piety (hyo), was
perhaps the most distinctly Korean element of this 'cult.' " Charles K.
Armstrong, *The North Korean Revolution, 1945–1950* (Ithaca: Cornell University Press, 2003), pp. 223–25.

Chongjin was 65 percent obliterated by aerial bombing during the
Korean War, according to a bomb-damage assessment prepared by the
U.S. Air Force at the time of the armistice. General William Dean, an
American prisoner of war at the time, described the towns he saw as
having been reduced to "rubble or snowy open spaces." Conrad C.
Crane, *American Airpower Strategy in Korea, 1950–1953* (Lawrence: Uni-
versity Press of Kansas, 2000), pp. 168–69.

As he did with cinema, theater, opera, and literature, Kim Jong-il fash-
ioned himself as an expert on journalism. See *The Great Teacher of Journalists: Kim Jong-il* (Pyongyang: Foreign Languages Publishing House, 1973).

On the various ways that North Koreans spy on one another, see
Lankov's *North of the DMZ*, "Big Brother Is Watching."

CHAPTER 4: FADE TO BLACK

On North Korea's economy before 1990, Helen-Louise Hunter's
Kim Il-sung's North Korea contains a wealth of information about the
wages and benefits North Koreans received. Mrs. Song told me that the
figures corresponded to those she remembered.

The historian Bruce Cumings writes: "An internal CIA study almost
grudgingly acknowledged various achievements of this regime: com-
passionate care for children in general and war orphans in particular;
'radical change' in the position of women; genuinely free housing, free
health care, and preventative medicine; and infant mortality and life expectancy rates comparable to the most advanced countries until the recent famine." Bruce Cumings, *North Korea: Another Country* (New York:
New Press, 2003), pp. ii–ix.

Bradley Martin in *Under the Loving Care of the Fatherly Leader* writes:
"Outside analysts' comparisons during that period bolstered Kim's
claim. One study shows North and South neck and neck at the time of
the 1953 armistice, with gross national product per capita of $56 and

$55 respectively. By 1960, the South at $60 had barely advanced—while the North's figure had nearly quadrupled to $208. . . . A Western academic's 1965 article entitled 'Korean Miracle' referred not to the South Korean but to the *North* Korean economy" (pp. 104–5).

For more on the North Korean economy, see Nicholas Eberstadt, *The North Korean Economy: Between Crisis and Catastrophe* (New Brunswick, N.J.: Transaction Publishers, 2007).

The gifts to Kim Il-sung are on public display at the International Friendship Exhibition, a museum in Myohang, north of Pyongyang. When I visited in 2005, there were said to be 219,370 gifts to Kim Il-sung and another 53,419 to Kim Jong-il. See a piece written by my colleague, Mark Magnier, *Los Angeles Times,* COLUMN ONE; "No Gift Is Too Small for Them: At a Fortress Museum, North Korea Shows Off Every Present Sent to the Kims, from a Limo Given by Stalin to Plastic Tchotchkes," November 25, 2005.

KCNA quote about food was carried by Reuters, September 26, 1992, "North Korea Angrily Denies Reports of Food Riots."

CHAPTER 5: VICTORIAN ROMANCE

North of the DMZ by Andrei Lankov (Part 8: "Family Matters") contains several essays about sex and dating in North Korea.

On Korean traditions, Isabella Bird Bishop's book contains a wealth of information about attitudes toward women and family life. The original 1898 edition is fortunately still in print. Isabella Bird Bishop, *Korea and Her Neighbors: A Narrative of Travel with an Account of the Recent Vicissitudes and Present Position of the Country* (Seoul: Yonsei University Press, 1970), pp. 37, 345.

CHAPTER 6: TWILIGHT OF THE GOD

See an excellent account of Kim Il-sung's death in Oberdorfer, *The Two Koreas,* pp. 337–45.

For the description of the mourning period, I reviewed videotapes of North Korean television coverage that were made available by the South Korean Ministry of Unification's library in Seoul. The most complete account in the U.S. press that I have found is T. R. Reid's "Tumultuous Funeral for North Korean: Throngs Sob at Kim Il-sung's Last Parade," *Washington Post,* July 20, 1994.

The classic referenced here is Charles Mackay, *Extraordinary Delusions and the Madness of Crowds* (1841; New York: Three Rivers Press, 1980).

CHAPTER 7: TWO BEER BOTTLES FOR YOUR IV

A nutritional study conducted by U.N. agencies in 1998 found that 62 percent of children under the age of seven had stunted growth as a result of malnutrition. By 2004, that figure had dropped to 37 percent, in part due to humanitarian intervention.

A train explosion on April 22, 2004, in the town of Ryongchon caused so many injuries that North Korea allowed foreign aid agencies rare entry into its hospitals to help out. Several aid workers who took part in those efforts have shared their observations. Barbara Demick and Mark Magnier, "Train Victims' Suffering Is Compounded," *Los Angeles Times*, April 28, 2004.

On North Korea's admission in 2005 of a food shortage: Kevin Sullivan, "North Korea Makes Rare Pleas After Floods Devastate Country," *Washington Post*, September 22, 1995.

The statistics here come from Nicholas Eberstadt's *The North Korean Economy*, p. 31. North Korea's economic data is notoriously unreliable, as Eberstadt notes in the chapter "Our Own Style of Statistics." In a submission to the United Nations in 1997, North Korea listed its own GNP per capita as $239. The export figures are also supplied by Eberstadt in "The Persistence of North Korea," *Policy Review*, October/November 2004.

For more on the effects of poor nutrition on children and the medical system in North Korea:

Central Bureau of Statistics, Institute of Child Nutrition, in collaboration with UNICEF and World Food Programme, *DPRK 2004 Nutrition Assessment: Report of Survey Results.*
"Medical Doctors in North Korea." *Chosun Ilbo North Korea Report,* October 30, 2000.

CHAPTER 8: THE ACCORDION AND THE BLACKBOARD

On North Korean propaganda in the school system, see Andrei Lankov, "The Official Propaganda in the DPRK: Ideas and Methods" (available at http://north-korea.narod.ru/propaganda_lankov.htm).

A recently published memoir by a North Korean defector has good descriptions of North Korean elementary schools. Hyok Kang, *This Is Paradise! My North Korean Childhood* (London: Abacus, 2007), pp. 64–65.

The examples used in North Korean school textbooks come from used books I bought in Tumen, China, at a shop near the border where North Korean defectors often sell their personal possessions. I've also reviewed the collection of textbooks at the library in Seoul run by the Ministry of Unification. The reading primer with the poem about killing Japanese soldiers was featured on Japanese television in 2007.

The Korean language uses name suffixes to indicate respect, or lack thereof. The ending *–nim* is polite; *–nom* is extremely rude. Thus North Korean propaganda often refers to Americans as *miguknom*, basically "American bastards."

The demand that Mi-ran's school finance the Kim Jong-il Research Institute was in keeping with a requirement imposed by the central government in the 1990s that institutions raise their own money. Even overseas missions were responsible for their own funding, which led to a number of embarrassing incidents in which North Korean diplomats were caught smuggling drugs, counterfeit money, and in one case ivory in an effort to raise money.

In Pyongyang, there are dozens of biographies of Kim Jong-il available, each more glowing than the next. For a more realistic treatment, see Michael Breen, *Kim Jong-il: North Korea's Dear Leader* (Singapore: John Wiley & Sons, 2004).

CHAPTER 9: THE GOOD DIE FIRST

There are several excellent studies of the North Korean famine that provided useful data.

Becker, Jasper, *Hungry Ghosts: Mao's Secret Famine* (1996; New York: Henry Holt, 1998). Becker was one of the first Western journalists to write about the famine in North Korea. The postscript of his book contains a chapter dedicated to the country.

Flake, L. Gordon, and Scott Snyder (eds.), *Paved with Good Intentions: The NGO Experience in North Korea* (Westport, Conn.:

Praeger, 2003). This collection focuses on humanitarian intervention in North Korea.

Haggard, Stephan, and Marcus Noland, *Famine in North Korea: Markets, Aid, and Reform* (New York: Columbia University Press, 2007). The authors of this authoritative study made the most sophisticated attempt to date to quantify the number of deaths caused by the famine and put the number at between 600,000 and 1 million. Hwang Jang-yop, the highest-ranking official ever to defect from North Korea, said that internal estimates put the number between 1 million and 2.5 million.

Natsios, Andrew S., *The Great North Korean Famine* (Washington, D.C.: United States Institute of Peace Press, 2001).

Smith, Hazel, *Hungry for Peace: International Security, Humanitarian Assistance, and Social Change in North Korea* (Washington, D.C.: United States Institute of Peace Press, 2005).

Andrew Natsios, who was vice president of the NGO World Vision during the famine, writes, "The bulk of food shipments did not arrive until after deaths had begun to subside," p. 186. Jasper Becker also deals extensively with the withdrawal of the aid agencies, in Jasper Becker, *Rogue Regime: Kim Jong Il and the Looming Threat of North Korea* (New York: Oxford University Press, 2005), pp. 213–17.

Amartya Sen, a Nobel laureate in economics, in his famous *Poverty and Famines: An Essay on Entitlement and Deprivation* (1981) pointed out the linkage between famine and totalitarian regimes. He observed that famines are caused not only by a shortage of food but also by inequalities in distribution that would not be possible in a democratic society because the hungry would vote out their leadership.

The propaganda claims that Kim Jong-il ate simple food are absurd. Throughout the famine Kim spent huge sums of his nation's wealth on regal meals. His epicurean tastes were made famous by a former sushi chef who, under the pseudonym Kenji Fujimoto, wrote a memoir in which he described going around the world to buy ingredients for Kim. When Kim traveled through Russia in 2001, consignments of live lobster and French wine were flown in for the leader, according to a book by a Russian official, Konstantin Pulikovsky. I wrote at some length about Kim's eating habits, "Rich Taste in a Poor Country: North Korea's Enigmatic Leader Kim Jong-il Demands the Finest Food and Drink," *Los Angeles Times,* June 26, 2004.

CHAPTER 10: MOTHERS OF INVENTION

The Kim Jong-il speech of December 1996, delivered at Kim Il-sung University, was originally reported by *Wolgun Chosun* (Monthly Chosun) in Seoul. It is quoted at some length in Natsios, *The Great North Korean Famine*, p. 99.

The World Food Programme also thinks biscuits were a convenient and nutritious way of supplementing the diet. As part of its aid effort in Chongjin, the U.N. agency used factories there to make micronutrient-enriched biscuits that were distributed to schoolchildren.

North Korea's markets are kept out of sight of foreign visitors. A North Korean with a hidden camera took a lengthy video of Chongjin's Sunam Market in 2004. The video, provided to me by Lee Hwa-young of Rescue the North Korean People, shows food in humanitarian-aid sacks being offered for sale. World Food Programme officials say it is possible that the sacks were merely being reused.

The market prices quoted in this chapter come in large part from the work of Good Friends: Center for Peace, Human Rights and Refugees, based in Seoul. The Buddhist-inspired organization has excellent sources inside North Korea and publishes regular reports under the title *North Korea Today*, available on the Internet at http://goodfriends.or.kr/eng/.

The coal miner was one of the subjects of a lengthy series of articles I wrote about Chongjin, "Glimpses of a Hermit Nation," *Los Angeles Times*, July 3, 2005, and "Trading Ideals for Sustenance," *Los Angeles Times*, July 4, 2005.

CHAPTER 11: WANDERING SWALLOWS

Andrei Lankov writes that the North Korean identification cards were designed to act somewhat like passports, restricting travel within the country (*North of the DMZ*, pp. 179–80).

The references to cannibalism come from Jasper Becker's *Hungry Ghosts*, pp. 211–19.

The description of the funeral comes from Andrew Natsios's *Great North Korean Famine*, p. 76.

CHAPTER 12: SWEET DISORDER

The title of this chapter is taken from Robert Herrick's poem "Sweet Disorder". *A Selection from the Lyrical Poems of Robert Herrick*, BibioBazaar, pp. 138–9.

Information about the North Korean criminal code comes from Yoon Dae-kyu, "Analysis of Changes in the DPRK Criminal Code," Institute for Far Eastern Studies, Kyungnam University, January 31, 2005. Portions of the code are also translated in Korea Institute for National Unification, *White Paper on Human Rights in North Korea* (Seoul, 2006).

Few defectors have emerged from the long-term political prisons that make up the North Korean gulag, so much of what is known is based on satellite intelligence and hearsay.

The most detailed account of life in the gulag comes from Kang Chol-hwan's *Aquariums of Pyongyang*. Kang spent much of his childhood in Yadok, the most notorious of the political prison camps.

Statistics and some of the terminology used for the prisons come from this meticulously researched human rights report: David Hawk, *The Hidden Gulag* (Washington, D.C.: U.S. Committee on Human Rights, 2003).

The 927 centers were a cross between homeless shelters and prison camps. Natsios estimates that between 378,000 and 1.9 million North Koreans passed through the camps over the course of a year. (*The Great North Korean Famine*, pp. 74–75).

Former Chongjin residents have differing accounts of when the purge of the 6th Army took place. Kim Du-seon, the former trade official, lived close to the military base in Nanam and told me in an interview on August 26, 2004, that the largest movement of military vehicles was in the fall of 1995.

The incident is mentioned in the following authoritative study of the North Korean military: Joseph S. Bermudez, Jr., *The Armed Forces of North Korea* (London and New York: I. B. Tauris, 2001), p. 202.

The information on students executed for streaking comes from *White Paper on Human Rights in North Korea*, p. 30.

CHAPTER 13: FROGS IN THE WELL

On the reading habits of North Koreans and North Korean literature, see Brian R. Myers, *Han Sorya and North Korean Literature: The Failure of Socialist Realism in the DPRK* (Ithaca, N.Y.: Cornell East Asia Series no. 69, 1994).

The quotation from the Russian economic treatise is based on Jun-sang's recollection. I was not able to locate the original book.

CHAPTER 14: THE RIVER

Family reunions were agreed to at the landmark summit between Kim Jong-il and Kim Dae-jung in June 2000 and commenced two months later. As of this writing, 16,212 Koreans have participated in face-to-face meetings and another 3,748 have seen one another through video links. More than 90,000 South Koreans remain on a waiting list to participate in reunions. South Korean Red Cross figures quoted in *Korea Herald,* May 13, 2009.

The most comprehensive study I have seen of North Korean defection is Stephan Haggard and Marcus Noland, eds., *The North Korean Refugee Crisis: Human Rights and International Response* (Washington, D.C.: U.S. Committee for Human Rights in North Korea, 2006).

CHAPTER 15: EPIPHANY

As of October 1998, only 923 North Koreans had come to South Korea. See Yonhap News report of October 11, 1998, citing figures from the South Korean Ministry of Unification.

The figures on East German defectors are quoted in Haggard and Noland, *The North Korean Refugee Crisis* (p. 54), and attributed to Albert O. Hirschman, "Exit, Voice and the Fate of the German Democratic Republic: An Essay in Conceptual History," *World Politics* 45:2 (1993).

Information about DVDs comes from a North Korean smuggler I interviewed in Bangkok in May 2005. He said that people brought videotapes into the country in the 1990s, but that the coming of the DVD boosted the business because the disks were slim enough to be hidden under other goods.

The lecture was published by the Chosun Workers' Party Press, April 2005. A copy was provided to me by Rescue the North Korean People.

CHAPTER 16: THE BARTERED BRIDE

The estimated number of North Korean women sold to the Chinese comes from Choi Jin-i, a North Korean poet and writer who defected to South Korea and was herself in an arranged match in China. I interviewed many women in Chinese villages near the North Korean border as well. "North Korea's Brides of Despair," *Los Angeles Times*, August 18, 2003.

There have been several excellent reports on the phenomenon:

Mucio, Norma Kang. *An Absence of Choice: The Sexual Exploitation of North Korean Women in China* (London: Anti-Slavery International, 2005).

Denied Status, Denied Education: Children of North Korean Women in China (New York: Human Rights Watch, 2008).

Revisions of the North Korean criminal code in 2004 slightly reduced penalties for illegal border crossing. See Haggard and Noland, *The North Korean Refugee Crisis*, p. 18.

Nongpo Detention Center is described in some detail in David Hawk's report *The Hidden Gulag*. The report also includes a satellite photo of the facility and other prison camps. Former detainees have said that it was common practice to kill babies born to the inmates, because their fathers were Han Chinese. Oak-hee said she did not know of infanticide taking place at the time she was there. She believes it is possible that the practice was discontinued in 2001 before her arrest.

CHAPTER 17: OPEN YOUR EYES, SHUT YOUR MOUTH

Information about how North Koreans think of defectors comes from a lecture entitled "How to Thoroughly Crush the Schemes of the Enemies Who Disseminate Unusual Lifestyles," Chosun Workers' Party Press.

On the various "planned escapes" out of North Korea, Blaine Harden of *The Washington Post* wrote, on November 18, 2007:

A low-budget escape through China via Thailand to Seoul, which requires treacherous river crossings, arduous travel on foot, and several miserable weeks in a Thai immigration jail, can cost less than $2,000, according to four brokers here. A first-class defection, complete with a forged Chinese passport and an airplane ticket from Beijing to Seoul, goes for more than $10,000. From start to finish, it can take as little as three weeks.

CHAPTER 18: THE PROMISED LAND

On the South Korean constitution and how it applies to the status of North Korean refugees, see Haggard and Noland, *The North Korean Refugee Crisis*. They write in their conclusion (p. 75), "If China's stance has been unconstructive, South Korea's could be described as ambivalent, even shamefully so."

The figures on the number of North Korean defectors settled in South Korea come from the South Korean Ministry of Unification and are quoted as well in the above report, p. 54. There was a notable increase in the number of defectors received in 2008, which might be the result of a more conservative government in Seoul. The two preceding governments, under Kim Dae-jung and Roh Moo-hyun, took great pains to avoid giving offense to Pyongyang.

The sociologist Yoon In-jin was originally interviewed for my story "Fleeing to Culture Shock," *Los Angeles Times*, March 2, 2002.

On the Hanawon reeducation program, see Norimitsu Onishi, "North Korean Defectors Take a Crash Course in Coping," *New York Times*, June 25, 2006.

The figures on the German economies come from Werner Smolny and Matthias Kirback, "Wage Differentials Between East and West Germany," University of Ulm and Centre for European Economic Research, Mannheim, March 17, 2004.

The most readable book about postwar South Korea is Michael Breen's *The Koreans* (New York: Thomas Dunne Books, 1998).

Before this book went to print, Oak-hee managed to get her daughter to South Korea, but was still in negotiations to bring out her son.

CHAPTER 19: STRANGERS IN THE HOMELAND

On the role of Christian activists in bringing out North Korean refugees:

Macintyre, Donald, "Running out of the Darkness," *Time*, April 24, 2006.
Reitman, Valerie, "Leading His Flock of Refugees to Asylum: A Missionary Helps North Koreans Flee via China and Mongolia," *Los Angeles Times*, October 27, 2002. The refugees featured in

this story from Erenhot, China, took the same route through Mongolia as Kim Hyuck.

On the role of religion in North Korea, see David Hawk, *Thank You, Father Kim Il-sung* (Washington, D.C.: U.S. Commission on International Religious Freedom, 2005).

On the subject of height, see Sunyoung Pak, "The Biological Standard of Living in the Two Koreas," *Economics and Human Biology* 2:3 (2004), pp. 511–18.

I wrote a long piece on the subject of stunting, "A Small Problem Growing: Chronic Malnutrition Has Stunted a Generation of North Koreans," *Los Angeles Times*, February 12, 2004.

The height difference plays a major role in North Koreans' difficulty in adjusting to life in South Korea. Don Oberdorfer writes of an incident in which two diminutive North Korean soldiers, aged nineteen and twenty-three, accidentally drifted into South Korean waters. They were overheard saying in a military hospital that they would never marry a South Korean woman because "they're too big for us." The soldiers were sent back to North Korea at their own request. (*The Two Koreas*, p. 314.)

CHAPTER 20: REUNIONS

Mi-ran's cousin was arrested and briefly served time in jail for fraud for falsifying passports. But the South Korean government ended up red-faced when the news reached South Korea that many former POWs and their families had escaped North Korea, only to be turned away by South Korean diplomats in China. South Korean veterans were outraged and the South Korean Ministry of Defense apologized. I wrote about one of these cases: "Fifty Years After Korean War's End, Ex-POW Returns Home," *Los Angeles Times*, December 25, 2003.

As of 2005, sixty-two former South Korean POWs had escaped North Korea across the Tumen River. Several hundred were believed to still be alive in North Korea.

Translation of the Sandor Petofi poem "Szabadság, Szerelem" by G. F. Cushing from the Corvinius Library of Hungarian History, http://www.hungarian-history.hu/lib/timeless/chapter23.htm.

EPILOGUE: WAITING

Eberstadt lays out the reasons he was wrong about North Korea's imminent collapse in "The Persistence of North Korea," *Policy Review*, October/November 2004.

Economic statistics are from the Bank of Korea, Seoul.

Information about the current state of the North Korean economy also came from the following:

Food and Agriculture Organization and World Food Programme (FAO/WFP) Crop and Food Security Assessment Mission to the Democratic People's Republic of Korea, December 8, 2008.

Stephan Haggard, Marcus Noland, and Erik Weeks. "North Korea on the Precipice of Famine," Erik Weeks Peterson Institute for International Economics, May 2008.

On U.S. aid agencies, see "Rapid Food Security Assessment. North Pyongan and Chagang Provinces, Democratic People's Republic of Korea." Mercy Corps, World Vision, Global Resource Services, Samaritan's Purse, June 2008.

On tensions at the markets in Chongjin: Good Friends: Center for Peace, Human Rights and Refugees, *North Korea Today*, no. 275, May 2009; "City of Chungjin Declares, 'Do Not Sell Any Items Other Than Agricultural Products,'" "Mass Protest Against Control over Commercial Activities at Chungjin," *North Korea Today*, no. 206, April 2008.

Also on market activity, see Kyungnam University, Institute for Far Eastern Studies, "New Restrictions on DPRK Market Trading," *NK Brief*, November 15, 2007. The institute quotes from an internal Workers' Party document it obtained, explaining the need for "a crackdown on markets that have degraded into hotbeds of anti-socialism."

BARBARA DEMICK is the Beijing bureau chief of the *Los Angeles Times*. Her reporting on North Korea won the Overseas Press Club's award for human rights reporting as well as awards from the Asia Society and the American Academy of Diplomacy. Her coverage of Sarajevo for *The Philadelphia Inquirer* won the George Polk Award and the Robert F. Kennedy Award and was a finalist for the Pulitzer Prize in international reporting. Her previous book is *Logavina Street: Life and Death in a Sarajevo Neighborhood.*

ABOUT THE TYPE

This book was set in Monotype Dante, a typeface designed by Giovanni Mardersteig (1892–1977). Conceived as a private type for the Officina Bodoni in Verona, Italy, Dante was originally cut only for hand composition by Charles Malin, the famous Parisian punch cutter, between 1946 and 1952. Its first use was in an edition of Boccaccio's *Trattatello in laude di Dante* that appeared in 1954. The Monotype Corporation's version of Dante followed in 1957. Though modeled on the Aldine type used for Pietro Cardinal Bembo's treatise *De Aetna* in 1495, Dante is a thoroughly modern interpretation of that venerable face.